Praise for
Relate to Others with Confidence:
A Guidebook for LGBTQIA+ People and
Those with a Different Label or No Label

"*Relate to Others with Confidence: A Guidebook for LGBTQIA+ People and Those with a Different Label or No Label* is both a probiotic and prebiotic for the LGBTQIA+ soul; its main focus is on finding powerful ways for our community to flourish that are often missing in the traditional 'diet' of existing literature. It takes the conversation about the lived experience and, most importantly, the unique needs of individuals within our community to new heights in an easily digestible and actionable way."

—El McCabe, president-elect of APA Division 44, Society for
the Psychology of Sexual Orientation and Gender Diversity

"A much-needed and outstanding resource to meet the clinical needs of sexually- and gender-diverse individuals. Brilliant!"

—Eli Coleman, professor emeritus, Eli Coleman Institute for Sexual
and Gender Health, University of Minnesota Medical School

Diverse Sexualities, Genders, and Relationships

Series Editors
Richard Sprott, California State University,
East Bay and President of APA Division 44
Elisabeth Sheff, Sheff Consulting

The Diverse Sexualities, Genders, and Relationships Series highlights evidence-based approaches to understanding and serving diverse individuals and families whose relational or sexual practices or identities have been marginalized and understudied; reports of emerging empirical research on these topics; and analyses of the latest trends in cultural and societal developments on the status and place of diverse sexualities, genders, and relationships. Books in the series emphasize the intersections of race, culture, age, social class, (dis)ability, and other factors that shape the social locations of relational, sexual, and gender minorities as they intersect with institutions in fields such as education, law, medicine, religion, and public policy.

The books in this series serve as sound and critical resources for the training and continuing education of professionals directly serving diverse communities in professions such as counseling, marriage and family therapy, social work, healthcare, criminology, human services and education. They are also useful for educators teaching undergraduate and graduate level university courses in anthropology, cultural studies, gerontology, psychology, sexuality studies, sociology, and women's and gender studies. Finally, these books interest educated laypeople who wish to better understand diversity among relational, sexual and gender minorities.

Titles in Series:

Love and Freedom: Transcending Monogamy and Polyamory by Jorge N. Ferrer
Please Scream Quietly: A Story of Kink by Julie L. Fennell
The Handbook of Consensual Non-Monogamy: Affirming Mental Health Practice edited by Michelle D. Vaughan and Theodore R. Burnes
Mental Health Practice with LGBTQ+ Children, Adolescents, and Emerging Adults in Multiple Systems of Care edited by Cristina L. Magalhães, Richard A. Sprott, and G. Nic Rider
Polyamorous Elders: Aging in Open Relationships by Kathy Labriola
177 Lovers and Counting: My Life as a Sex Researcher by Leanna Wolfe
What Is Compersion? Understanding Positive Empathy in Consensually Non-Monogamous Relationships by Marie Thouin
Feel Secure in Yourself: A Guidebook for LGBTQIA+ People and Those with a Different Label or No Label, edited by A. Lee Beckstead, Jacks Cheng, Sulaimon Giwa, Mark A. Yarhouse, and Iva Žegura
Relate to Others with Confidence: A Guidebook for LGBTQIA+ People and Those with a Different Label or No Label, edited by A. Lee Beckstead, Jacks Cheng, Sulaimon Giwa, Mark A. Yarhouse, and Iva Žegura

Relate to Others with Confidence

A Guidebook for LGBTQIA+ People and Those with a Different Label or No Label

Edited by

A. Lee Beckstead

Jacks Cheng

Sulaimon Giwa

Mark A. Yarhouse

Iva Žegura

Part of the LGBTQIA+ Peacemaking Book Project

ROWMAN & LITTLEFIELD
Lanham • Boulder • New York • London

Published by Rowman & Littlefield
An imprint of The Rowman & Littlefield Publishing Group, Inc.
4501 Forbes Boulevard, Suite 200, Lanham, Maryland 20706
www.rowman.com

86-90 Paul Street, London EC2A 4NE

British Library Cataloguing in Publication Information available

Library of Congress Cataloging-in-Publication Data
Names: Beckstead, A. Lee, 1966– editor. | Cheng, Jacky Li-Yang, editor. | Giwa, Sulaimon, editor. | Yarhouse, Mark A., 1968– editor. | Žegura, Iva, editor.
Title: Relate to others with confidence : a guidebook for LGBQTIA+ people and those with a different label or no label / edited by A. Lee Beckstead, Jacks Cheng, Sulaimon Giwa, Mark A. Yarhouse, Iva Žegura.
Description: Lanham : Rowman & Littlefield, 2024. | Series: Diverse sexualities, genders, and relationships | Includes bibliographical references and index.
Identifiers: LCCN 2024005864 (print) | LCCN 2024005865 (ebook) | ISBN 9781538190432 (cloth) | ISBN 9781538190449 (paperback) | ISBN 9781538190456 (epub)
Subjects: LCSH: Sexual minorities—Life skills guides. | Confidence. | Resilience (Personality trait) | Interpersonal relations.
Classification: LCC HQ73 .R453 2024 (print) | LCC HQ73 (ebook) | DDC 158.2086/6—dc23/eng/20240407
LC record available at https://lccn.loc.gov/2024005864
LC ebook record available at https://lccn.loc.gov/2024005865

Contents

Acknowledgments

A. Lee Beckstead, Jacks Cheng, Sulaimon Giwa, Mark A. Yarhouse, and Iva Žegura

Thank you for reading this guidebook. We hope the ideas, experiences, and skills shared here will empower you in some meaningful way. The 110+[1] contributors to this book project attempted to find agreement about their chapter topic(s) to help a wide range of people. This has been a group effort, and we know we have not covered everything. We will disappoint, but hopefully not offend or invalidate. We hope you are inspired to learn more about these issues, including through our companion chapter e-resources and online resource lists.[2]

The LGBTQIA+ Peacemaking Book Project was designed to be inclusive, research based, affirming, and comprehensive. Each guidebook was overseen by five coeditors chosen for their distinct and diverse areas of expertise. Each chapter was coauthored by three to 15 clinicians, researchers, or community leaders who also hold divergent viewpoints, sometimes politically opposing. We hope these diverse perspectives and checks and balances against prejudice will help you and other readers appreciate the commonalities and differences between and within cultures, communities, and nations. We want to explicitly recognize that the issues addressed in these chapters are not limited to specific age-groups. Older adults, with their unique experiences and challenges, are an integral part of the diverse communities we aim to serve.

To promote collaboration between communities, we have brought together coauthors and coeditors who have been at odds in the clinical literature, professional debates, and legal disputes. We have conservatives and progressives who feel differently about same-sex marriage and parenting, and we have proponents and opponents of LGBTQIA+-affirmative approaches and "conversion

---

[1] It is difficult to say how many contributed to this guidebook and book project. Some might have contributed to the development of a chapter topic or provided feedback on a draft, or their contribution may be in the companion e-resource, given how the final content was divided. We also included content from coauthors who ended the collaboration for various reasons but allowed their contribution to remain in the chapter.

[2] www.FindingCongruence.com

therapy." Rather than take sides, contributors agreed to pool their resources for a collective inquiry to clarify what works and doesn't and for whom. The reason for this respectful adversarial collaboration (Kahneman, 2003) is to promote individual and community health and flourishing.

Those with differing viewpoints often meet to debate each other's ideas. These experts are rarely in the same room without this opposition. Academics and researchers rarely collaborate with mental health counselors, and researchers rarely translate their findings into self-help resources for the general public. This book project and these chapters serve as *that room* where experts along many spectra have come together to improve the common good and help a wide range of readers regarding sexual/gender diversity.

One safety guideline proposed by contributors to engage in this process is acknowledging that all coauthors and coeditors participated in this book project independently of their various affiliations. All ideas and skills in this book project do not necessarily represent all the contributors' viewpoints or reflect the viewpoints of their various affiliations. Collaboration in this book project does not necessarily mean coauthors and coeditors agree with or promote the work or views of the other contributors or the ideas or strategies presented in the other chapters.

With these diverse ideas and skills, we want a broad readership that includes (a) readers who feel resolved about being LGBTQIA+ but want more self-love and confidence in relationships and when responding to stress, rejection, and prejudice; (b) readers who are questioning or distressed about their sexual orientation or gender identity and are coming out or considering it; and (c) academics, clinicians, researchers, religious leaders, parents, and other providers and individuals who want to learn updated and common-ground ideas and skills about sexuality, gender, race/ethnicity, faith/purpose of life, emotional health, resilience, and relationships.

We should address how we arrived at using the LGBTQIA+ acronym. It was popular in the 1990s to say "GLB" to indicate everyone who is not exclusively heterosexual. It then became popular to say "LGB" to center lesbian women's experiences and then add "TQIA" to recognize more aspects of sexual/gender diversity. Lesbian, gay, bisexual, transgender, queer, intersex, and asexual/aromantic can be considered overarching categories that represent multiple sexual and gender identity subcategories. Each identity label, however, can also be perceived as a distinct and binary label (for example, you are transgender or you are not transgender), which does not speak to everyone's experience. Some individuals prefer more specific sexual and gender identity labels (for example, androsexual, heteroflexible, transmasculine, agenderflux). Some prefer the term *queer* because it is inclusive of queerness in the sense of both gender identity and sexual orientation. The terms *sexual/gender diversity* and *sexual/gender minorities* remove labels to reflect intersecting continuums and identities. A plus sign was added to the LGBTQIA acronym as an attempt to acknowledge this spectrum of diversity. Coauthor Dr. Candice Metzler noted the following about using LGBTQIA+ to describe a population:

> This approach largely emerged as a way to consolidate political power to gain visibility, inclusion, and protection. This categorization has created conflict for people who (a) do not want to be associated with other experiences/subgroups within the framework, (b) do not feel included within this group, or (c) feel like their experiences are overshadowed by more dominant and visible experiences within the group.

In this book project, we use "LGBTQIA+" because many use these labels to self-identify and experience community. They also highlight a broad range of sexual and gender diversity. Yet we recognize that some individuals have different sexual/gender minority identities not represented by this term. We ask readers who do not identify with "LGBTQIA" to respond to "LGBTQIA+" as if it includes your identity. This request applies also to those who do not identify according to their sexual attractions or gender experiences. We will also use "sexual/gender diversity" and "sexual/gender minorities" throughout because we consider all these terms as similar and representing people who are sexually, gender, and relationally different and diverse and stigmatized, marginalized, and disadvantaged because of it. This acknowledgment is crucial as it reflects the reality that individuals of all ages can face challenges related to autonomy, agency, and informed decision-making.

To recognize our collective responsibility, the lead coeditor Dr. Lee Beckstead acknowledges working on this book project in Utah, a gathering place for Indigenous peoples. This land, named for the Ute tribe, is the ancestral homelands of the Shoshone, Paiute, Goshute, Navajo Nation, and Ute tribes. Dr. Beckstead acknowledges their painful history of genocide and forced removal from this land. He hopes to honor and respect the Indigenous people still connected to this land. Coauthor Jim Struve expressed the importance of this acknowledgment in this way:

> Every community owes its existence and vitality to generations and ancestors who contributed to their hopes, dreams, and energy that led to this moment in our history. Some were brought here against their will, some were drawn here from distant homes pursuing hopes or fleeing violence and poverty, and some have lived on these lands from time immemorial. This guidebook offers guidance for healing harms inflicted on people because of their gender or sexual orientation or both. As you read this guidebook, we invite you to acknowledge that we are not the first generation to confront toxic harm and violence.
>
> Take a moment to reflect on ancestors who preceded us and the legacy of historical harm and violence inflicted on many generations of individuals who also wanted to express their authentic identity. Also, consider harms and

violence that have similarly been perpetrated against the authentic identities of Mother Earth and our environment.

We encourage you to go beyond the words in this book and take concrete steps for personal investment in the *congruence of words AND actions*. Beyond digesting the words that fill the pages of this book, "we must be the change we wish to see."

We hope the following helps you with what you need regarding sexual/gender diversity.

Chapter 1

Live Assertively

Paul Linden, A. Lee Beckstead, Jeannie
DiClementi, Julia Mackaronis, Jim Struve,
Eduardo Morales, and Tim van Wanrooij[1]

This guidebook aims to educate and help readers manage conflicts, losses, and discrimination and live truer to themselves—in whatever way feels authentic and healthy to them. This chapter highlights ideas and skills for creating safety and responding assertively to challenges and emotional distress. We focus on the following:

1. Experiencing and understanding boundaries as the learned, skilled behaviors by which a person controls the world inside and around them to create safety and comfort
2. Understanding how to cocreate safety while exploring boundaries
3. Understanding what assertiveness is and is not
4. Developing knowledge about and skills in being assertive
5. Applying assertive behaviors in conflict situations

We hope these ideas and skills will help sexual/gender minority (LGBTQIA+) individuals, including those with other sexually queer identities (polyamorous, kink/BDSM, etc.), develop resilience and live more self-directed, healthful, happy lives. Those not LGBTQIA+ may benefit from these ideas and skills by becoming more loving and powerful in how they meet their own needs, respect their limits, and respond to conflicts, including with LGBTQIA+ individuals.

By nature, we humans seek control and try, in our own ways, to meet our needs for safety, connection, and nourishment. As we mature, innate temperament and life experiences shape how and if we meet our needs. Unfortunately,

---
[1] Silvia L. Mazzula, PhD, contributed to an earlier chapter draft. Jacob Z. Hess, PhD, reviewed earlier drafts, participated in the dialogue, and supported the vision of more open-hearted attempts at working together. We also thank Annette S. Kluck, PhD, for providing chapter feedback and sharing her ideas.

as children and as adults, many of us experience neglect or trauma or both, and our needs are not satisfied. We may experience powerlessness and, on that basis, fail to develop strategies for living as well as we can.

Part of the human makeup is to respond to challenges, threats, and distress with flight, fight, freeze, or collapse. These reactions create a feeling of control and safety and help us survive. They can also create more distress, separation, oppositional thinking, and dehumanization, especially if they become habits we use indiscriminately. It is essential to distinguish the *feeling* of safety from the *actuality* of safety. Creating the feeling without the actuality is not enough on its own.

People who are stigmatized and marginalized in society will often experience additional distress from being devalued, disadvantaged, and attacked by people who have more social power (power derived by their position in society) (Hsieh & Ruther, 2016). Being stigmatized and marginalized generally makes people feel powerless, unsafe, and unwell (Mallory et al., 2023). However, throughout history, people in stigmatized and marginalized groups have developed unique strategies for safety, expression, and connection.

Take a moment to appreciate how your innate reflexes, personality, and willpower have helped you survive. As Paul Monette expressed, "Somehow applaud [yourself] for simply having survived it."[2]

This chapter will teach skills to reduce the intensity of your emotional distress, which we discuss later as actions you do in your body. You may or may not be aware of much, all, or any of that process, and training will improve your awareness and control. We hope these skills help you face and resolve conflicts and find freedom—from discrimination, rejection, intimidation, and unjustified shame/guilt. It is vital to remember that some oppressors are so cruel and powerful that attaining freedom is not a realistic goal, at least at the moment. Assertiveness skills are essential, however, in maintaining emotional balance when dealing with tyrants and ultimately creating peace for ourselves and others.

What Are Boundaries?

For coauthor Linden, boundaries are skilled, learned behaviors by which you attempt to control the world and your internal experiences to achieve comfort and safety. It may sound strange and an unfamiliar way of thinking about boundaries, but a boundary is not an abstract term or an object but a promissory note. Boundaries are actions and take practice. You don't simply *have* boundaries. You must *do* boundaries. You do behaviors to enforce what you need and prefer. Implicit in this metaphor of doing a boundary is

---

[2] Interviewed by Mark Thompson in his book *Gay Soul* (1994, p. 25).

protecting yourself from something or someone. For example, a fence around a yard or borders between countries are not boundaries. They are statements of what somebody will do if you do something they don't want. If you set foot in their backyard, they will do something to enforce their desires. The consequence of disobeying makes the fence work. Having a sense of your personal space and personhood involves knowing what is okay for you and what is not. But that is not a boundary. It is a preference. Expressing your preferences to someone, accompanied by a statement of how you will achieve those preferences, is a boundary. You don't have effective boundaries if you can't or won't enforce your preferences and meet your needs. Talking is not enough; you have to act.

"Setting a boundary," then, involves reflecting on and clarifying what you want/need from someone, expressing it as a direct request, and making sure to the extent possible that the person understands the request and what you will do if the person doesn't give it to you, and then having the skills, resources, and will to do it. If you want respect and a person won't give it to you after you express this request, then you do what you need to experience respect elsewhere, even from yourself. How can you minimize the effects on you of other people not respecting you? "Having better boundaries" means identifying the actions that give you more control of yourself and your environment for your safety and comfort. When we say, "You do boundaries," we hope it moves people toward a sense of response-ability. Getting better at assertiveness means figuring out or learning behaviors more effective at attending to your reactions, needs, and limits and practicing those behaviors until you get good at them.

What Is Power?

There are many forms of power. *Generic power* refers to behaviors that apply in every life situation, which include body awareness, full breathing, and a clear voice. *Specific power* refers to actions that relate to a particular situation in which you need specific skills to achieve specific results. For example, breathing well will help you calm down and be more alert and effective in every situation, but learning to drive a car will not teach you how to fly an airplane. You enact specific power by doing the actions that are the particular requirements for power in that situation. If you are thirsty, getting a sandwich doesn't solve the problem. If you have the power to get a sandwich, you might still be powerless to get a drink. Power is specific. You are powerless or powerful only in reference to what you need to do in a particular situation.

Powerlessness, therefore, is not the absence of power. It is an assessment and comparison of your resources and those of someone else's or of a particular situation. The solution to powerlessness is to learn and do now what you couldn't do in the past. The term *power* can be the opposite of powerlessness when we learn how to face and defeat a former attack or threat.

People often think power is negative because they have witnessed only brutality and experienced that power as hurtful. However, from Linden's perspective, power is not negative. Negative use of power is negative. Power by itself is neutral. Linden uses the term *power* to refer to the beautiful, life-affirming, creative, and ethical ability to control what is happening in and around you. When kindhearted people think power is negative, they refuse or neglect their power. They would often rather be victims than perpetrators. If you do good things with your power, such as protecting yourself and others, helping people to grow, giving freedom, being friendly, and creating community, that power is used for good, and you are neither a victim nor a perpetrator.

Also, from Linden's perspective, there's nothing wrong with attempting to control others. It's how you do it, why, and the results that matter. It's normal to try to control others, and we do it all the time. If you're polite and friendly, that usually is an effective form of control. If you want someone to pass the salt, being polite instead of brutal has a much better chance of getting the salt and having the meal go well. That is power, and it is not weak. People often think being polite is being weak, but it is usually a good way of getting what you want more efficiently and effectively.

Cultures typically define how and why to behave appropriately. Politeness is one example. Our power can come from legal, governmental, and financial structures and from the ways we've been taught to treat each other. All of these behaviors may or may not evolve or change over time. However, we hope the better ways of behaving that we embrace become normal for the culture over time. It is necessary to practice these behaviors until they become easier and more available.

Linden uses the word *emotions* to refer to actions we do in our bodies. He uses the word *feelings* to refer to the experience of these actions by the person doing them. For example, *anger* is a noun, but anger is an action and a process, not a thing. We "do" anger by raising our voice, tightening fists, scowling, and so on. The feeling that we call anger is our internal experience of these behaviors. "Releasing anger" is a metaphor because anger can't be released. You can hold an object up and release it, and it will fall, but what are you releasing when you try to release an emotion? You don't release a process; you replace it. You don't stop running; you start walking. We have to *do something* to replace the experience of an emotion. For example, when we notice we are *doing* anger, we can release our tense muscles and breathe deeply, which will create a feeling of relaxation and a different type of control and power.

You achieve this relaxed power by focusing on yourself (rather than on others) and it will enable you to better manage the following:

- your body, temperament, beliefs, expectations, feelings, values, needs, limits, passions, interests, roles, actions and reactions, the consequences of your actions and reactions, and more.

This power is the basis for creating safety in your life and for being safe when you state clearly where others' responsibilities lie:

- their body, temperament, beliefs, expectations, feelings, values, needs, limits, passions, interests, roles, actions and reactions, the consequences of their actions and reactions, and more.

Boundary statements indicate how you protect what is yours and the intersection with how others protect what is theirs, including their choices. Awareness of behaviors as boundaries allows you to find others with similar boundaries while recognizing that what is important for you and works for you may not be of value and possible for someone else.

The behaviors we use to establish our comfort and safety can shift depending on the nature of the situation and context. A person can have different boundaries and sets of behaviors with romantic partners, coworkers, family members, neighbors, and seatmates on a plane, up to a point. You can take your awareness of yourself and your needs and limits into all situations, but what you disclose or express to others can depend on the situation. The context or role helps determine the physical and psychological behaviors, such as beliefs and attitudes, that are expected and appropriate for that particular context.

Cultural Differences in Boundaries

Expectations are value statements of what a person would or should do in specific situations. People's expectations will be different from each other. These expectations can differ for different groups, and cultures have different beliefs about how people should behave. A person's perception of their boundaries is the values and expectations of the person's culture.

One of the differences in cultural worldviews is the importance of the individual versus the collective. Individualism and collectivism are different scales, not opposite ends of the same continuum. Some cultures and relationships value both individuality and collectivism. People who primarily endorse individual worldviews have more freedom and choose who and what to let in and out of their lives for the sake of diversity. They can decide who and what is best for them and their life. People who primarily endorse collective worldviews prioritize the group over the individual. There is less freedom to choose who and what is in their inner and outer social circles. For them, family, loyalty, duty, community well-being, social harmony, unity, and self-sacrifice may take more precedence than uniqueness, self-determination, and competitiveness (Shulruf et al., 2007). Furthermore, self-worth, identity, and happiness for those who endorse collectivist worldviews can depend on roles and relationships and being attentive to the needs of others rather than on meeting individual needs. People from collectivist cultures benefit from the dialectical thinking of appreciating contradictions as not opposites but interdependent, complementary, and inseparable (valuing the yin and yang) (G. Liu & An, 2021).

A third cultural viewpoint is collaborative, which is different from collective or individualistic because this cultural perspective is not controlled or limited by the goals of the individual or the collective whole. Both can be indifferent to social inequities (Suh & Lee, 2017). Instead, attention and sensitivity to others and those in "out-groups" and to collective wellness and wholeness are expected to lead to more individual and collective awareness, empathy, and growth. Collaborative norms are interdependent, communal, and dialectical (both/and) and therefore (a) are inclusive of innovative resolutions that sometimes match things that would otherwise not coexist, (b) create opportunities for opposites to find overlapping intersections and synergy, (c) foster creativity for win-win strategies and solutions, and (d) expand capacity beyond either/or solutions by creating third, fourth, fifth, and more options. As Blume (2020) noted about many Indigenous cultures, people who value interconnectedness do not express individuality at the expense of others but promote self-actualization to advance their well-being and the well-being and actualization of others and the community. Regardless of culture, however, people with a strong sense of self are more likely to act assertively and speak up for themselves and others (Aoki et al., 2017).

Learning Safety and Control

As a martial artist, coauthor Linden has a different perspective on creating and maintaining boundaries. He has been practicing and teaching aikido, a nonviolent Japanese martial art, for 50 years and using his practice as a laboratory to study the body in movement and conflict. His understanding of boundaries is closely related to the question of safety. One of the ways that he demonstrates this to his students is to punch them in the stomach (lightly, of course). He then asks them why their stomach hurts. The obvious and usual answer is that he punched them. Of course, that is quite true, but it is not helpful.

He then asks his students to punch him. When they try, he blocks the punch. He teaches them that there are two forms of safety. One form of safety comes from the other person not attacking you. The second form of safety comes from your skilled ability to protect yourself. This means that you must have the physical, emotional, and cognitive skills to protect yourself if the other person tries to do something to hurt you. The first kind of safety is how the world might ideally be, and the second is how the world is. We shouldn't have to protect ourselves and our boundaries; we should be safe by virtue of nobody wishing to attack us. We hope families and societies are built around this type of safety, and we also want to empower people to create safety for themselves right now.

The issue of domination and privilege is related to safety and control. It is important to note that the distinction between appropriate or inappropriate domination is measured less by abstract ideas of good and evil and more by the degree to which a behavior undermines or helps the self-determination and health of the recipient. Therefore, an individual who is overfunctioning as a friend, helper, parent, or ally may contribute to the dynamics of harmful domination. Well-intentioned individuals who are not sensitive or responsive to the limits and needs of others may overstep boundaries and intrude. No matter their motivation, their behaviors are negatively imposing and interfering rather than helpful.

From a martial arts point of view, it is appropriate and necessary to learn self-defense.[3] Self-defense skills involve increasing awareness of what happens in one's body during the conflict. Linden's approach to teaching aikido includes specific exercises for helping people experience how emotions/body actions, such as anxiety, rage, guilt, shame, spacing out, and numbness, make it difficult to focus our attention and move smoothly and efficiently. It is counterintuitive, but if fighting is necessary, the best state to fight out of is one of kindness, relaxation, and stability. Achieving this physical-emotional state takes practice. It includes taking time to stop conflicts in action, set aside the actual problem, and find control by balancing breathing, body, and movement. The exercises detailed later in the chapter will show how.

Safety Issues in Exploring Boundaries

It's important to face powerlessness and pain to understand and live positively with them. However, it can be difficult to understand and learn better ways to respond to distress and conflicts if you are not safe or do not feel safe. We believe some guidelines are essential in creating interpersonal and personal safety. You can decide whether these suggestions will be helpful to you in dealing with conflicts with others.

- Keep your body calm and open as you dialogue your differences.
- Listen carefully to the entirety of what others say instead of assuming their positions, beliefs, values, and behaviors.
- Use your curiosity to understand the person better. Ask questions to become familiar with the perspective the other person inhabits. Given that all

---

[3] "Martial arts" is a vast category and often a gendered practice. For example, Louie (2014) talks about martial arts' relationship with manhood and masculinities in Chinese culture and the bilateral influence with Western masculinities.

our viewpoints are limited, be curious about how your limited viewpoint impairs your ability to see the other person's perspective.

- Take time to understand how the conflict affects each other and search for mutual needs and shared goals.
- Extend your curiosity to explore whether differences might have degrees of congruence, be complementary, or have added value if allowed to coexist.
- Clarify terms. Often people do not speak each other's language. Consider cocreating a list of labels or jargon that others might perceive as demeaning, isolating, or dismissive. It can be helpful to ask, "What does that word mean to you?" to develop understanding rather than expand the vocabulary deemed off-limits.
- Appreciate differences to recognize cultural and personal assumptions that guide and misguide discussions.
- Appreciate differences to promote learning and more options for growth. Appreciating differences allows people to respect and value each other and brainstorm mutually beneficial solutions, even when they do not share perspectives.
- Engage with the other person for mutual brainstorming to explore beyond binary solutions—searching for third, fourth, and more options.
- If or when someone becomes discouraged and wants to drop out of engaging, asking a compassionate, neutral third party to help understand disagreements and explore win-win options may help in the decision to keep engaging or end the relationship.

Resolving disagreements requires creating space for discomfort and sharing meaningful perspectives and experiences in the discussion. Yet many individuals are too scared of bringing verbal or physical violence on themselves by saying the "wrong things" to the wrong people. Because it can be challenging to know who's "safe," it's difficult to speak out on important topics. If your goal is never to cause other people to feel uncomfortable or you're worried about what others will do to you with their discomfort, then you can hardly say anything. Discussions about climate change, religion, racism, immigration, COVID-19, mpox, abortion, and gun control carry clear signals that potentially threaten those who might disagree. Some people fear having any conversation about the rights of LGBTQIA+ people for similar reasons. Voluntary segregation and vigilant separation sometimes result when people want to feel safe from those with different views.

As mentioned earlier, "feeling safe" and "being safe" are different. For example, people who have been traumatized often develop coping strategies that amount to anesthesia or numbing, but being numb, people can't act to create actual safety. In contrast, something may feel unsafe because it reminds you of a traumatic past, although you are safe in the present. Opening up may feel unsafe, but this openness may be the foundation for becoming safer. Openness helps you be more aware of the boundaries of others and yourself, strengthening your resilience by helping you make more informed decisions. But if you are open to others yet unable to protect yourself from attack or internalizing their negativity, then being open can be unsafe.

When you plan to dialogue with someone, especially about a controversial and conflicting topic, take time together to define safety guidelines before starting the dialogue. If a predialogue discussion isn't possible, negotiating safety guidelines during a conflict may be a constructive path forward and cool the tension between opponents. What do you need from others during a conflict? What can you offer so that difficult conversations are productive? What do you need from yourself so that difficult conversations can be safe and productive? A collaborative strategy helps manage difficult situations.

What Assertiveness Is

The word *assertive* does not conjure positive connotations for some people. It may reflect the self-promotion, pushiness, and even recklessness associated with advocacy across the political spectrum. Assertiveness is very different from a bullying attitude of "I'm going to speak my damn mind, no matter what people think," unhindered by social restraints and empathy. Similar to *power*, when people use the word *assertive*, they often mean aggressive, self-centered, and hurtful actions. With these actions, these people are trying to secure their personal needs at the unjustified expense of those around them. When that happens, the person is *using* another person and operating with aggressive actions.

When members of marginalized groups make their opinions and needs known, they are often accused of being aggressive. This dynamic is present in most situations involving people with different levels of social power; the person with less social power is ignored or labeled as aggressive if they assert their viewpoint and needs. This dismissal and oppression happen to some minority groups more than others (Cortina et al., 2013). Women, for example, are often victims of gender-based power differentials. Men, in general, talk over, interrupt, or ignore women while women are talking (Chira, 2017). When men make their opinions known, they are seen as assertive, whereas women are often accused of being aggressive for the same behavior. Similarly, Black men are perceived to be aggressive due to racism and negative stereotypes of them throughout many systems, including the news media and prime-time television (Najdowski, 2023).

We want to use *assertiveness* to represent ethical and life-affirming ways of presenting oneself and living based on the integration of power and love. Assertiveness is the ability to act on one's behalf, based on awareness of one's needs, limits, feelings, thoughts, and values, while allowing the same for others. A primary example of assertiveness is when we speak our needs, feelings, thoughts, limits, and requests in a clear, kindhearted, firm, and respectful way and are open to hearing those of others. Acting assertively offers a better chance of interacting successfully with people who disagree with us and provides an option for those who don't want to be aggressive by being insensitive or be passive by assuming a victim role.

In this definition, we need to acknowledge that systemic oppression expressed through daily microaggressions weakens people significantly (Fattoracci et al., 2020) and limits their ability to be assertive. For instance, when people are often treated poorly for their racial/ethnic and sexual/gender identity, they feel unsafe speaking out in certain environments and may have fewer places that provide safety.

Sometimes, people act passively in a manner that is not directly to their benefit because they are more introverted or highly caring and agreeable (Kammrath et al., 2015). They may be sensitive to the energy, feelings, needs, and behaviors of other people or situations. Other times, people may become overstimulated. Their perceived "passivity" results from emotional flooding and being overwhelmed by confusing information and strong sensations. For others, their perceived "passivity" may result from cultural norms that value harmony and emotional control. Hence, passivity may represent power, emotional maturity, strength, and values of connection, balance, and respect in relationships. In such cases, speaking up or disagreeing is counterintuitive and may conflict with cultural values. Some aggressive people might be expressing their cultural and family values. Others may be reenacting the dynamics of those who have hurt them. Consequently, they may have internalized and embraced dominance and control as a survival response.

Developing the skills to think of and act for oneself while thinking of and acting for others is a sign of relational maturity. Passive-aggressiveness, instead, incorporates both the harmful and unstable behaviors of aggressiveness that involve choosing for and demeaning others with the ineffective and unstable behaviors of passivity by being indirect and allowing others to choose for you.

Assertiveness, in contrast, incorporates the powerful behaviors of being self-determined and direct while incorporating the loving behaviors of being sensitive to self and others. Assertiveness represents both self-respect and respect for others (Hotta, 2013). Aggression and passivity are primarily self-protective behaviors that often lead to experiences of isolation, while assertiveness opens up the potential for authenticity, connection, and understanding. A person's ability to be engaged and assertive predicts their happiness, especially when they feel a sense of self-efficacy in meeting their needs (Hasannia, 2017).

Now we turn our attention again to a discussion of power. Power without love tends to be cruel. Love without power tends to be ineffective. Again, we want to use and reimagine words with a bad reputation (*power*) while preserving the meaning of *power* for people who don't want to manipulate others and don't want to be pushovers. Here we prefer to differentiate by using the word *power* for ethical, compassionate behavior. With this definition, a person can be strong, loving, and powerful. Linden refers to this capability as a *centered state* that we can achieve in different ways (Linden, 2018):

- Speaking structurally, the body is balanced and strain free.
- Speaking functionally, this state allows stable, mobile, and balanced movement.
- Speaking psychologically, this state involves staying anchored in internal self-awareness while simultaneously reaching out into the world.
- Speaking spiritually, it integrates the body states of power and love.
- Speaking ethically, this creates an awareness of and concern for the effects of one's actions on the well-being of others.

With a centered state and other assertiveness skills, you can rely on yourself as your power source. As a client of coauthor Beckstead noted, "Power (ethical, compassionate behavior) is a choice. It doesn't need to be earned, is not a competition for a limited resource, is available to everyone, and does not come from outside myself. It is something I can choose to do or not do. It's always available."

Mindfulness skills allow us to act assertively by giving us more ability to choose what we focus on and observe instead of judging our experience and that of others. Our human mind can develop this kind attention (Siegel, 2019) and loving awareness (Kornfield, 2018). Centered-state and mindfulness skills can give us a calm openness to recognize and understand our thoughts, feelings, needs, and limits. This mind-body awareness leads to accountability and self-direction. As Wade (2021) explained,

> Mindfulness gives us the courage and compassion to look our own emotions and worries in the face without fear or defensiveness or judgment, to cut through our own instincts for self-protection so that we can see our own hearts honestly, our goodness and flaws, and so we can use that knowledge in the world to be who we say we are. To both recognize and actualize in ourselves who we aspire to be. (p. 93)

A calm openness offers the space to understand the behavior and intentions of others by mindfully asking about and hearing about their beliefs, feelings, needs, and limits. This ability allows a person to understand misunderstandings, differentiate thoughts from emotions, and get emotionally close to someone without losing independence (*differentiation of self*) (Hung & Chan, 2022). From a place of calm openness and mindful intention, dialogue can happen, and we can think and feel to grasp different people's contradictory perspectives and allow for curiosity and mutual empathy (Jordan, 2000).

Dialoguing differs from debating and trying to win an argument by proving you are right and the other person is wrong. The primary purpose of dialogue should not be for conformity, agreement, or even peace but for clarity that will help differentiate yourself from others. Often, differentiation implies rightness or wrongness, such as, "I am right, and you are wrong" or "I am different and therefore wrong." However, being different does not mean someone has to be wrong. Developing self-awareness and valuing perspectives allow for brain-storming solutions that consider all views, needs, and limits.

Assertiveness skills can help you and the other person engage in a dis-agreement without becoming disagreeable. If you are stable and compas-sionate, you will not be controlled by an insult, rejection, attack, negative emotion, misunderstanding, or other types of conflict. Assertiveness, there-fore, can be an intra- and interpersonal protective factor (Vagos & Pereira, 2016). Assertiveness also includes the wisdom not to say anything when you know it is unsafe or unproductive. Perhaps the other person does not respect you or is not open to change despite your requests. Assertiveness skills will be a foundation for understanding the other person's actions and limitations. This foundation will help you make decisions based on collaboration and equality/equity.

Speaking your truth even when the other person won't hear you can also be assertive. This is called nonaggressive resistance because speaking out reclaims your space, states your feelings (particularly to yourself), and reinforces your values and needs. This assertion allows you to protect yourself, reject what does not fit you, and set limits. Advocating for yourself promotes nonconformity and diversity and helps you see yourself as being as worthy as others. Acts of non-acceptance characterize civil rights movements. Mahatma Gandhi adopted the term *civil disobedience* from Henry David Thoreau to describe his life strategy of acting nonaggressively by refusing to cooperate with injustice. For Gandhi, civil disobedience was based on a devotion to truth (Teach Democracy, 2024). People engaged in social justice are focused on disrupting the social flow for a larger goal of equality. As Shirley Chisholm, the first Black woman elected to the United States Congress, expressed, "If they don't give you a seat at the table, bring a folding chair." As organizer, activist, and U.S. Representative John Lewis expressed, "Do not get lost in a sea of despair. Be hopeful, be opti-mistic. Our struggle is not the struggle of a day, a week, a month, or a year, it is the struggle of a lifetime. Never, ever be afraid to make some noise and get in good trouble, necessary trouble." Advocating for oneself, however, can result in losing friends, family, communities, lovers, jobs, business relationships, or, for some, one's life. If you desire mutual respect, asking for this in relationships can sort out those who don't have assertiveness skills and enable you to seek out others who want mutual respect.

However, for some, family loyalty and respect are important cultural val-ues. Asserting oneself is viewed as an act of rebellion and disrespect. People in this situation must decide whether advocating for themselves and others during minor disagreements fits them rather than the collective value. Consequently, to maintain harmony, they may assert themselves only when their boundaries are violated or someone else is in danger of harm (Mitamura, 2018).

Assertiveness is directing your energy to develop who you are. In this way, assertiveness is not just about self-determination but includes forgiveness, grieving, humility, and respect. All are loving, powerful responses to conflicts. Each requires skills to remain open and loving while facing pain. The mind-body state of being open and soft helps people live with and accept the unacceptable and contemplate things they don't want, such as disappointments, traumas, deaths, losses, rejection, disapproval, and mistakes. Instead of rejecting what can't be avoided or has already happened, people can learn to acknowledge and adapt by deciding where to invest their energy. Instead of wasting energy resisting what you can't control, spend time being curious about the reality of the situation and having compassion for how something happened.

Assertiveness skills, therefore, can provide you with compassionate strength to not stay stuck on feelings associated with a negative event. Forgiveness involves understanding, learning, and recovering from offenses. Humility and grieving involve letting go of what you cannot have. Humility, grieving, forgiveness, and assertiveness give you the compassionate power to move in your direction within the limitations of what you cannot change.

Which Skills and Knowledge Must a Person Have to Be Assertive?

When studying assertiveness, the body's responses are often ignored but are an important source of sensitivity. For Linden, training to respond to attacks nonviolently made it very clear that feelings of violence and other emotions are physical actions in the body. The quickest and most efficient ways to make deep changes would require working directly with the body.

People generally do not have the skills to regulate the body as a foundation for conflict resolution. Even people who have learned the skills will not find them available in an actual conflict—unless they have consciously practiced them regularly.

Part of the difficulty in managing emotions is that English is set up with a passive stance. For example, one may think, "You made me so mad when you stepped on my pet turtle." This common language implies that the offended party is powerless over their emotions. You indeed stepped on my turtle, but if I remember that emotions are actions that I do in my body, then it is clear that you stepped on my turtle, and I made myself angry at you and what you did. Other people do not have to be in control of our emotions. If we give them that power, they will be in control. With more awareness and tools, we have more possibility of self-regulation and choosing what we do in our bodies within the limits of what's possible on any given day. It is our responsibility to choose the emotions we do. Using assertiveness tools for emotional distress can mitigate social conflicts and unnecessary suffering.

The five skills detailed below are straightforward, easy, and broadly practical based on clinical and training experiences. These skills are simple enough that people can learn them easily, use them effectively immediately, and even teach them to others. They are neither philosophy nor psychology. They are based on physiology. The skills reliably produce similar results for almost every person. As we noted earlier, emotions are actions we do in the body. So, to live assertively, start with the body as your foundational resource. We all have a body, and we can access it with practice.

Recognizing the Distress Response

Assertiveness is difficult because we are biologically and culturally predisposed to defensiveness, resistance, and aggression—or toward resignation, passivity, and spacing out. How is this expressed in the body? When challenged, stressed, or overwhelmed—by anything from playing a difficult piano piece or trying to deal with an angry boss to a violent assault or a serious injury—our natural tendency is to constrict or collapse. We constrict or collapse our attention, breathing, posture, vision, and movement. This distress response is usually experienced as fear, anger, frustration, worry, effort, strain, shock, weakness, resignation, numbness, or dissociation. Linden made up the word *smallify* to describe the action of getting small, whether that smallness is a clenched fist, shallow breathing, body numbness, narrowed viewpoint, or seeking to be invisible to self and others. Becoming small is common in all distress responses, from fear to dissociation to anger and other similar reactions.

These powerful physical reactions can take over the rational mind and compassionate heart and move our thinking and acting toward oppositional and violent ways of dealing with challenges. This reduces our awareness of the other person, and we often dehumanize the other person and ourselves, resulting in more distress.

Just as you cannot dig a hole in the water, you cannot stop being angry. Instead of trying to suppress anger, start doing a more useful behavior. Employ compassion or a behavior that is collaborative and respectful. The antidote to the physical state of smallness is centered expansiveness. Calm alertness and compassionate strength move our thinking and acting toward reasonable, empathic, and peaceful ways of handling conflicts. Living in the present with relaxed awareness, compassionate curiosity, and humility breaks the chains that bind people to reenacting their dysfunctional past.

Caution

When the distress response gets locked into the body, this is known as the trauma state. You should be aware that in any group of 25 people, there are likely to be some survivors of sexual victimization, identity oppression, minority discrimination, or other traumas. Body awareness exercises can sometimes trigger people into painful emotional states. These five skills are also effective for empowerment in trauma recovery work. However, working with trauma is delicate and requires professional skills and understanding. We advise providers and instructors to assess participants and clients for trauma history before using these techniques. The three guidelines described in the next paragraph may be helpful when engaging others in experiential exercises (and may also be helpful in everyday life). If you are concerned that you may become triggered by reading about and practicing body awareness, keep breathing, stay relaxed and steady, and consider seeking qualified professional help.

Three safety guidelines for exploring self-awareness include (1) if you don't want to do an exercise or answer a question, feel free to decline and skip it; (2) if you are wondering why a therapist/teacher/facilitator is asking or asserting something, feel free to ask; and (3) whatever your response is to a question or an exercise, it is information to understand. Assertiveness is acceptance without judgments of inferiority, badness, or disgust. That doesn't mean everything is acceptable; assertiveness is built on a foundation of kindness, humility, and effectiveness.

The knowledge of your body's responses is important for understanding your life. However, some people have learned to be very disconnected from their bodies, so their body awareness is limited. Some gender-diverse individuals suffer from gender-body incongruence, so paying attention to gendered parts of the body may be aversive. If you have learned to distrust or not feel what you are feeling, then be gentle with yourself and allow time and patience as you practice and develop the ability to notice, observe, and stay connected to yourself. With these guidelines in place, we invite you to expand your body awareness at your own pace and explore if the following skills can help you act with more power and love.

Five Body-Oriented Assertiveness Skills: Developing a Centered State

Skill #1: Relax the Core

Some people experience relaxation as dangerous because they learned it feels safer always to be on guard and responsible. This trauma state is like driving with the parking brakes engaged. It cannot be a long-term solution because the constant stiffness is tiring and ineffective and restricts personal growth. It becomes impossible to keep some things in and others out. Hypervigilance is sometimes believed to be a state of increased awareness. Actually, this is a state of reduced awareness because it is usually a constricted, tense, always-on-guard, fatigued energy searching only for dangers, and the body's inner state is ignored. When some people think of relaxation, they think about being zoned out and limp. Linden defines relaxation as an appropriate effort to get the job done. A relaxed core allows you to do as much and as little as you need. This section will teach you how to develop a relaxed core. We invite you to consider the following exploration.

Drop or soften your tongue if it has been pressed to the roof of your mouth, and let it hang without effort in your mouth. What do you notice happening in your body? Some people feel the muscles relax around the face, jaw, neck, or shoulders. If you don't notice those muscles relaxing, try tightening your tongue to the roof of your mouth and then softening it. What do you notice happening in your body, if anything? Now let your shoulders hang loose. Imagine you have cotton balls under your armpits and imagine releasing the cotton balls and dropping your armpits, and notice the effect on your body. Now bring the movement of breathing into your belly. Try to bring your breathing even into your lower back. What do you notice happens when you bring your breath as low as possible? Now let your legs hang loosely from their joints. Drop your pelvic floor muscles. Let the muscles around your anus and your genitals open up. What did you notice happening in your body? Though some people experience openness and relaxation as vulnerability, it is easy to demonstrate that it frees the body for more effective movement. To test this, experiment with tightening your tongue, shoulders, belly, and anus and walk around the room. Then loosen these areas and walk around the room. How would you describe the difference? Which is easier? Which is more empowered, centered, and balanced? Which is safer?

When you inhale, where is the movement in your body? Up into your chest, perhaps? And perhaps your stomach contracts? That is fear or startle breathing. Instead of forcing your breathing into some externally prescribed pattern, when you inhale, feel the gentle movement of expansion in the belly, the chest, and the back so that they all move simultaneously. When you exhale, allow the body to sink inward. When you let the core of your body get soft and open, you will feel the movement of breathing throughout your body. This relaxed breathing will counteract anxious panic breathing. Notice the difference between breathing with your whole body soft or tightening your belly and breathing high into the chest. Observe the effects on your body, feelings, and thinking when you try both types of breathing.

Skill #2: Smile Inside

Most people have something or someone that makes them happy or something or someone they love or who loves them. This can be a family member, a friend, a child, a pet, a passion, a flower, a favorite food, a favorite song, an idea, a memory, a place, or an accomplishment. Some people may have to search hard to find something positive, but there is almost always something. For example, Linden worked with a client who felt his life consisted only of pain. The author asked the student to consider that we gain wisdom through pain. That's the good news. The bad news is that there's more good news coming. That brought a smile to the student's face.

Spend a moment thinking about whatever it is that makes you smile inside. What happens in your body? Most people experience an expansive warmth, especially in their chest. Try walking around as you carry this smile inside with you. How is this experience different from walking around angry or afraid? Some people believe their anger keeps them safe. Are you more powerful when embodying love or anger or fear? Most people notice that when they do anger and fear, it weakens their body.[4]

Consider using an inner smile during a conflict to stabilize your body in compassionate power. Imagine how this could affect your relationship with your opponent. Would it help you avoid reacting to the other person's fear and anger with your fear and anger? Use this loving feeling to anchor yourself when thinking about difficulties in your life or when faced with a challenging situation. Use your inner smile to project love at others as a protective force for yourself. Here's an example from a participant who attended a workshop with Linden:

> I was at a meeting called by an industry regulatory organization. There was a lot of vocal resistance to some of the suggestions. The regulator was being very hard-line, accepting no "excuses." We stopped for a break, and as I got a coffee, I started a conversation with the angriest of the objectors. I kept checking that my body was relaxed and tried maintaining an "inner smile" while listening and talking to her. When we all returned to the table, she spoke calmly and reasonably, and the meeting ended with some compromises being accepted by all. The regulator had seen me talking to my "opponent" and thanked me for my behind-the-scenes input, which had transformed the atmosphere. He said everyone was asking what he had put in the tea!

Skill #3: Shine

Imagine you are a star, firefly, or light bulb. What do you do? You shine and glow. Feel all of your skin radiating outward in every direction as far out as

---

4   See a video demonstration of this at https://www.youtube.com/watch?v=OeZF9zfu3yg.

you wish or can. How does that feel? Most people experience this as expansive, spacious, and calm. Some people find it easier to imagine reaching their awareness outward in six directions toward something tangible. These directions are below you, above you, to your right and left, and toward your front and back. Imagine breathing and reaching out in all six directions for something you desire or that is symbolically meaningful. If expanding and extending your awareness beyond your body is difficult, then return to smiling inside and focus on where and how you feel this love in your body. Try letting that feeling expand, glow, grow, spread, and extend from your heart through your body to grow into personal strength and loving action. Focus on this feeling as long as you want.

Here's an example from a workshop participant:

> I have been teaching your techniques to call on internal courage before talking to others or in preparation for hearing unwelcome words. . . . Yesterday, a woman from a small town in Saurashtra region of Gujarat [India] called me up to report on her experience. She has been having difficult relations with her brothers and their families. They tend to look down upon her husband and spread rumors about them. It is stressful when she encounters them on the street without notice. She tends to feel like not looking at them or running away. This time, though, she handled it differently. She did the six-direction-reaching [Shining] when she saw an older brother coming her way. After that, she handled the situation without the usual panic and went about her way. She repeated the same experience when encountering her younger brother, who has a sharp tongue. She was quite pleased and hopeful when she talked on the phone.

Skill #4: Power Sitting

The development of personal power starts with postural stability. Stand in front of a chair and get ready to sit down. With each hand, touch your hip joints, where the legs bend at the top of the pelvic bowl. Imagine a line from the hip joints to the tailbone. Push your tailbone back and down along that line. This will lean your torso slightly forward and to a sitting position. This way of sitting down creates a solid posture without effort. Most people feel calm, alert, and dignified in this posture.

Here is how a workshop participant described the benefit of power sitting:

> During a local chapter meeting of an anti-racist and social change group, I led about 40 attendees in one of Paul [Linden]'s exercises: Power Sitting. After demonstrating how to perform

Image © 2023 by Joshua Brown. Printed with permission.

the exercise with two volunteers, we broke into groups of three and spent ten minutes learning how to sit powerfully. Seeing the look of pleasant surprise in their eyes and hearing their laughter when they realized they were easily resisting the full weight of someone leaning against them was satisfying. Once we had reassembled in our seats, one attendee asked, "So how is this exercise practical?" Before I could respond, another attendee said, "Well, I could see how if I'm in a meeting and I'm feeling myself getting irritated or collapsing emotionally, I can readjust so that I am sitting in this way that makes me feel strong and safe. Feeling that way, I am much more likely to act compassionately and confidently in the face of a verbal conflict."

Skill #5: Power Walking

There is a standing equivalent of the sitting posture. Paying attention to how you naturally or unconsciously walk can be helpful. Walk around barefoot and observe how your legs and feet move your body forward. Many people swing a leg forward, using the weight of the leg to drag their body forward. Some people put a foot on the floor out in front of them and use it to pull themselves forward. Others feel that when their foot is behind them, they use it to push themselves forward. People often notice that their gait and walking change depending on their mental state.

Next, stand with your feet together and jump up in the air. To jump up, you push down. This can be applied to walking. Push to the rear with the back leg to walk forward more efficiently. One way to experience this is to have a partner stand behind you and hold you back as you walk forward. Your partner pulls back and offers resistance to your walking. They should use enough resistance to be useful but not so much that you can't move forward. You will notice that you move forward by pushing backward with the rear leg. People generally notice that when they walk with awareness of the thrust of the feet down and back, their walk becomes more erect, precise, purposeful, and energetic. It is mechanically more efficient, powerful, and more psychologically confident and alert.

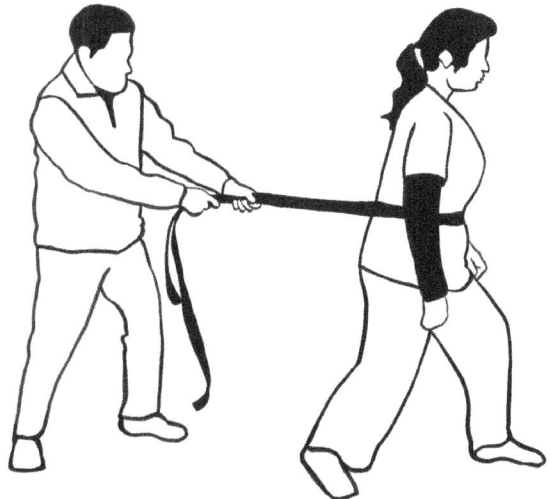

Image © 2023 by Joshua Brown. Printed with permission.

Remembering the Somatic Skills

A key to assertiveness is owning your space, which is helped by the body's actions of stability, spaciousness, and kindness. However, when you are over-taken emotionally by something in yourself or your environment, it can be dif-ficult to remember to use the body awareness techniques that you have learned in this chapter. There is a simple sentence that will help: ***Relaxed love shines powerfully.*** The first three words will remind you to relax your tongue and core and breathe, smile inside, and radiate the love outward. The last word covers the two power stances when sitting or moving.

Of course, there is more to assertiveness than body openness, love, and power. Another element is self-defense. It is much easier to speak up for yourself when you know you can protect yourself within limits, of course, against physi-cal attacks and verbal insults.

Developing Cognitive Self-Defense

People with stigmatized and marginalized identities often have to face other people's judgments about them, and experiencing and internalizing these judg-ments can be painful and damaging. Rejection can hurt emotionally and physi-cally, and the shame and pain it causes can box people into passive, aggressive, or passive-aggressive reactions.

Self-defense against verbal attacks is much the same as protection from physical attacks. Body-oriented skills that develop calm alertness and compas-sionate power create a grounded presence. This provides the foundation for cognitively staying separate from harmful assertions and staying true to oneself. Suppose we can relax and stabilize ourselves in our own experience and beliefs. In that case, we can examine whether the rejection is because of what we did or how others are judging our self-expression. Understanding the logic of lan-guage can be very helpful in creating and maintaining these boundaries. It will put words to your experience in a clearer and more organized fashion and help you detect false assertions.

An assertion is a statement about something; for example, "The cat is on the couch." It's important to know the accuracy of assertions. The cat may not be on the couch. She may be in the kitchen, eating the salmon you wanted for dinner. Accurate assertions are road maps that tell us how to act to achieve a purpose. The statements "This is a red pillow" and "This is a beautiful pillow" both seem to have the same language structure, but the second statement is more about the values of the person making the statement than the pillow.

Many people have internalized statements such as, "You are worthless," believing such statements are accurate and true. However, these statements are not about the person being told they are worthless. Add "to me" with value assertions: "You are worthless *to me.*" Without those last two words, the structure of this value statement makes it easy for people to accept it as a true statement about them. Cognitive self-defense allows an individual to understand that valuing is an action done by someone. Being told you are or are not worth something is not about you but about the individual who is "worthing" you. The hearer needs to evaluate the accuracy of the statement *for the listener.* In this actuality, the listener is a witness to themselves. With this understanding of the logic of assertions, the listener is free to think for themselves as they are worthwhile to themselves and do things that represent their worth to themselves, like finding others who will value them.

Similarly, when someone does not feel "good enough," it typically means they were conditioned to believe their worth, value, and safety are based on their performance. This usually leads to failing impractical expectations and judging themselves negatively because of this impossibility. We may try to please someone who cannot be pleased and not understand that everyone is "not good enough" to accomplish this unrealistic expectation. Understanding the logic of assertions, you are free to evaluate if you are good enough to meet realistic and practical expectations, your goals, or someone else's. For example, you might say, "I am good enough for me." Accepting our realistic limitations and those of others frees us to invest in more compatible people and activities where we feel good about ourselves.

Cultural attitudes can restrict people's ability to accept or reject beliefs and direct their own lives. This cultural pressure can arise from many competing certainties, including religious, philosophical, political, or familial. People can feel ashamed to go in a specific direction in many circumstances. One strategy to remedy this cultural pressure is to help people recognize the interpretive nature of our experiences. We must interpret and make sense of this information beyond simply receiving input and data from various sources. The story we tell about our experiences (Brown, 2017) is our choice and something we can determine based on what feels right to us and is ultimately good for us.

One test of any belief system or identity is what you do in your body as you live the values associated with that belief system/identity. It's not absolute, but the values, beliefs, and norms that lead you to relaxed muscles, free breathing, stable posture, ease of movement, calm alertness, and compassion will likely be healthful, constructive, and life affirming. Remember, though, that past trauma can prompt you to avoid beneficial things. If your sexual, gender, faith, and cultural expression is distressing, examine which values, beliefs, and norms provide you with health and stability. The outcome of this practice is relative to individuals' deepest commitments and distinct views on what is most important for them. While diverging in these broader matters, the coauthors of this chapter are united in advocating for a gentle, mindful approach to holding in mind competing expectations and directing one's own life.

Yielding and Adapting: Yes, And

Keeping yourself in the body state of power and love will provide the steadiness needed to speak and act confidently. Understanding the logic of assertions and value statements will help you develop independent thinking and reject lies expressed by aggressive or misinformed individuals. These skills will help you act according to what is healthful for you in your perceptions, needs, limits, and values.

There is another skill that helps deal with conflicts and verbal attacks. The basic aikido strategy for dealing with a physical attack is to feel where the attacker wishes to move and then join that stream of movement to assume control. Improv comedy describes this approach as "Yes, and . . . ," which means that the receiving improviser acknowledges what the other improviser says and expands on it in a direction that the receiving improviser chooses to go. The aikido technical term for this is "yielding." Yielding is the opposite of surrendering or attacking. When we yield, we keep our body open and are aware of and sensitive to the other person's experience and actions, and go along with the person for a while. If we go along with and pay attention to what the person is expressing, we will come to understand better their experience and can decide if we want to think that way or not. We then can use our power to do what we want and not waste energy in opposition, avoidance, collapse, or submission.

A *yielding-adapting, yes-and* mindset is based on using skills of acknowledging facts, while keeping our body relaxed, loving, and open so that we can respond to the present situation in an ethical and effective manner.

You may benefit from becoming distinctly aware of the differences between you and the other person: *Yes-No-And* (for example, *Yes*, I understand and know this will work for you, *No*, that doesn't work for me, *And* instead, this other thing will work for me.). Adding a *no* to your response may help you understand more clearly what doesn't work for you. You don't have to worry about the other person's opinions. Instead, your task is to separate your opinions and decide what you want to do. Yielding is different from being passive and allowing someone or something to control you. Being firm and stable is different from brutally trying to control someone else.

You must be relaxed, balanced, strong, and soft to yield and adapt to an attacker's movement. The verbal equivalent is not fighting back against the words of the attack. For example, if your boss says you wrote a terrible proposal, you might not want to say, "That's not right. It's an excellent paper! I did a lot of work on it!" It would probably be more useful to say, "I understand you're upset. I will gladly redo it if you help me understand what you need." You aren't agreeing that you did something terrible or are terrible. You are asserting how and where you want the discussion to go. Instead of being focused on changing your boss's mind, you are accepting your boss's experience while validating your experience. You are joining with the person but not colluding with their false idea of you (Martin, 2023). Yielding-adapting is a way of not resisting or submitting but eliciting help from your "opponent." Of course, this would be very unlikely to work well with an abuser. But it may help with people who don't understand you or are prejudiced against you. Regardless of the other person's response, you invest your energy in affirming yourself and what you will do to meet your needs.

We can use a similar yielding-adapting approach to respond to what happens inside us. For example, when a person feels worthless, almost undoubtedly they learned to think they are worthless from how someone treated them. If they say, "I am NOT worthless," that directly fights against the attacker's opinion and puts energy into the statement the person is resisting. Suppose someone tells themselves an affirmation such as "I am valuable" to stop or get rid of the feeling of worthlessness. In that case, the person is fighting the statement and wastes energy on an internal battle. Agreeing with a false evaluation is acting passively. When we either surrender to or fight our negative feelings, we strengthen the old stimulus-response connection. What do you notice happens in your body when you respond negatively to your experience? Do you feel freer and more empowered? Most likely, you are reinforcing the distress response and smallifying some aspect(s) of your mind-body. We'll describe below (under "Frying Words") how to use body openness to express negative self-beliefs and replace the distress response associated with those beliefs.

Regarding affirmations, explore how it feels to respond to your internal experience with a yielding-adapting response. Consider keeping your body open and saying, "*Yes*, I will, for now, feel I'm worthless, given my history and what was done to me, *and*, I know currently or would prefer to believe I am worthwhile to me." This allows for acceptance, flow, and self-direction. This loving, self-determined attitude reflects what you wish your reality would be and saying it will provide you with constant reminders to work toward it. You are strengthening your own message to yourself. Affirmation is a way to practice how you want to treat yourself. In this way, you do not have to get others to agree with you. Saying it to yourself sets the stage: This is the message I want to believe and what I need to live better. This self-directed focus gives you more control over those things that can be controlled by you. Affirmations, like values, provide direction and can be soothing and reassuring when a person feels shame/anxiety or oppression. Affirmations help people develop their identity and guide their actions.

Similar to a traffic intersection, yielding-adapting promotes diversity. It allows others to "go their own way" (say *Yes* to their reality/autonomy) while you remain focused on the direction that is best for you (*And* for me). Another way of saying this is "Instead of fighting evil, start good" or, as we mentioned earlier, instead of trying to stop a behavior, start doing a more useful behavior. Responding to distress needs to include de-escalating fear, shame, and anger. Yet de-escalation is not a negative process of stopping feelings. Instead, it is a positive experience of jump-starting awareness, kindness, and power.

Martin Luther King Jr. (1957) expressed it this way: "Returning hate for hate multiplies hate, adding deeper darkness to a night already devoid of stars. Darkness cannot drive out darkness; only light can do that. Hate cannot drive out hate; only love can do that." As trauma specialist Francine Shapiro (2017) described, "There is more power to the statement 'I am loveable' than to 'He will love me.'" Viktor Frankl (1946), a Holocaust survivor, described it in this way: "Everything can be taken from a person but one thing, the last of the human freedoms—to choose one's attitude in any given set of circumstances, to choose one's own way."

Assertive, yielding-adapting actions often seem small and may not get immediate results, but they likely are good for you, and you never know what effect they have down the road.

Applying Assertiveness Skills

The following exercises are designed to help you practice assertiveness. Living assertively takes continual practice and intention. These exercises aim to develop your ability to stay connected to yourself, understand the other person/situation, and adapt positively.

Saying No

The stronger your sense of self, the more likely you can refuse what doesn't fit you. Feeling confident in saying no can give you more power and freedom to say yes to what you like. Another way of saying this is that *yes* has no meaning if *no* is not an equal option. For example, it is empowering to learn verbal and physical skills to protect yourself from being touched—whether you want the particular touch or not. Once you can say no, you are free to say yes to which touch you prefer. A *no* response is assertive by differentiating experiences and defining limits. The following exercise will increase your awareness and protection of boundaries by noticing how it feels to say no.

Explore what you do in your body when you say no. Then notice what you do in your body when you say no accompanied by whatever gesture feels right for you. Finding the gesture that feels the most powerful and true for you may take time. Does it feel different in your body if you say no without the gesture? Now bring up feelings of anger and explore how it feels to say no. Next, feel afraid and explore how it feels to say no and how you experience *no* when feeling guilty. Each emotion is a set of physical actions in the body. It takes practice to notice and feel the differences between the different emotions.

Now, explore how it feels to say no using the body-mind skills described earlier. These were (a) relax your core by dropping your tongue, armpits, breath, belly, and pelvic floor and letting your legs hang; (b) smile inside by thinking of something/someone you love; and (c) shine, expand, and grow that loving feeling. Remember to put your body in the state created by power sitting and power walking. What do you notice when you say no from a place of relaxed, loving openness? Which feeling (anger, fear, guilt, or love) gives you power and makes your *no* response stick? How do you think others would respond to each different feeling? Which experience felt like you were protecting yourself versus rejecting someone?

The next exercise may help you recognize your boundaries by noticing *when* to say no. This exercise requires you to pair up with someone who also wants to increase their body awareness regarding boundaries. Decide who will be person A and who will be person B, and stand at least 10 feet apart. Person A will walk slowly toward person B. Person B will indicate when they want person A to stop by saying, "Stop." Then, person A will return to the original position, and person B will walk toward person A until person A tells person B to stop. Share how you determined when you expressed stop. Was it something outside of you (for example, the look on the other person's face, a typical distance, or a mark on the floor)? Did you notice anything happening in your body as the other person approached?

Return to your starting positions and take turns moving toward each other, but use your body as a reference by noticing which internal reactions tell you to say, "Stop." These reactions indicate your boundary. Do your boundaries change when you feel angry, afraid, and guilty, or when practicing relaxed core, smiling inside, shining, power walking, and power sitting?

What if the person doesn't stop? If you shrink and withdraw, then you will feel intruded upon. If you are kind, strong, and calm, the other person can't invade your psychological space. The person can get physically close to you but not invade your space. From a self-defense point of view, when the attacker gets close to you, you are getting equally close to the attacker. The person who has the resources to own and control the space is the one whose space is not getting invaded. If you must fight, this peaceful state will enable you to think and move in a relaxed, coordinated way, and you will fight better.

You can test this in real time. This is accomplished by working as a pair with a trusted friend. You will take turns "slapping" the other's face with a tissue. Before you start the exercise, it is essential to adjust it to the needs of each partner. Ask permission to "attack" and how fast or strong your partner wants the attack to be. And, it's perfectly permissible and admirable for a partner to say they are not ready for this exercise yet. When you find a partner, explore how you and your "attacker" feel when "attacked" by a tissue while doing anger, guilt, and fear versus relaxing your core, smiling inside, shining, and power walking and sitting. Which state feels secure and powerful?

Frying Words

Many people have experienced situations that are associated with a painful, negative self-belief, such as "I am broken," "I am less than," "I am a failure," "I am helpless/powerless," or "I am inadequate." Notice what you do in your body reflexively when you think of that evaluation. Most likely, it will be some variation of the distress response and smallifying some aspect(s) of your mind-body. The negative evaluation is linked to the old situation in your memory and body. Saying or thinking the negative belief will call up the old body reactions, and the body reactions will call up the belief. You can break the link between the belief and the body reactions by saying the negative belief in an expansive/empowered body state and "fry" the old stimulus-response connection. In a centered state of expansiveness, kindness, and power, explore what happens when you say the negative belief clearly, loudly, and joyously. You are not agreeing with the negative words but building a new stimulus-response connection in which remembering the statement or old assault reminds you to be in your power and embody love in the present. Here you can use all the earlier exercises in stability and expansiveness. Once people have built the new connection, they can think and talk about the statement or past event/assault without the statement of the past event/assault reminding them to reject themselves and be victims as they were in the past. For coauthor Linden, acceptance and forgiveness are accomplished by thinking about something unacceptable and having the skills to feel calm, loving, open, and self-directed.

Options for Self-Development

Next we will introduce additional skills to help you move in your direction by adding to your ability to experience a variety of personal, powerful, and expansive responses.

First, something you can do when you recognize you are emotionally triggered is bring your attention to the present moment, your surroundings, or something meaningful to you. Presumably, you are triggered by reexperiencing something painful or unresolved from your past. The pain comes from doing reflexively in the present what you learned to do in the past, such as rejecting yourself with a negative self-belief. You can liberate yourself from the "shame/trauma vortex" of the past by putting your attention and focus on what stabilizes you. You can focus on your breath, your favorite music, or nature. You can express a prayer or personal affirmation. Some drop their attention to their feet for a sense of grounding and feel the pull of gravity. See how it feels to feel the pressure of pushing on the ground. Feel the earth supporting you (see "Skill #5: Power Walking" above), or feel rooted like your favorite tree. If you are sitting, feel your body being supported by the chair.

What happens in your body when you look for and enjoy your favorite color or look for what interests you in your surroundings? You can expand your sense of self by using your hearing and sense of smell to add to what you see and feel. When eating, pay attention to how each mouthful tastes, the food's textures, flavors, colors, and aroma. How does each compare to other foods on the plate? How does the flavor of this spoonful compare to other spoonfuls? What happens when you mix flavors? Moving to a different level of awareness, how does each bite of food affect your whole body? Does your feeling about a food come from feelings about your body? If you pay attention to what you feel about a food, does that feeling affect the rest of your whole body?

How do you want to respond during stressful situations? Which words, self-beliefs, and values nurture and empower you? Practice creating a centered state and saying inwardly your affirming phrase (for example, *I have value, I have worth, I belong, I'm okay/fine as I am, I matter, My feelings/needs/limits matter, I'm equal, I have myself, I can make choices about my body, My body belongs to me, Their reaction is not about me*) and notice the impact on your internal state. When you express a true statement in a centered state, that will liberate you from unhealthful habits.

Our values, ethics, and philosophy of life and what motivates us are all expressions of our identity—who we are and who we want to be. Living from self-informed values will give you self-direction. Acting from self-informed affirmations will direct you away from your distress responses and toward facilitating what's important for you. Our online worksheet[5] provides a list of values from which to choose your life direction. To identify your core values, think about how you want to feel about yourself at your 90th birthday party. What happens in your body when you focus on an affirming self-belief or value that is important to you? Paying attention to your physical responses may help you sort through which beliefs and values are beneficial to you and you choose to practice and make yours.

Another way to live by affirming self-beliefs and values is to make them part of your daily time management. What would people notice if they saw you

[5] Found at FindingCongruence.com.

living your affirming values? What would your life look like if you expressed your affirming self-beliefs and values? Which activities and long- and short-term goals do you need to schedule that would represent these self-beliefs and values? How would it feel in your body if you lived these self-beliefs and values more fully? What will you enjoy most when you live these self-beliefs and values? How would it affect others if you lived these empowering self-beliefs and values? How would living these affirming self-beliefs and values affect your ability to deal with distressing situations?

Similar to *Relaxed love shines* and embodying the value of love in a relaxed state, explore how it feels to relax your core and live a value or do an activity (for example, relaxed play, relaxed eating, relaxed eroticism, relaxed pleasure, relaxed acceptance, etc.).

Pick one or two options from the above to explore and practice during nonstress times. This practice will establish a habitual body response to get through difficult situations.

Conclusion

Living assertively means promoting self-determination, diversity, and connection and avoiding unnecessary harm. This life philosophy allows a person to define and live what feels authentic and right based on that person's faith, sexual, gender, racial/ethnic, and cultural identity while allowing others to do the same, as long as boundaries are respected. Assertiveness represents the ability to be self-aware and sensitive to others to promote interdependence and engagement. This dual awareness allows people to feel separate and together.

We advocate for relationship dynamics that allow for individuality and togetherness and social environments that make legitimate space for differences and sameness. We believe a cultural structure that celebrates safety, equity, and diversity can coexist with strong—even conflicting—personal convictions. Well-practiced assertiveness skills allow people to hold space for conflicting convictions (no matter their nature or origin). Assertiveness also includes evaluating assumptions and convictions and expressing our concerns with clarity and power. Across the ideological spectrum, including religious and nonreligious, some convictions are false, mistaken, and harmful, and someone living assertively would not stand idly by without offering a more humanizing response.

We encourage everyone in communities, families, and relationships to promote kindhearted power and assertiveness in their interactions. Not recognizing power as different from brutality leads to problems—one being that victims and kind people often push away their power to avoid being aggressive. More examples of compassionate, ethical power are needed. We hope the ideas and skills offered here promote awareness, strength, peacemaking, and growth.

Chapter 2

Find Places to Belong: You Do You

Frances Aranda, Samuel Skidmore, A. Lee Beckstead, Iva Žegura, Christopher H. Rosik, Jay Jacobsen, and João Carvalho

This chapter will focus on identity development and coming out, especially the potentially challenging dynamics of living authentically. We emphasize the value of social inclusion, belonging to oneself, and building a support system with similar and diverse others. We highlight coming out safely and which transitional stages develop a person's sexual/gender personal-social identity. We also highlight nuances for racialized[1] sexual/gender minorities.

Coming Out and Belonging

The first steps of coming out involve internal processes that present a personal coming-out story. Often, this period of self-reflection is followed by heightened awareness and realization about feelings that are authentic to the person—or a lack of sexual attractions—that the person has had for some time. Self-realization can occur during sexual experiences and lead to disclosure (*sex centered*) or through education and self-reflection and lead to disclosure and then sexual experiences (*identity centered*) (Bishop et al., 2020). Some cisgender[2] heterosexual and LGBTQIA+ individuals also come out as polyamorous,

---

[1] Racialization is the process by which individuals and groups are inevitably assigned color. People are not colored. The assignment of race to people became a means to a goal, a mechanism to legitimize dispossession, destruction, and exploitation of resources from people whom White colonizers judged to be inferior and underdeveloped. The use of the phrase *people of color* avoids an examination of this colonial history, which continues to this day, whereas the use of *racialized* allows for such examination.

[2] Cisgender individuals are those whose gender matches their sex assigned at birth. Transgender/nonbinary individuals are those whose gender does not match their sex assigned at birth.

nonmonogamous, and/or sexually interested in objects, kink, role-playing, group sex, and so on.

The gap between self-awareness and disclosure may be brief or extended and represent the person's level of shame about their diversity and their social safety in being different (Russell & Fish, 2016). One study of Christian sexual minorities with theologically conservative religious beliefs in U.S. colleges found a four-year gap between self-awareness and disclosure (Yarhouse et al., 2018). The person's (a) romantic/sexual experiences and degrees of same-gender and other-genders attractions (Katz-Wise et al., 2017) and aversions, (b) degree of gender nonconformity, (c) sociohistorical education/socialization, and (d) beliefs about gender and sexual orientation (Tierney et al., 2021) will affect their self-labeling and timing of disclosure (S. K. Goldberg et al., 2020).

Coming out should be a process of choice for sexual/gender minorities to decide if, when, and how that happens within their social circles and networks. In our complex societies with diverse cultural backgrounds, coming out involves obstacles connected with other identities and marginalized, intersecting experiences, such as race/ethnicity, nationality, immigration status, religion, age, career, and disability. For example, some sexual/gender minorities prioritize their traditional religious identities over any sexual/gender identity and come out by acknowledging to themselves and a few safe people that they experience some degree of same-gender attraction or gender incongruence, but only when they can locate such persons within their family or faith tradition. Therefore, coming out can be (a) an ongoing gradual *scaffolding process* of indirect communication that facilitates and also inhibits authenticity and reconciliation (Jhang, 2018) or (b) happen suddenly by choice or by being forcefully outed.

Self-actualization and other concepts of authenticity ("living true to yourself") are culture-bound. Self-actualization can be embedded within a Western colonial concept of the individualistic self, while family belonging and harmony can be a central organizing principle of identity in collectivist cultures. Traditionally religious sexual/gender minorities in the United States and abroad would likely identify more with the latter collective emphasis for structuring their identity. People with similar commitment levels to religion tend to have similar values within and across countries (Atari et al., 2023). Therefore, being authentic and "true to oneself" can be in the direction of desires (*internal congruence*), ideals (*purpose/goal congruence*) (American Psychological Association, 2009), or both. Many Indigenous cultures consider self-actualization through interpersonal, community, and earth actualization (Brown, 2014). *Probeing pride* is a state of celebration and delight in one's own and others' authentic ways of being and relating, which can heal relational trauma (Benau, 2022).

Community connectedness can clarify a person's self-concept and direction in life and reduce fears of being open about one's stigmatized sexual/gender identity, which can positively affect well-being (Kavanaugh et al., 2020; F. Li et al., 2021). Self-identifying can help with finding similar others, but connecting within the LGBTQIA+ community can be disheartening for those whose interests and bodies are not valued. Status concerns, rejection, and pressure to be and act like other LGBTQIA+ individuals can cause more suffering (*intraminority community stress*) (Pachankis et al., 2020). Those disillusioned with their efforts to connect may need to create their own networks and groups and talk with community leaders about how to do this.

Above all, we do not want to reinforce expectations that you or anyone *should* come out, especially if your personality prefers to be private or you have reasons not to disclose. As Claude Louis expressed (Louis & Browne, 2023), "Your identity is your own. It is okay to come out and not to come out if doing so jeopardizes your family and community lifelines and resources."

- As you reflect on the above, what is most relevant to your identity development, relationships, well-being, and belongingness?

Applying a Sexual Identity Coming-Out Model

The sexual identity formation model developed by Vivienne Cass in 1979 offered six transitional stages accompanying the coming-out process. These stages can be circular and not necessarily linear or consecutive. Many factors, such as personality, culture, structural discrimination, privilege, sociohistorical contexts, and life circumstances, will affect how or if they are experienced. This model has its critics on the left and right (Goodrich & Brammer, 2021; Yarhouse & Sadusky, 2021). For example, Cass's model does not account for the increased fluidity in contemporary sexual experiences and identities and has a latent bias against sexual minorities who prioritize their religious identity over sexual identity. We highlight Cass's model here for your examination of how accurately it fits your sexual-social identity formation.

- As you read the following, reflect on how you would adapt Cass's model to fit your experiences.
- How would you describe your stages of coming out and sexual identity development?

Cass's stages include (a) identity confusion, (b) identity comparison, (c) identity tolerance, (d) identity acceptance, (e) identity pride, and (f) identity synthesis. The main issue of the first stage is that the person is unaware, in denial, or confused due to false information and a lack of accurate information and options about sexual/gender diversity. Rationalizations are made to manage conflicts, confusion, discrimination, and gaps in knowledge and experience. The second phase is marked by the person noticing how they are different and similar from peers and others, especially regarding social status and what they prefer and don't like. This comparison acknowledges the possibility of being "not normal," "not straight," and "not valued." During this comparison, the person may worry about loss and harm from being labeled with a stigmatized social identity. They may try to fit in by copying others and trying to stop their "bad" feelings and behaviors to "earn" approval, worth, safety, and belonging. They may reject themselves in the hope of avoiding rejection from others.

Identity tolerance is marked by the person being able to reflect on their experiences and feel an increase in acknowledgment and acceptance of experiencing and enjoying their sexual/gender diversity. Although confusion about sexual/gender diversity decreases, the person may experience or fear increased isolation and alienation as their self-awareness and self-concept become increasingly different from societal norms and expectations. During this period of identity tolerance, a person often contacts members of the LGBTQIA+ community to connect and explore who they are with similar others.

The period of identity acceptance brings the sexual/gender minority person to the resolution of most of their questions about their identity. They have now acknowledged their sexual attractions (or lack thereof) and gender expression as part of who they are and may have increasing contact with the LGBTQIA+ community. If these experiences are positive, the person can enjoy identity pride and feel worth and value in being who they are and part of the LGBTQIA+ community. Identity pride comes from appreciating the intrinsic worth and accomplishment of being a sexually/gender-diverse person, regardless of identity label. Each person decides how much they will engage and merge their life into LGBTQIA+ community events. The side effect of this immersion may be that the person has less contact with the cis-heterosexual community. They may also feel anger toward or reject the cis-heterosexual community. Some experience *hetero-phobia* and are untrusting and avoidant of cis-heterosexual individuals, which can also affect their emotional relationship with LGBTQIA+ individuals (Haldeman, 2006). Others encounter racism and other forms of discrimination within the LGBTQIA+ community, which can cause similar anger toward and disengagement from the LGBTQIA+ community (Giwa, 2022). They may seek other routes to develop community and relationships, such as racial affinity groups.

With more personal and social security, the identity synthesis period allows sexual/gender minorities to integrate their sexuality and gender with other aspects of themselves. Sexual orientation and gender become interwoven positively with their whole identity. Anger they may have felt toward their community may motivate them to assertiveness and self-protection when the community feels unsafe or lacking in understanding. Feelings of superiority from pride may be resolved into wisdom, resilience, compassionate anger, and activism. This strength enables LGBTQIA+ individuals to live their whole self with others, or at least in ways that fit them and are possible and to navigate more comfortably within and between social groups. Some may focus on building *communities of resilience* out of a sense of social responsibility and collectivist values (Chiongbian et al., 2023). People attracted to multiple genders or to no one and whose gender experiences don't fit social binaries will need to build resilience as they navigate identity denial and illegitimacy within monosexual, cisgenderist settings (Thöni et al., 2022).

Overall, this process of self-acceptance, identity affirmation, authenticity, and community building can help LGBTQIA+ individuals feel more congruence, strength, and peace between their public and private selves.

Understanding the Additional Coming-Out Processes for Gender-Diverse Individuals

Trans/gender-diverse individuals likely come out twice, first with their sexual identity and then their gender identity. During or after transition, the trans/gender-diverse person may come out a third time about a new sexual identity that matches their current gender expression (Rowniak & Chesla, 2013). Some trans/gender-diverse individuals detransition, retransition (Durwood et al., 2022), or "course correct" (Eckert & McLamore, 2023) after adopting a specific gender identity, learning more about themselves, and finding a new identity that fits better. They come out again about their realized and more livable gender identity (Sanders et al., 2023).

The terms *transgender* and *gender nonbinary* refer to people whose gender identity—how they experience their gender—is different from their gender assigned at birth. Some transgender/gender-diverse individuals experience distress from the incongruence with their gender and physical body (*gender-body dysphoria*). Some experience congruence with their physical body but incongruence between how they express their gender and cultural gender expectations (*gender-role dysphoria*) and how others perceive their gender and treat them (*social dysphoria*). The terms *transgender* and *gender diverse* describe a whole range of people and take many forms, from binary trans men and trans women to individuals who identify as gender nonbinary or expansive, agender, genderfluid, pangender, neutral, genderqueer, androgynous, gender bender, drag queen/king, a person with no gender label, and more.

Gender transition processes can involve three levels, each involving benefits, risks, and side effects: (1) reversible interventions (experimenting with gender expression; changing social identity to be more aligned with one's gender experiences; considering the need, safety, risks, and benefits of hormone blockers), (2) partially irreversible interventions (using cross-sex hormones), and (3) irreversible surgeries. A trans/gender-diverse individual who transitions must also worry about how society regulates people's gender expression and involve legal action to change their gender designation in personal documents.

There is controversy regarding whether social and medical transition for gender-diverse youth is reversible and safe. For example, if minors socially transition, research suggests many will move on to medical transition compared to gender-diverse minors who are not socially transitioned. Some interpret this to mean that early transitioning is the primary cause of gender-diverse youth later using medical transition. However, early transitioning youth may suffer from more significant gender incongruence than gender-diverse kids who are less compelled to transition. The experience of significant incongruence, whether a youth transitions early or not, will inevitably lead a youth to consider social/physical transition. Yet, many gender-incongruent youth later identify with their birth sex.

It is important not to lump all gender-diverse youth into the same gender category and identity trajectory. Each gender-diverse individual will need to consider if social transitioning and medical interventions will shut down or open up options for their well-being (Chang & Chakrabarti, 2023). We do not have sufficient research to make definitive conclusions about many or most cases. This should change in the next 10 years as a significant number of adolescents (especially those assigned female at birth) who socially and medically transitioned during the past decade age into their 20s.

Above all, the very process of social transition is a visible coming-out process. The gender-diverse identity becomes more evident and relevant to the social field of a gender-diverse person. If this sociocultural field is rigid and restrictive, then every individual existence that falls between the gap between two strict gender categories will suffer some form of minority stress. Gender stigma involves a risk of violence motivated by rejection and neglect of gender-diverse individuals. There are additional risks and coming-out processes for gender-diverse individuals in a marriage and intimate relationship. These risks can vary from relationship problems due to social stigma to inflexibility and lack of knowledge navigating changes in gender expression, roles, appearance, and sexuality. Coming out about being gender diverse can involve violent outbursts or passive-aggressive reactions of transphobia from the other partner while negotiating expectations of who does the emotional work in the relationship (Zamantakis, 2022).

Regardless, trans/gender-diverse individuals "must find ways to make sense of their bodies, their fantasies and desires, and their sexual practices" (Devor & Dominic, 2015, p. 195) within their intimate relationships within a binary social context of biological sex, gender, and sexuality. Dating for intersex individuals, for example, can involve a process of (a) feeling good about their gender presentation and genital appearance and function; (b) disclosing and describing their intersex condition; and (c) navigating stigma, reproduction, and family concerns (Frank, 2018). Each new relationship for trans/gender-diverse individuals has risks of rejection and violence and potential hopes for connection and support.

Suppose the gender-diverse individual decides on hormonal treatment or gender-confirmation surgery. In either case, the individual has to reach out to institutions as their coming-out process often includes coordinating an interdisciplinary team: mental health professionals, a general practitioner, an endocrinologist, a gynecologist and urologist, a specialist in sexual medicine, a vocal therapist, a surgeon, a social worker, and a laser-hair removal practitioner for those who are transfeminine, as well as from institutions that provide legislative support to change their legal name and designation of gender in personal documents. This can be highly demanding, costly, confusing, overwhelming, and traumatic for many gender-diverse individuals, especially when institutions and providers reflect societal transphobic prejudices. Each contact not made according to professional standards and humanizing ethics can result in increased gender dysphoria, retraumatization, and further diminishment of trust and disconnection from society.

In medical and mental health care, there are some insurmountable problems globally. These relate to uncovered costs of gender transition by health insurance, lack of educated professionals, and lack of protection by the legal system to ensure each gender-diverse person has access to time-appropriate treatment and legal protection. The EU LGBT Survey points out that 21% (one in five trans respondents) indicate having experienced inappropriate curiosity when accessing health-care services, and 17% say their specific needs were ignored (European Union Agency for Fundamental Rights, 2014). It would be in the best interest of both professionals and their trans/gender-diverse clients if professional societies and institutions would implement in their guidelines and ethical codes specific paragraphs about comprehensive care of gender-diverse patients concerning their human rights. The specific national guidelines for each profession, if they are to be made, should consist of ethical and professional recommendations based on up-to-date scientific knowledge and best-practice recommendations to avoid the slightest possibility of culturally and socially prejudicial belief systems coming from the side of authority. Research and policy committees should include professionals with differing political affiliations to reduce groupthink biases. Our political culture wars distract from developing common-ground recommendations and safe, person-centered interventions for the wide range of individuals who experience gender diversity.

When trans/gender-diverse individuals enter a medical and mental-health setting for services related to their gender-transition process, they require a diagnosis of *gender dysphoria* or *gender incongruence*. This diagnosis is used to address and improve mental and sexual health, which may lead to a transition for the achievement of appearance and social congruence. The scientific stance regarding gender and sexual orientation identities is clear: these identities are equal in status and ability for well-being to cisgender and heterosexual identities. Although there is an elevated level of co-occurring mental health disorders among trans/nonbinary individuals (Valentine & Shipherd, 2018), a trans/nonbinary identity should not be considered and treated as psychologically unhealthy. Yet the lack of specific diagnostic categories could lead to limited health-care provisions from—and education of—medical providers and mental health workers.

Recognizing, accepting, and valuing oneself as gender diverse is a nonlinear process that can repeat and last for years. Each gender-diverse individual has their own concept of and need around the transition process and living more authentically. Yet framing this developmental process as a "transition process" may set up one type of congruence that may not fit others' experiences, particularly those more conservative and/or nonbinary. Indeed, most trans+ U.S. adults in 2015 did not use hormone therapy or gender-confirming surgeries, only 44% and 25%, respectively (National Center for Transgender Equality, 2022). Most did make a social transition. Above all, medical transition should not be required to be recognized by one's gender.

Aaron Devor (2004) described a model of transgender identity development of "witnessing and mirroring," which considers multiple minority stressors and could be considered for all gender-diverse individuals.

- How much does the following fit your experiences with personal/social gender congruence? What narrative better fits your gender coming-out story?

1. *Abiding anxiety* is when the individual feels constant conflict and preoccupation about gender. Intrusive thoughts and feelings of "not being right" about their gender role, gender expression, or body appearance can be felt from early childhood and during puberty or when the individual begins awareness of their body, social role, and gender.
2. *Identity confusion* involves doubts about one's initially assigned gender and gender role. The feeling that one is different from same-sex peers leads to questioning whether they are in the right assigned gender category. Some children may feel certain that they have been given the wrong gender. They can spontaneously verbalize a wish to be another gender to their caregivers but may not have the language and understanding of what that means for them. The adults they depend on may discourage and convince them that this is not the case or just a phase, and confusion and isolation get reinforced.
3. *Identity comparisons* involve the trans/gender-diverse individual seeking to understand possible alternative gender identities and communities. The fact that their gender was attributed to them at birth based on the morphology of their genitals is not questioned. They may hyperfocus on living their gender assigned at birth and expressing their expected gender role. Some may hide, mask, lie, and overcompensate. A harmful barrier to this process is not having anyone also going through it and, therefore, not knowing which

questions to ask and which experiences to pursue and avoid (Pulice-Farrow et al., 2023).

4. *Discovery of trans/gender-diverse experiences* involves learning that trans/gender-diverse people exist. This discovery occurs early or late in life, depending on social circumstances. Many describe knowing their gender before they found a name for their experiences. Some describe coming across media about a trans/gender-diverse person or character, or they were searching the internet and finally found the right words and representations for their experiences after years of uncertainty, shame, and confusion. Most trans/gender-diverse individuals will recall this period as a turning point.

5. *Identity confusion about a trans/gender-diverse identity* involves doubts about its relevance to the person and how much it means to them not to be gender stereotypical. This questioning leads individuals to reflect on their chosen name (Russell et al., 2018), pronouns, and personal gender appearance and expression. Individuals will seek additional information on gender and what it means to be gender diverse.

6. *Identity comparisons with trans/gender-diverse individuals* involve connecting with more trans/gender-diverse individuals and comparing themselves to gain more definitive conclusions about their gender identity and options.

7. *Tolerance of a trans/gender-diverse identity* is when the person identifies as "probably" transgender or another gender category that better fits them.

8. *Delay before acceptance* happens when minority stress and personal/family stressors cause individuals to pause and address other needs. Some may recapitulate and seek more information to confirm their identity. They may look to others with whom they are close who are not trans/gender-diverse to validate and accept them and for those who are trans/gender diverse to confirm that they belong together. Hope during this period may come from thinking about future transition steps and believing others someday will accept them as trans/gender-diverse and affirm their gender (Lindley & Budge, 2022). Exploration, evaluation, and differentiation help consolidate the individual's understanding of their gender diversity and identity.

9. *Acceptance of a trans/gender-diverse identity* occurs when the individual has firmly established their gender identity and may open up to others about that acceptance. By this point, the trans/gender-diverse individual has reflected a lot on their anxieties, gender dysphoria and euphoria, traumas, and options to say openly, "I am transgender (or the gender category that fits them), and my pronouns are. . . . I accept this about myself, I love you, and I want us to be in this space together" (as described by Ty Browne in Louis & Browne, 2023). Individuals who suffer gender-body dysphoria, at this stage, may feel, "I'm not right, but I'm not bad."[3]

10. *Delay before transition* involves learning more about the transition process, weighing and balancing priorities and risks/uncertainties about social transition and medical interventions to decide what fits needs and circumstances

---

[3] As expressed by a trans women client of Beckstead considering gender-confirming surgery.

(Butcher et al., 2023) and problem-solving how to realize their transition and organize support systems. Many find support and options through talking with other trans/gender-diverse individuals about changing names, clothing, and pronouns; understanding medical transition and aftercare; and learning how to navigate conversations and relationships around gender (Lindley & Budge, 2022). Examining any gender shame from believing one is inferior and not equal due to not looking and acting a certain gendered way will be important in living more authentically and confidently.

11. *Transition* involves acting on an informed decision to undertake different activities to actualize personal/social gender congruence. This includes open conversations with loved ones and close contacts and may involve changes in the social presentation of self, psychological education, psychotherapy, hormonal treatments, legal documents, or surgical procedures of gender affirmation. Due to different medical conditions, financial resources, and health-care options, some have to delay medical interventions (for example, if someone has breast cancer or severe congenital heart malformation) and will pursue available transition options. Living between surgeries can be mixed for some transgender individuals due to decreased gender dysphoria and increased gender euphoria for some aspects but increased gender dysphoria for others and increased attention to their body.

12. *Success of posttransition living* is accomplished when the person feels satisfied and comfortable (enough) with the level of congruence between their gender identity, appearance, and expression and their social and intimate relationships. They must still navigate others challenging their gender and expression. Self-acceptance and identity affirmation provide resilience and purpose to these social challenges and discrimination.

13. *Integration* may be an invisible period for gender-diverse individuals with a binary gender (man or woman) who merge with cultural gender norms and conceal their past and transition. Others who are gender nonbinary will experience additional minority stressors of binary normativity, interpersonal invalidation, and the burden and mental/emotional labor (Matsuno et al., 2022) to advocate for their unique expression as they seek to be integrated equally into society. Living authentically in one's gender, however, can foster a sense of shared humanity and connection with others (Tebbe et al., 2022). Many who medically transitioned may need to integrate continual use of such methods in their life.

14. *Pride*—this stage is marked by a personal appreciation for gender diversity and valuing one's gender experiences and resilience. This pride may motivate some to be more open and political to support others struggling with stigma and gender diversity. This can involve social activism and community building from any of the following (Lindley & Budge, 2022):

- supporting others with their emotions while they navigate transition
- volunteering at organizations that support trans/gender-diverse youth and adults
- wearing accessories that state pronouns and welcome diversity

- being active in educating the public (for example, participating as a "human book" in a living library whereby one's experiences enable students to learn about sexual/gender diversity)
- advocating for safety and health care for trans/gender-diverse individuals, and more

Due to social risks from violating gender norms, Devor's model highlights how trans/gender-diverse individuals first integrate their gender identity and then consider how "proud and open" they want to be about being gender diverse. For trans/gender-diverse individuals in unsafe binary-gendered cultures, Pride may be an inward strength from feeling good about themselves as they navigate gender expression in everyday life. They may avoid discussing their gender identity or decide how to explain/validate themselves with the people around them. Some find relief in people and places that are accepting and permissive, where more differences and diversities are represented and they don't have to fight for recognition.

It may be difficult for some to find the type of support they need if the emphasis in trans+ social groups is on transition and appearance when the individual is looking more for emotional connection about other interests, needs, and conflicts. Some may experience jealousy, resentment, or defensiveness in trans/nonbinary groups about medically transitioning. Some create their community by connecting to neighborhoods, organizations, or friends that reinforce belonging, well-being, protection, and socialization (Abreu et al., 2021). Some cannot find safe people and settings where they can be vulnerable and themselves.

Each LGBTQIA+ setting will have its cultural gender norms to violate and unsafe gendered spaces and activities to avoid (Lindley & Budge, 2022). As one research participant described, "Trans inclusivity and acceptance isn't necessarily a given in all LGBTQ+ spaces, so the feeling of being in that kind of generalized space isn't as immediately comforting as being a cis person in this space" (Pulice-Farrow et al., 2023, p. 5). This research highlights how the sociopolitical identity of trans/gender-diverse individuals intersects with their racial/ethnic, gender, sexual, disability, income, immigration, age, and faith identities and shapes their experiences of community and belonging. This research highlights the importance of feeling like "members of a community" and how interactions with others who share a similar identity can increase *feelings of community*, while connecting with others increases *feelings of belonging*.

Coming Out and Belonging as a Racialized LGBTQIA+ Individual

Racialized LGBTQIA+ individuals live within four social environments: their family, ethnic community, LGBTQIA+ community, and society. While each community fulfills fundamental needs, integrating all four environments is almost impossible for racialized LGBTQIA+ individuals because of the negative attitudes toward multiple minority identities. The intersectional oppression and lack of complete support and acceptance in these social environments may require more effort in identity development and maintenance.

- How would you describe (in a few words) your family, your racial/ethnic community, your LGBTQIA+ community, your nationality, and society overall? How interconnected and independent are your communities?
- How much can you express and share important aspects of yourself, including your gender identity, sexual orientation, sexuality, nationality, and race/ethnicity, in these settings?

Discrimination for being LGBTQIA+ can be more psychologically damaging than discrimination from racism for racialized LGBTQIA+ individuals because of the impact of stigma and isolation that can occur (Drazdowski et al., 2018). Experiencing racism within LGBTQIA+ communities is associated with lower levels of belongingness and higher levels of internalized heterosexism (*I wish I weren't LGBTQIA+*). This disconnection from self and the LGBTQIA+ community can be more pronounced for those who are multiracial (Felipe et al., 2022) or bisexual/fluid (Pistella et al., 2016). While this assertion may have validity for some, the proximity to Whiteness can also afford multiracial individuals access to certain benefits and opportunities within LGBTQIA+ communities that are typically withheld from LGBTQIA+ individuals whose skin color noticeably differs from that of White people.

Racialized sexual/gender minorities indicate that race/ethnicity is just as important as their sexuality and gender (Giwa, 2022). So how does a person negotiate multiple identities in societal groups that do not embrace all their identities? For example, how do racialized sexual/gender minorities who prioritize their traditionally religious identities find their places to belong when they are viewed disparagingly by their family and religious, ethnic, and LGBTQ+ communities? People also may not have agency or choice in being able to identify themselves. People are more often assigned/perceived based on social norms (for example, a "feminine" man is considered gay even if he does not self-identify as gay). Similarly, people can have a congruent or divergent identity and experience with the primary culture (for example, a person may be culturally Christian versus Muslim in a Christian-dominant country).

Most of what is known about disclosure of a sexual/gender minority identity is based on White LGBTQIA+ populations. As a result, little is known about the struggles and strengths of negotiating multiple minority statuses by racialized LGBTQIA+ individuals. Morales (1989) indicated that attitudes toward sexuality and gender differ within racial/ethnic communities and play a major role in determining how individuals behave within their family and social environments. Morales termed the loyalties for racialized LGBTQIA+ individuals to one community over another as "conflicts in allegiances." Potential factors that hinder disclosure are traditional gender roles, parental reactions, community closeness, traditional religious values, and the importance of religiosity and spirituality among ethnic minorities (A. Gonzalez, 2019). Conflicts in allegiances and lack of safety can be felt in conservative political families regardless of religion. These cultural factors can contribute to the need for racialized LGBTQIA+ individuals to hide their sexual/gender identity from their social networks and those they love.

Traditional Gender Roles

One area of potential conflict for racialized LGBTQIA+ individuals is traditional gender roles, which are embedded in some ethnic cultures and often conflict with the lived experiences or roles inhabited by racialized LGBTQIA+ individuals. Gender roles are strictly defined in some cultures based on strong traditions and stereotypes. Traditional gender roles are hierarchical in many ethnic cultures, giving men positions of power while women maintain subservient roles (Fukuyama & Ferguson, 2000). The Latine culture provides one example of divergent male and female gender roles: Latine individuals use the term *machismo* (dominance, manliness, and virility) to describe the masculine role and *marianismo* (submissive, self-sacrificing, and pure) to describe the feminine role (Reyes, 1998). As a result, Latina women are not expected to be interested in sex other than as a duty to their husbands. In contrast, Latina sexual minority women are accused of celebrating female sexuality and flaunting forbidden sexual behavior by partnering with other women. The mere presence of Latina sexual minority women in the family and ethnic community threatens the dominant Latino male hierarchy (Fukuyama & Ferguson, 2000; Reyes, 1998).

In contrast, the Black community is largely matriarchal and defies the traditional stereotypes of masculine and feminine roles (Fukuyama & Ferguson, 2000).[4] Black women play critical roles in keeping Black families together and supporting Black men. This can be problematic for Black sexual minority women because their behavior defies traditional family roles by not including

---

[4] Inverted gender roles illustrate the significance of ethnic/racial cultural dynamics layering and meshing with queer experiences.

and caring for Black men in the same way as their heterosexual female counterparts (Loiacano, 1989). This may be one reason that Black sexual minority women may be wary about coming out to family and Black friends (Bridges et al., 2003). Ironically, Bowleg et al. (2003) reported that Black sexual minority women equated happiness with freedom from gender roles.

Parental Reaction to Coming Out

One of the main factors influencing disclosure among LGBTQIA+ individuals is the fear of parental rejection. Parents' emotions can range from shock, doubt, guilt, anger, and embarrassment to overt rejection. Some of the more extreme reactions include estrangement, violence, and even threats of murder. Parents often ask, "What did I do wrong?" as if they were not good parents, were too lenient, or favored another child too much. Parents may blame each other for not providing an adequate role model. Sadly, parents may even respond by ejecting their LGBTQIA+ child from the home or rushing them to a psychiatrist to "correct" their sexual/gender expression. For these reasons, LGBTQIA+ individuals must evaluate whether the disclosure cost is worth the risk of harmful reactions and consequences. Because disclosure is risky, LGBTQIA+ individuals have legitimate reasons to be concerned about their well-being.

Parental acceptance is empowering for anyone. However, for racialized LGBTQIA+ individuals, parental acceptance allows them to maintain their rich cultural upbringing and be sheltered from societal/community rejection. Accepting parents are also more likely to provide support. Yet "support" may not be a one-size-fits-all proposition. Some traditionally religious parents may provide positive support that falls short of a full endorsement of an LGBTQIA+ identity, and parents may feel torn between supporting their child or supporting their religious/cultural values. To address this conflict, the Family Acceptance Project researches which parenting behaviors are helpful and harmful to the health of the sexually/gender-diverse child. They are dedicated to empowering ethnically/racially and religiously diverse parents of LGBTQIA+ individuals to interact with their children in ways that align with parents' cultural values and strengths without needing to change cultural beliefs. Please see their website[5] for many helpful resources.

Family and Community

Family units and communities are vital to racialized/ethnic minority groups because of the shared experiences of oppression they have overcome and continue to manage (Fukuyama & Ferguson, 2000). This means that when

---

[5] Family Acceptance Project, https://familyproject.sfsu.edu/.

racialized sexual/gender minorities come out to family members, it can extend beyond just the family, as many racial/ethnic individuals often reside in communities where people share similar cultural aspects, such as history, language, and customs. Where they shop, worship, socialize, and more are enclaves of communities unto themselves. Family and community are so enmeshed that it is impractical to distinguish between them when navigating disclosure and identity development. Family and racial/ethnic communities can provide racialized LGBTQIA+ individuals with cultural strategies and resources to combat racism and other social stigma but also reinforce sexual/gender stigma and discrimination.

The ideology often used to describe the context for many ethnic groups is called collectivism. Collectivistic orientation is prevalent in the histories and cultural traditions of Asian, Pacific Islander, Latine, and Black Americans. Generally speaking, collectivists are concerned about harmony and well-being in their interpersonal relationships, particularly within the family. Claude Louis explained, "As an individual, I suffer, but with community, I can thrive" (Louis & Browne, 2023). Collectivists are very attentive and responsive to the needs of others and are often willing to sacrifice their individual goals to promote the collective or family (Kaniasty & Norris, 2000). The reliance on family is routinely credited with a decreased involvement with support networks outside the family (Chávez & Guido-DiBrito, 1999). This may be a similar dynamic for conservative religious community members whose reliance on their religious community reduces their LGBTQ+ social networks but not their peer-group support networks (Yarhouse & Zaporozhets, 2022).

For Latine families, social networks are generally based more on biological ties, whereas Black Americans emphasize extended family, which frequently includes a variety of nonbiological linkages (Gaines, 1997). Latine individuals reverently refer to "*familismo*," the importance of family (Reyes, 1998). The family unit is where cultural beliefs and resilience are developed and nurtured. An individual's value system is shaped and reinforced in the family setting, which is usually extended and reflected in the norms of the broader ethnic community (Morales, 1989). The individual who finds themself at odds with significant swaths of their community's value system will need to determine their own path of identity development, even if it is to conform and find purpose in these conflicts.

Many racialized LGBTQIA+ individuals invest in family interests and sacrifice individual wishes (Bridges et al., 2003). For example, showing unconditional obedience to parental authority (**authoritarian filial piety**) is associated with Chinese LGBQ+ individuals' perceived pressure to marry heterosexually and their internalized homonegativity (F. Liu et al., 2023). Despite homophobic attitudes in racial/ethnic communities, racialized LGBTQIA+ individuals remain firmly attached to their cultural heritage and view their racial/ethnic identity as primary (Bowleg et al., 2003; Giwa, 2022; Parks et al., 2004). A study by Merighi and Grimes (2000) on Black, Mexican, and Vietnamese American gay males discussed the difficulties and conflicts that resulted from their desire to respect their cultural upbringing while trying to establish their LGBTQIA+ identity without harming their family's image in the eyes of others. The Asian American and Pacific Islander (AAPI) cultures refer to this as "saving face," which is avoiding humiliation and embarrassment for one's family. According to Hunt and Huang (2020), several Asian cultures will tolerate displays of same-gender affection if there is no open discussion of one's sexual identity. It is important to highlight here how identity and behavior can be separate (for example, men who have sex with men who don't think of themselves as gay or bisexual, being on "the down low"). Coming out publicly as a sexual/gender minority person goes against the AAPI value of "saving face." Hunt and Huang state that coming out draws the focus to the individual and their needs rather than the needs of one's family and community. This may bring "loss of face" to their parents, who may feel humiliated by their child's disclosure to the community. This focus on the self contradicts collectivistic values and processes.

- How much do your cultural heritage, upbringing, and family dynamics resonate and not resonate with the above?

Although some families might risk "losing face" within their social networks by overlooking what they believe is deviant behavior, they only do so to maintain family continuity. This level of family tolerance should not be confused with acceptance. Tolerance is often gained at the price of living in silence for racialized LGBTQIA+ individuals (Greene, 1994; Parks et al., 2004). "Tolerance" can result from staying silent about identity and sexual/romantic relationships. Tolerance can be an action and only reluctantly offered with a contract that "We'll no longer directly attack you but tolerate you, but you have to keep your queerness out of our lives and associations." Tolerance and not being treated differently disappear once the queer person's queerness is introduced into the tolerators' community dynamics. Living with secrets can contribute to one's emotional burdens (Pachankis, 2007).

Greene (1994) stated that racialized LGBTQIA+ individuals could experience greater opposition to their sexual/gender minority identity in their ethnic group than in the dominant culture. Serious conflicts between family members may erupt if racialized sexual/gender minority individuals openly disclose being LGBTQIA+.

As a result, racialized LGBTQIA+ individuals must learn to "code switch" across rigidly defined communities (family, ethnic, LGBTQIA+, and society). They frequently report not feeling part of any group completely, leaving them at greater risk for isolation, feelings of estrangement, and increased psychological vulnerability. The potential cost of disclosure among racialized LGBTQIA+ individuals becomes more significant than for White LGBTQIA+ individuals because a meaningful aspect of their identity is not fully supported within all their environments.

- How much do you "code switch" and change how you communicate and interact within your social contexts? What are the costs and benefits to you in doing so?

Religion and Spirituality

Religion and spirituality are important to many ethnic families and communities. Catholicism and Evangelical Protestantism are the predominant religions practiced among Latine and Black Americans, and both are often vehemently against homosexuality. Differences can exist among congregational and denominational levels (Lefevor et al., 2020). However, the belief that homosexuality is a sin and goes against God deters many Catholic Latine and Protestant Black LGBTQ+ individuals from being open about their sexual experiences or gender identity to family members, church members, and religious leaders (Bridges et al., 2003). Many religions publicly condemn same-gender relationships and gender-diverse behaviors, causing conflicts between LGBTQIA+ individuals and their families. LGBTQIA+ individuals who identify more with their sexual/gender identity than their ethnic identity risk being alienated from their church.

Despite the negativity, religion and spirituality serve as a source of resilience and moral compass for many racialized sexual/gender minorities. One study (J. J. Walker & Longmire-Avital, 2013) found Black LGB young adults who reported greater religiousness and higher internalized homonegativity (IH) were also more resilient. This may reflect the possibility that high IH among some traditionally religious individuals is an expression of high religious devotion rather than shame or self-loathing.

Racial/Ethnic Differences and Risks in Disclosure

Disclosure within the family may be due to how much family members are homophobic/transphobic and prioritize family lineage, family obligation, reproduction, and traditional gender roles (Son & Updegraff, 2023). Family values that promote family closeness, family importance, and family unity may encourage some racialized LGBTQIA+ individuals to be more open to family members.

The fear and loss of support from their kinships and communities may make racialized LGBTQIA+ individuals apprehensive about coming out. Studies have found that a lack of support from crucial social networks is associated with psychological distress (K. McDonald, 2018). One study found that initial and current acceptance of one's sexual minority identity was lower for family members than other network members, thus increasing the risk of psychological distress (Aranda et al., 2015). It is likely difficult to maintain quality relationships with family and community members who do not accept one's sexual/gender identity (Beals & Peplau, 2006). Attitudes of one's social environment could limit or encourage an individual's participation in LGBTQ+ subcultures and influence the construction of their sexual/gender identity and self-acceptance (Frable et al., 1997; Vincke & Bolton, 1994).

Can racialized sexual/gender minorities who prioritize their religious identity find positive support within their religious communities? It seems possible, if not necessarily the norm. Certainly, there can be ostracization for admitting same-gender attraction or plans to transition genders. However, more, if not most, support can be lost by claiming an LGBTQIA+ identity, which may be viewed as a rejection of the religious identity prioritized by their support system.

Clearly, cultural factors make it difficult for racialized LGBTQIA+ individuals to be authentic and belong. Racialized LGBTQIA+ individuals can share their racial/ethnic identity experiences with their families and ethnic communities. However, a sexual/gender minority identity is not a commonly shared identity within their family and ethnic communities. Racism within LGBTQIA+ communities further marginalizes racialized LGBTQIA+ individuals. Because of the changing demographics of the United States, research on the effects of multiple identities has become more crucial, especially for Asian and Latine groups, which are two of the fastest growing racial/ethnic groups (Budiman & Ruiz, 2021). With studies showing racialized LGBTQIA+ individuals are less likely to come out, their risk for distress may be more significant.

A person can gain *cultural pride/resilience* from their racial/ethnic/faith culture by using the spirit, stories, strengths, rituals, and activities of their culture(s) for guidance, comfort, embodiment, strength, and dignity (Elm et al., 2016). Strategies that strengthen stigma resilience include practicing self-love, developing kinships with people who support your many identities, being role-flexible in different contexts, believing you can resist and change oppressive situations/environments, and enhancing a personal connection to one's spirituality and purpose in life (Wilson & Miller, 2002). Research suggests that discomfort within the LGBTQIA+ community, however, may only be reduced for racialized LGBTQIA+ individuals who have high sociopolitical involvement (Le et al., 2023).

Hope to be seen as a whole person for all sexually/gender-diverse individuals will require social changes that value diversity, equity, and inclusion. These social changes would need to develop safety support systems with similar and diverse others. As one research participant described, "'It feels really good to be acknowledged, the different parts of who I am to be acknowledged. . . .

It feels really good just to have those different parts of me be acknowledged as a whole' (Hispanic gender non-conforming person, 18)" (Pulice-Farrow et al., 2023, p. 6).

Conclusion

Coming out is a lifelong process of self-acceptance and decisions about openness and adapting, and as such is not something that happens at one point in time. The tasks of coming out are often described as prerequisites to true belonging to oneself and others. Among the benefits of coming-out experiences is a heightened sense of connectedness, even if the person is only truer to themselves, in whatever diverse manner they conceptualize this. Sexual/gender minority/LGBTQIA+ individuals who find places to belong allow others to see another aspect of themselves and invite others to act more authentically. As such, coming-out experiences and places to belong are empowering resources for personal, relational, and community trust, strength, and growth.

Chapter 3

Develop Your Sexuality and Understand Consent

Jordan Rullo, Alex Rivera, Nathalie Huitema,
Don L. Braegger, A. Lee Beckstead, Alison Feit,
Josephine Pui-Hing Wong, and Kersti Spjut

This chapter will explore how to develop *person-centered sexuality* through the intersecting lenses of social identities rooted in gender, faith, race/ethnicity, disability, age, and other life dimensions. We hope to underscore the value and nature of individual, complex experiences of sexuality. The chapter will also highlight, along with our companion e-resource, specific tensions in the experience of sexuality, as it is impacted by culture, politics, social media, and power relations; this has profound implications for the meaning of consent.

Research on Healthy Sexuality

Sexual health—often defined as the intersection between healthy sexual identity development, healthy sexual behaviors, and healthy sexual relationships—is a concept coined by the World Health Organization in 1975, where it was deemed to be an essential component of general health and well-being (Edwards & Coleman, 2004). In the early 1980s, with the advent of the HIV/AIDS epidemic in the United States, interest in sexuality took on national prominence, with an immediate impact on the health of the queer community. Thus, for many years, the gold standard for sexual health did not consider any specific positive goals for health and well-being but instead was defined as the elimination of any sexual risks and the absence of sexually transmitted infections (STIs). As the ways we understand healthy sexuality have changed throughout the years, in this chapter, we hope to discuss some of the societal factors that have limited our understanding of what sexual health can be and how it is transforming. We also will highlight the meaning of consent and how it plays an essential role in sexual health development.

Structural Conditions That Create Sexual Health Disparities

People who are stigmatized and marginalized for their age, sexuality, gender, race/ethnicity, neurodivergence, disability, health, or other fundamental aspects of their identity experience particular challenges in developing a "healthy sexuality" (Pollitt & Mallory, 2021; Roberts et al., 2020). Prejudice, bullying, and lack of positive role models, social safety, and relevant sexual health education programs can result in an atmosphere of neglect, restriction, and oppression of LGBTQIA+ youth (Tordoff et al., 2021). These individuals grow up in a complicated and confusing social environment, hiding aspects of their actual identity from others and sometimes finding themselves in sexual relationships that do not resonate with their true sexual desires or lack of sexual desires.

Unlike socially sanctioned heterosexual relationships, LGBTQIA+ youth are often forced to determine basic aspects of relational connection (such as self-esteem development and maintenance, safety, and intimacy) without the benefit of social information about the nature of healthy and meaningful romantic and sexual relationships. As a result, LGBTQ+ youth are more likely than their heterosexual peers to engage in risky sexual behaviors, such as developmentally inappropriate early sexual debuts, higher rates of sexual abuse, and less consistent use of condoms and contraceptives (National Center for Health Statistics, 2011). Research has shown that these behaviors can be attributed to a lack of safe social outlets, limited access to sexual health options, and internalized self-rejection (Saraff et al., 2022). Some federal, state, and institutional policies lack inclusive, comprehensive sexual health education, which presents further challenges for developing a person-centered, relational sexuality.

An additional challenge is that many states provide sexual education that is focused on an "abstinence-only" model, which provides little actionable information for this population. Such sex ed initiatives are often driven by "traditional values" but have harmful effects on sexual risk for teens. For example, they provide incomplete information and do not delay initiation of sexual intercourse or change risky behaviors (Society for Adolescent Health and Medicine, 2017). The current political environment makes it uncertain how many states will require education about non-cis-heterosexual identities in the near future. Many states may seek to embrace school curricula with more inclusive standards for sexual health education. In contrast, other states have made—or are at the cusp of making—such education illegal.

Given these challenges, where do positive models of queer sexual behavior and identity come from? Family inclusion and acceptance of LGBTQ+ identity can be an excellent source of stability. Research suggests that it helps reduce sexual risks, counters negative societal messages, and improves overall self-esteem and general health (Ryan et al., 2010; Saiz et al., 2021). In addition, resilience and positive role models are often acquired through affirming friendships, intimate relationships, mentors, reliable sex education, and broad-minded community resources (for example, inclusive religious centers and community support groups). Online resources can promote community identity and health, but as the internet is a complicated place, sometimes teens are also exposed to erroneous information that distorts reliable and scientifically based information as to the nature of gender and sexuality.

The term *healthy* to describe sexuality can be problematic because it sets up a binary implying that there is an "unhealthy" sexuality, which is rooted in statistical norms and expectations. The power relations embedded in these norms are often invisible. We suggest using words like *flourishing sexuality* to encompass a broader swath of social identities, senses of self, spirituality, relationships, ethics, and sexual practices. *Sexual authenticity* (Guyon et al., 2023), *integrity*, *wellness*, or *well-being* (Lorimer et al., 2019) are other terms that have been suggested, as they imply that each individual can make a personal decision about a sexual life that works for them and can be facilitated and celebrated by the larger system of family, community, and society. Regardless of the precise terms used, research from the past three decades suggests that a broad and robust definition of positive sexuality has been lacking for quite some time and that the addition of such is likely to improve overall mental health (Goldfarb & Lieberman, 2021).

Understanding the Nature of Consent

The term *consent* can be nebulous, and its meaning continues to evolve across disciplines. As early as 1996, the social sciences began to define sexual consent as mutual agreement of sexual behaviors between sexual partners, without coercion (Muehlenhard et al., 2016). Ideally, this definition works best when each new sexual act is verbally agreed on by the participants involved. Another emerging and essential aspect of this research is the importance of highlighting that a mere lack of physical resistance does not imply consent to sexual activity (Tilley et al., 2020). These additions to consent were essential steps in stating the need for mutuality and accountability in sexual relationships (*sexual assertiveness*).

In the following decades, the understanding of consent has expanded to include components of desire, willingness to engage in sex without desire, interpersonal dynamics of the relationship, and the need for clear and explicit verbal and nonverbal communication (Marcantonio et al., 2022). Additional goals include that partners aim for sensitivity to reading one another's signals and the need for consent to be revocable at any time if an individual no longer feels comfortable. Research has found that *unwanted* sexual encounters are cor-related with levels of the participants' sexual desire, ambivalence, sexual asser-tiveness, compliance, and the context of the relationship and situation (Darden et al., 2019). brown (2019) described how sexual consent can be pleasurable: "Consent means saying yes on your own terms. Giving permission or agreement for something to happen" (p. 165).

As we attempt to define consent, sexual flourishing, or whatever term feels most comfortable for each individual to develop relational secu-rity, it is important to note that such definitions arise from and may be restricted by White heteronormative (Hobaica & Kwon, 2017), nondis-abled expectations.

> Disabled people's sexual and intimate lives teach us that sex and pleasure are not merely about penetrative, goal-oriented sex. Disabled people have sex and receive pleasure in many ways and spaces that general society does not recognize or approve. . . . Sex for disabled people often means throwing out the norms and working with a partner to discover what their body can and cannot do, what they do and do not enjoy. . . . We would all benefit from such an approach that takes each partner's body, each sexual interaction, as new, figuring out what is best with this person in this moment, given how their body feels, what's on their mind, etc. (Schalk, 2019, p. 148)

As these sentiments resonate very much with us, in this chapter, we similarly hope to broaden perspectives, increase person-centered sexuality, and include at least a few of the voices not typically acknowledged by mainstream sexual culture and institutions.

Several Stories of Sexual Development

The first section below is a narrative of a client of coauthor Beckstead, with permission from the client, and the second section is a personal account of coauthor Braegger. After these, the third-person stories[1] that follow provide more diversity for readers to learn about the various ways to live an authentic sexuality and understand consent.

Questions to keep in mind as you read these accounts:

- How are their experiences similar to and different from yours?
- Which emotions and thoughts come up for you as you read their experiences?
- Which strengths did you see in each example, and what would you wish for each person?

---

[1] They are based on a compilation of experiences from people coauthors have encountered in our clinical practice, empirical research, and personal lives. Personal facts were changed to protect identity. The stories and names are not connected to any specific person.

- Which ideas and strategies could help you develop your sexuality, understand consent, and act more sexually assertive and authentically?
- How would you write and describe your sexual/gender history, development, and future?

Remember to care for yourself and how emotionally regulated you are when reading the following sections. If you feel lightheaded, dizzy, not present, angry, or fearful, you are probably doing *fear/startle breathing*, which is usually tight, shallow, or rapid. This constricted way of breathing could be related to previous painful experiences and a sign you are heading into deep feelings you should be careful about. You might decide whether or not to *skip any of the following sections* for now, take a break, or continue reading. If you're feeling any discomfort and you want to continue reading despite that, it would probably be helpful to practice some *breathing-awareness skills.*

Start by paying attention to how you are breathing. Breathing in a relaxed way means letting your tongue, throat, armpits, chest, belly, and pelvic floor (the web of muscles around the anus and genitals) hang loose. A relaxed core will allow your breathing to go downward into the belly, which will expand gently as you inhale. There will be some expansion in the low back and pelvic floor, but it will be smaller. When you exhale, just let the breath fall out like a sigh. Don't force it. These breathing-awareness skills will help you any time you feel anxious, including having sex or reading this chapter.

A Transsexual Woman Trapped and Powerless

Tammy relates that, before hormone therapy, she would ruminate nightly on using a potato peeler to take off her skin, and those ruminations stopped early on with hormone therapy. Since puberty, she had felt betrayed and violated by her body's physical changes. Her body hair really bothered her, and she did not like how physically big she felt. But now, Tammy relates that noticing her thinner wrists while driving or typing has given her a sense of relief. She describes that her gender dysphoria was constant before hormone therapy, and she would have a distressing thought every 10 minutes about how much she hated her body. She relates that she can now recognize (parts of) her face and her arms, chest, and legs as (mostly) her body, where before they felt foreign or alien. Being sexual, even aroused, still reminds her of having a male body, and she has to dissociate at times to be intimate with her wife to prevent panic attacks. Other times, she focuses on sensual touch to avoid distressing contact with her genitalia.

She describes liking having a more feminine silhouette and being treated more congruently, especially at work. She also relates not dissociating as much since taking hormones, when before she would go catatonic and be unresponsive because she could not deal with distress triggered by gender dysphoria. She relates that her skin now feels like her skin since taking hormones, and, consequently, she can focus on her body to help settle and ground herself when stressed. Before hormones, she could not find a spot on her body that didn't trigger gender dysphoria, shame, and self-hatred.

She also relates not missing erections at all and feeling so happy that they went away with hormone therapy. She describes her sex drive as being in a better, healthier place since taking hormones, and she can now feel sexual desires and not feel distressed about them.

She describes still feeling much dysphoria and embarrassment for her genitalia and tries not to think about them. She describes her genitals as always feeling ugly and "in the way." She relates feeling angry that she even has to deal with her genitals because other women do not have the same experiences and because she hates to be stuck between genders. Her genitals make her feel separate from women and like an alien and a monster. She also loves swimming and misses it so much and is not able to swim as long as she has her current genitalia because she does not feel safe and does not feel comfortable around other women in the locker room. Tammy relates that she knows she will never be "whole," but she wants to get to a place where she feels okay and is as good as she can be.

Tammy's wife says Tammy is happier since taking hormones, and Tammy has noticed she is singing to herself all the time now and in a good mood most of the time. She describes enjoying her work since taking hormones and socially transitioning, when before she was isolated and really depressed and lonely. Tammy describes feeling better, more herself and authentic, and no longer a liar. She sometimes feels like a monster but less often than ever before. She wants to live a long, happy life in which more people will have known her as female than as male and that the male part will be only a memory. She states that she is done presenting as male because it never did serve her well. While on a recent visit to a cemetery, it occurred to her that she might one day be buried beneath a tombstone that would state "Tammy—Mother," and that brings her a great amount of comfort.

In contrast to this happiness and congruence, Tammy is stressed about finances and how paying for her upcoming gender-affirming bottom surgery will affect her family. She also relates feeling stressed with the bureaucracy of the medical system and waiting on insurance and authorities, not being in control of deadlines, and trying to arrange for surgery in the new year with her work's Flexible Spending Account funds expiring and her insurance deductible resetting. Tammy also has to travel out of state for this surgery, and planning has been difficult. She relates worrying about how to solve all these problems when nobody in power feels the same urgency that she does, with the solution to her distress only happening within a small window of scheduling surgery and aftercare. She describes feeling trapped and helpless with so many people having control over what happens to her body. She expressed, "People don't understand the gravity."

She relates that this distress and loss of body autonomy feels similar to junior high when it was dangerous to be different, she had to trivialize her suffering to appear normal, and she couldn't do anything about it but hide and change how she dressed. She relates that this caused a lot of bullying anyway, including rejection from her mother. Her mother tried to help by saying, "If you didn't dress so weird, you wouldn't get beaten up." She also describes struggling with the current political messages that trans people are perverts and sinners or, in contrast, trans people shouldn't change but be okay the way they are. She also describes feeling social pressure to look attractive enough to be taken seriously as a woman but avoid being overly sexual and being labeled a "groomer." While she is supported by her wife in seeking gender-affirming bottom surgery, Tammy worries how it will affect their relationship as transitioning has ended relationships in the past.

Gay/Bisexual Cisgender Man Coming Out Late in Life

To borrow a phrase from fundamentalist Christianity, I feel "born again"! I am hardly a "new creature in Christ Jesus," as I attribute no special powers to that presumed historical wise man, and my general disbelief in God puts me firmly in the agnostic camp. But the phrase and concept fit my rebirth as an out and proud gay man.

This "rebirth" occurred just five years ago at the wonderful age of 54. Before that time, I was a devout Mormon or a member of the Church of Jesus Christ of Latter-day Saints. I served a two-year mission to Alabama at the age of 19. I married a woman in one of the holy Mormon temples and wore the sacred undergarments night and day. I dutifully paid 10% of my gross annual income in tithing and still managed to provide for seven children. (It was our job as righteous Mormon husband and wife to bring as many spirits to earth as possible into our LDS home so they did not have to go to a home where they would not be raised Mormon.) Suffice it to say that I was "all in"! One hundred percent was not good enough for me. I gave 120% of myself to the Mormon church and followed its inspired leaders as men of God who personally communicated with and spoke for Christ.

The problem was I knew from a young age that I was different. I did not understand what all the fuss was about girls. They held little interest for me. But other boys and men were beautiful and wonderful and amazing in so many ways! My church leaders said that I was not gay but had same-sex attraction and that God had given this challenge to me as a test. As long as I never acted in sexual ways with another man, it was all good—but if I did succumb, God would be very displeased, and I would be excommunicated from his chosen church and people!

After 20 years of doing all that was prescribed by my Mormon therapists and ecclesiastical leaders—with no diminishing of my attraction to men or increase of attraction to women—I finally had to disagree with the "inspired" Mormon prophets who insisted that my attraction to men was perverse and a thorn in my side to overcome.

My six-month faith transition began as I wondered if these church leaders were inspired and ended with my jettisoning not only the Mormon church but all organized religion and God himself! (The Mormon God is cis-male!) My no longer giving any credence to what religions say about the LGBTQ community of individuals made my "rebirth" so much easier. I could totally and completely rid myself of those decades of voices that said sex with another man was vile, perverse, and disgusting. (My test sampling had certainly indicated that it was the opposite!) If there is no bearded old White man in the sky who dictates where I may put my penis, then why not enjoy what feels natural and right for me? The transition from a homophobic religious zealot to a wonderfully happy, sexually active gay heathen was, at times, a challenging one. Still, I can honestly say that the last five years have been the happiest and most rewarding of my life.

So here are some things that I have learned along the way in no particular order of importance. Use what has meaning and value to you and leave the rest behind:

- I do not see a gay/straight world or even one with 50 shades of "bi" thrown in. I believe humanity presents a wonderful scatter graph of potential healthy sexual expression. I really like these words by Alfred Kinsey: "Everyone is different. The problem is most people want to be the same. They find it easier to simply ignore this fundamental fact of the human condition. They are so eager to be part of the group that they will betray their own nature to get there." I am no longer willing to betray my nature to fit in.
- While I am now accepting of my sexual orientation, it is just a part of the wonderful complex person that I am.
- I no longer seek approval and validation from those who cannot or will not give it to me.
- It is all just data. Nothing in life has any innate meaning or judgment of worth, only what we assign to it (or allow others to assign to it).
- If you believe in God, develop a personal relationship with him/her/them. Stop relying on others to define who/what God is and how divinity feels about you.
- It takes planning, compartmentalizing, and good boundaries, but it is possible to balance a personal sexually active gay life with being the father of seven adult children.
- I wish someone had told me that educating myself about and protecting myself from STIs would be up to me. While asking every new sexual partner's status and most recent testing date is always desirable, it is best to assume and act as though every new sexual partner can infect you with something unless proven otherwise. There is much more to be aware of here than HIV, syphilis, gonorrhea, chlamydia, and mpox. For example, while not common, giardia can be an STI if your partner has it and you rim your

partner. It can be scary sometimes, but safer sex is about understanding, minimizing, and accepting risks.

- Happiness as a gay man need not be predicated on my finding the perfect guy and having a monogamous relationship. Those who have gone before us have fought hard for the right to marry, but do not feel the need to conform to cultural biases of marriage and monogamy if they hold little value to you. Nontraditional relationships are much more common among LGBTQIA+ individuals. Polyamory is a thing, and "compersion"[2] is amazing for those who feel it.
- There will be just as much judgment and shaming coming at you from within the LGBTQIA+ community as there was/is outside of it, and it can be even more toxic and harmful as it comes from within the "family."
- The hookup and dating apps are here to stay, and while there are many negatives about them, they can be the source of many good friendships and perhaps even a partner.
- Knowledge is power and readily available. Reddit/askgaybro, YouTube stars, and Google searches can produce answers to questions you don't even know you had! If you have a travel budget, going to Provincetown or Fire Island or events like the Miami White Party or Folsom Street Fair in San Francisco can also be educational and fun.
- Speaking of Folsom Street—give kink a try! In my sexual journey, there are things that I would have never thought I would enjoy that are now some of my favorite activities. And the individuals in some of the subculture groups are some of the nicest, most accepting, and welcoming I have found. Ya never know until you try it!
- Get help for your emotional challenges, preferably from a therapist who understands where you've come from and where you want to go.
- Find support groups until you can create your support network. Pride Center groups and Facebook groups are all very helpful. Take time to create your family of choice.
- Get help for your physical/sexual issues. Sexual challenges will happen, especially as you age. It can be frustrating when you find yourself with an opportunity to be sexually honest and authentic for the first time in your life. Don't accept anything less than the best sex that you can have. I had resigned myself to being a total bottom due to erectile dysfunction issues but found a new and fantastic sexual life as a true versatile man due to an instant two-hour erection in a syringe (look up TriMix). Versatile men do have twice the fun! Ask your health-care provider for information about medication options and behavioral strategies (mindfulness) to help with performance anxiety.
- Last but certainly not least of all: Have fun! Sex is meant to be enjoyable. If aspects are not for you, then look into why that is. There is nothing "wrong" with you—you are not broken. Remember that it is just data to be processed and acted on or not. I know that I have had a great sexual

---

2 The ability to be happy and celebrate your romantic/sexual partner enjoying sex or being romantic with another person.

encounter if I have laughed out loud at least once during it. I recently had the experience of a partner and me bursting spontaneously into laughter at the same time—it was better than a simultaneous orgasm! (Which is not as easy to accomplish as porn suggests!)

Be happy and horny—if you are not both, focus on one and see what happens with the other!

Young Adults From Racialized and Immigrant Communities

Living in a predominately White society, young people from racialized and immigrant communities experience many challenges in exploring and embracing their sexualities. They often experience tension and confusion as they receive conflicting messages from different aspects of their life: media images/messages are highly racialized and sexualized; school sex education is mostly heteronormative and risk based; sex education at home is expressed in messages of "silence" or "don't do it"; and there is peer pressure to experience sex, especially among young men. Furthermore, racism and xenophobia construct discourses of White/Western sexual practices as "liberal and progressive" and sexual practices of ethnoracial minority communities as "conservative and backward." These discourses deny that patriarchy, sexism, and homophobia exist in all communities but manifest differently in different communities. They also create stereotypes and self-rejection, making it difficult for racialized young people to embrace their sociocultural identities and make informed sexual decisions.

Some Examples of These Challenges and Strengths

Aatifa, aged 18 and self-identified as Muslim, made a personal choice not to engage in sexual intercourse until she finished university and got married. She resented that her choice was often viewed and stereotyped by others as not "really" her own "free" choice but "oppression" from her family and communities. She recalled that premarital sex was presented as the norm in school sex education, and discussions of diverse values and perspectives were predominantly absent. She rejected the myth that young Muslim people did not engage in premarital sex when she knew that some of her friends were sexually active. She also rejected the myth that there are no queer youth in the Muslim communities because she had friends who self-identified as queer. She advocated for bringing young people, parents, teachers, and faith leaders together to have open dialogues about sexuality and value-guided decisions.

For Kai, sexuality was never easy to talk about in his Japanese American family, let alone coming out. His parents were first-generation immigrants and felt strongly that sexual issues were private. They regularly reinforced the idea that he should be considering marriage to an Asian woman, and he felt pressure to fulfill their visions for him. In high school, Kai knew he was attracted to men and women but had little reference for what this meant for his identity. At dinner one night, he decided to ask his mom how she would feel if he was gay, just to test the waters. This was met with immediate anxiety and his mother's words, "I would probably kill myself." Going to college changed things for Kai. He became friends with other second-generation Asian American students who identified as LGBTQIA+. He began using the terms *bisexual* and *queer* and had his first intimate relationship with another racialized man; it all led to painful but essential conversations with his mom about his sexuality. He wanted her to know his authentic self, as difficult as that was. With time, he learned he didn't need to reject his Asianness or sexuality to be wholly Japanese American.

Jasmine grew up in a conservative Catholic household. She went to the Confraternity of Christian Doctrine, took communion, was confirmed in middle school, and attended a Catholic high school. The messages were clear throughout her life: being gay is a sin. When she began to realize she felt different in middle school and much more so in high school, this was incredibly scary. Jasmine tried to ignore her attraction toward women. Ignoring worked through high school and most of college until it no longer worked. In her senior year, she met her first girlfriend, and dating, romance, and sexual intimacy felt right for the first time. However, she was terrified others would find out and, as a result, kept her girlfriend a secret from her friends and family. Even holding her girlfriend's hand in the car was off-limits because someone might see!

It took years for Jasmine to feel comfortable coming out to friends, colleagues, and eventually her family. Her family took years (10!) to support Jasmine. During the decade she and her family were distant and trying to reconcile their differences, she left the Catholic Church and found a new spiritual community, the Unitarians, who were more accepting of her. Although she openly identified as lesbian, she still found herself uncomfortable around a group of lesbians, at lesbian functions, or if someone she didn't know correctly guessed she was a lesbian. She'd wonder, "How did they know I was lesbian?" Underneath this question was a fear that if people identified her as lesbian, and lesbian equals disgusting, then people would see her as disgusting. Jasmine also felt disgusted when she saw lesbian women in public, watched movies or shows about lesbian women, and even after sexual encounters. One day, her friend, who identified as lesbian, noted this when they were watching *The L Word*. Her friend asked, "Why do you think this is disgusting? This is us." This was when Jasmine realized her internalized homophobia. The hatred and disgust she was taught to feel about gay people growing up led her to feel hatred and disgust toward other lesbians and herself as a lesbian.

This realization of hating herself as a lesbian opened the door to finding a therapist who helped her challenge the old negative messages she learned about the gay community and understand new, healthy messages. It was only through challenging the negative societal stereotypes about the lesbian community, challenging the negative messages she learned about her identity, and surrounding herself with friends and communities that supported her that Jasmine could finally embrace her sexual identity and feel comfortable with her sexual self.

Using the Sexual Health Model

Now that you have read examples of evolving and personal definitions of sexual health, integrity, and consent, it may be helpful to understand which aspects of life are involved in developing sexuality. To answer this, we can turn to different models informed by research. There are nearly a dozen unique models, but they all have a few things in common. Specifically, most models are multidimensional, meaning they define health and wellness based on many dimensions, not just the presence or absence of sexual risk or sexual dysfunction. Second, these models consider the whole person and incorporate how sexual health impacts you biologically and psychologically within your relationships, society, and culture. And these models are individualized. They provide a framework or outline for sexual well-being, not a prescription for what you should or shouldn't do sexually. That's what you get to decide.

One of the most comprehensive and widely used models is called, not surprisingly, the Sexual Health Model (Robinson et al., 2002). It includes 10 areas a team of researchers created based on sex education curriculum and research on sexual attitudes, behaviors, and sexual risk factors. This model emphasizes three crucial points. First, consider sexuality in the context of your culture, which could mean your race/ethnicity, faith, sexual/gender identity, or other identity. Second, understand that how you define your sexual health may look different than the sexual health of someone else, and that is okay. This is called *sexual pluralism*, meaning there are many ways to experience sexual wellness. Finally, you get to decide what is sexually healthy for you. You define your sexual values, morals, beliefs, and expressions. You don't, however, get to choose the consequences of your choices, so choose wisely.

Sexual Beliefs and Values Card Sort

For each area of the Sexual Health Model, you will hold a set of sexual values, whether you are conscious of them or not. For example, under "Talking about sex," your sexual value may be honesty. You can think of a value as a compass that guides you. It differs from a goal in that you cannot just check off a value on a to-do list. You can't simply check off the value of honesty and say, "Phew! Glad I got that off my list." We unconsciously reference our values all the time!

The Sexual Beliefs and Values Card Sort can help you identify the sexual beliefs and values most relevant to you now. This exercise contains 63 possible sexual values, and it is up to you to narrow down these cards to your top five values. While many people struggle with eliminating dozens of positive values to obtain a top five, remember that these five core values are intended to be guiding principles you prioritize in your sexual health decisions, not the *only* guiding principles in your life. Try to identify five sexual values to help simplify your sexual decision-making. To do this:

1. Print the Sexual Beliefs and Values Card Sort pages (which can be downloaded from www.FindingCongruence.com). Cut out each card.
2. On the floor or a large tabletop, lay the headers on the first page (Not at All Important to Me, Very Important to Me, Somewhat Important to Me) side by side. Place each of the beliefs and values cards below their corresponding header based on importance to you.
3. Once complete, discard all the cards in the Not at All Important to Me and Somewhat Important to Me columns.
4. With the remaining Very Important to Me cards, rank and prioritize how important these are to you. Condense this column to 10 cards.
5. Now condense this pile down to five cards. These are the top five most essential sexual beliefs and values to you. How do you feel thinking about these sexual beliefs and values?
6. Consider your current sexuality, sexual practices, and sexual behaviors. Are these congruent with your top five sexual beliefs and values?
7. If not, how so? And what do you want to do about this?

Take a moment to answer the following questions to get familiar with your sexual values:

1. Which values did I learn from my family, culture, friends, media, sexual experiences, or other sources? How did these values affect my sexual development?
2. Do I adopt the values of others around me, or do I tend to form my values despite what other people think?
3. Do I consider values that have proven true over long periods and in different cultures, expecting them to work well for me?
4. What does it mean if my values differ from my community? How does this make me feel? How does this shape my behaviors?
5. Are these values congruent with how I see myself/what is important to me? If not, which values would facilitate my identity development? Which values do I want to inform my current and future sexuality?

If you struggle to clarify your sexual values, you are not alone. The following section highlights principles that may help clarify your sexual values further.

Understanding Six Core Sexual Health Principles

Using recommendations from the World Health Organization, the Pan American Health Organization, and the World Association of Sexual Health, two therapists, Braun-Harvey and Vigorito (2016), identified six principles of sexual health:

1. Consent: Permission to be sexual with oneself and others. In other words, all parties in a sexual interaction voluntarily choose to engage with one another and agree on which sexual acts to engage in.
2. Nonexploitation: The easiest way to describe nonexploitation is by defining exploitation. Exploitation typically happens when one person has more social or physical power/influence over another and uses that power to manipulate, deceive, or coerce sexual activity. Exploitation also happens when a person betrays trust, disregards a relationship agreement, or violates a relationship agreement without the other knowing (for example, an affair). Thus, nonexploitation is when partners (a) share equal power and decision-making and control over their own body, (b) have honest communication about what works and doesn't for each person, (c) keep their relationship agreements, and (d) inform each other if they cannot keep an agreement.
3. Protection from sexually transmitted infection and unwanted pregnancy. This principle does not say you must use protection. Instead, you should be aware of the risks and benefits of using and not using protection in order to make a thoughtful decision.
4. Honesty/transparency: Sexual integrity can flourish with communication about wants, desires, needs, limits, sexual health status (HIV, HPV, herpes, etc.), and histories.
5. Shared values: Communication with self and partners about sexual values, sexual motivations, and goals of sexual activities/relationships can help sexuality flourish.
6. Mutual pleasure: Sexuality can be healthy and flourish by enjoying reciprocity in giving and receiving pleasure.

As you read these descriptions, how do they relate to what you want for your sexuality?

Ten Components of Sexual Health

Now that you have spent some time thinking about your sexual values, the Sexual Health Model and accompanying questions below may help you further develop a clearer understanding of which values, behaviors, and experiences are best for you.

1. Talking About Sex: The foundation of consent and developing person-centered sexuality is knowing and communicating your desires and limits and feeling comfortable enough doing so.

    a. How comfortable am I talking about sex? With a partner? With friends? With family? Which judgments about sex affect how I feel talking about sex? How do I want to feel about myself when I talk about sex?
    b. Where did I learn to talk, or not talk, about sex? Which messages/beliefs about sex most helped or harmed me?
    c. Which words do I use when I talk about sex? For example, sexual nicknames, medical terminology, or language that fits me and my body parts?
    d. How much do I know about my sexual body, turn-ons, and limits?
    e. How much and in which ways do I teach my sexual partner(s) about my body, turn-ons, and limits?

2. Culture and Sexual Identity: Your culture (family, generation, religion, ethnicity, geography) likely has shaped how you experience sexuality and consent.

    a. How has culture influenced and not influenced my sexuality? Do I want it to?
    b. How can I use my cultural values to develop my sexual integrity and wellness and a flourishing and authentic sexuality?
    c. What messages have I received from my culture(s) about sex? Which ones help me connect to myself and others, and which ones disconnect me from myself and others?
    d. How can I use my cultural values to reinforce asking for sexual consent?

3. Sexual Anatomy and Functioning: A significant component of sexual health is physical health and functioning. It is essential to understand how your sexual anatomy works, what it looks like, and what is considered a biologically healthy response.

    a. Am I familiar with my sexual anatomy and how different parts of my body function?
    b. How do I feel about my body, including the sensual parts and genitals?
    c. Do I have realistic expectations for how my body should function sexually at my age?
    d. Do I have realistic expectations for how my partner's body should function sexually?

4. Sexual Health Care and Safer Sex: Sexual health is a part of one's general health. This includes regular checkups with a health-care provider, especially if you notice changes in your body or sexual function.

    a. When was the last time I had a complete physical?
    b. Do I know my options for preventing a sexually transmitted infection (STI)?
    c. Can I name six to eight STIs? If not, I need more education.
    d. Do I know the signs of various STIs?

e. Do I know which STIs can be transmitted during oral sex?
f. Am I aware of PrEP for HIV prevention? Am I aware that there are programs that can potentially help me get it at no cost?
g. Am I aware that using PrEP only helps in HIV prevention and does not protect against contracting other STIs?
h. Am I aware of DoxyPEP, a postexposure preventative treatment for several STIs, but not all of them?
i. Do I know what changes in my body warrant going to the doctor?
j. Do I know which sexual acts are associated with the highest risks of infection?
k. Do I know where I can get free or low-cost STI testing?

Ask a health-care provider about the above for current information.

5. Challenges: Common barriers to developing sexual integrity and flourishing include a history of sexual trauma, chemical use (alcohol, drugs), difficulties with emotion regulation, and out-of-control or out-of-balance sexual behaviors.

a. Do I experience any of these barriers? If not, which barriers (if any) might I experience when developing an authentic sexuality and well-being?
b. Do I ever need to drink alcohol or use drugs to feel comfortable being sexual? How well do I respect my limits with substances during sex?
c. Have I ever dissociated (checked out of my body) when being sexual? Have I sought professional help with this?
d. Have I considered the advantages and disadvantages, both psychological and physical, of sexual abstinence until marriage or relationship trust or commitment?
e. Are there aspects of my sexual behavior that feel out of control? Are there negative beliefs about myself, sex, and relationships that I need to address directly to experience more sexual satisfaction?
f. Do I need to learn or develop skills to understand my emotions and needs and respond assertively to my impulses when I'm upset (Rahm-Knigge et al., 2023)?
g. Do I need to consider that I have an asexual sexual orientation and that there is nothing wrong with being asexual?

6. Body Image: Developing self-acceptance and understanding how culture influences your idea about your body are essential to developing sexual wellness.

a. How do I relate to and feel about my body sensations?
b. How have my culture(s)/society/media shaped my relationship and judgments of my body?
c. How do I think others view my body? How does focusing on others' views affect how I relate to my body? How does this focus and relationship affect my sexual pleasure (Poovey et al., 2022)?

7. Masturbation and Fantasy: Masturbation, or self-pleasure, regardless of how it fits in your belief system, is one way to practice safe sex. Getting to know your body and sexual responses, coupled with fantasy, is one option to learn what you enjoy and find sexually arousing.

   a. What are three to five words to describe how I experience masturbation? And why?
   b. What are my beliefs about masturbation or self-pleasure?
   c. What do my cultures say about masturbation and self-pleasure?
   d. Do specific fantasies fit within my sexual values or outside of my sexual values?
   e. Has frequent masturbation or porn use trained my body to respond sexually in only one way, making it more difficult to respond well to a sexual partner?
   f. How can I engage with my sexuality with more mindful attention, acceptance, curiosity, enjoyment, self-compassion, self-appreciation, self-respect, and grace?

8. Positive Sexuality: Healthy sexuality includes experiencing pleasure, not experiencing sexual pain, feeling sexually empowered and not ashamed, and having the independence to learn and experiment sexually and consensually with oneself and others.

   a. What role does giving and receiving pleasure play in my eroticism, romance, and sexuality?
   b. How do binary and rigid gender roles and expectations, heteronormative sexual scripts, and communication impact the sexual pleasure of me and my partner(s) (Harvey et al., 2023)?
   c. What role do shame, guilt, pride, and humility play in my sexuality?
   d. What does it mean for me to feel and act sexually empowered and assertively?
   e. What does it mean for me to experiment sexually? What is the purpose, and does it fit within my sexual values?

9. Intimacy and Relationships: Intimacy is described as closeness/togetherness. A sexual relationship is one way to experience intimacy with another person; however, it is only one of many ways (spiritual, recreational, emotional, etc.). Sexuality can be experienced with or without intimacy and along a spectrum of ways to be sexually intimate.

   a. How much are emotional connection and commitment vital to me in a sexual experience and relationship? Do my values and sexuality allow me to have sex or enjoy sex without an emotional connection and commitment?
   b. What other ways do I need to be intimate (feel close/together) beyond sexual or physical?
   c. How does my gender-role expression affect my sexual expression, intimacy, and relationships?

10. Spirituality: Spirituality may encompass a formal/current faith or religion, your moral and ethical sexual beliefs and values, or your purpose in life. Your spirituality may match closely with how you experience your sexuality, or they may be at odds. Moral incongruence and traditional religiosity, for example, are predictors of negative feelings about porn use (Štulhofer et al., 2022). If there is a discrepancy between these areas of your life, exploring how best to resolve these issues for you will develop your sexual congruence (Griffin et al., 2016).

    a. What are my moral and ethical sexual beliefs and values? Where and how did I learn these?
    b. Considering the moral/ethical sexual beliefs and values I learned as a child, do I still believe those today? If so, why and how do they affect my sexuality, relationships, and feelings about myself?
    c. Is my sexuality congruent with my spirituality and philosophy of life? How can my sexuality provide a positive meaning in my life?
    d. What is my idea of experiencing spiritual sexuality and sexual spirituality?

We encourage you to use your values and the 10 areas of the Sexual Health Model and the Six Principles of Sexual Health to guide your understanding of what is essential to you and the sexual well-being/flourishing of your partner(s). What is important to you currently and how you understand your sexuality may differ from when you were in your teens and 20 years from now. Your definition of sexual wellness and integrity may evolve as you age, engage in relationships, and learn about your body and as your sexual responses change through life.

The Expiration Date on Sexual Consent for Older LGBTQIA+ Adults

When the question of consent is discussed, it is predominantly in the context of younger people. The lack of research focused on sexual development and sexual expression in older LGBTQIA+ adults has resulted in an "unseen minority" of the 21st century (de Vries & Herdt, 2012). Without visibility, older LGBTQIA+ adults are not appropriately considered in policies, general discourse, and health-care settings (Syme, 2021). Consequently, this not only affects their daily lives but also influences the way they receive health care. This written piece on sexual consent for older LGBTQIA+ adults will discuss the history of this cohort, as well as the consequences of this history, namely, stigma and ageism.

Historical Bias Leading to Current Ageism

To understand how consent is formed in the lives of older LGBTQIA+ adults, it's important to realize that they came of age when same-gender/queer relationships were not just stigmatized but criminalized (Fredriksen-Goldsen & Muraco, 2010). The oldest cohort moved into adulthood in approximately 1952, when homosexuality was officially listed as a sociopathic personality disturbance that could be cured. At the same time, they were routinely harassed by law enforcement and federal politics. One particular case of harassment led to the historic Stonewall rebellion in New York in June 1969. It was not until 1973 and 2013 that homosexuality and a transgender identity were respectively removed from the *Diagnostic and Statistical Manual of Mental Disorders* as psychiatric disorders.

Around the start of the civil rights movement in the 1960s, increasing numbers of younger LGBTQIA+ people gradually started to come out. However, the discriminatory and violent history to which they were subjected resulted in some older generations remaining in the closet even as they aged. Already part of the "silent generation" who worked hard and stayed quiet and loyal, this group of LGBTQIA+ individuals had to find a way to survive in a cis-heteronormative society to prevent being alienated by family and community and fired from their jobs. They grew up understanding that they had much to lose and little to gain from being LGBTQIA+. Since many older LGBTQIA+ adults did not disclose their orientation, their lives have remained largely unseen, resulting in a lack of sexual agency. Reynolds (2021) emphasized that sexual consent is a multifaceted process of communication and interaction between sexual partners. It is unlikely that this unseen and silent generation of LGBTQIA+ adults is experiencing and receiving their total sexual consent capacity.

Not only did the older LGBTQIA+ cohort face challenges in their early lives related to sexual identity, they also encountered additional difficulties stemming from ageism. In contemporary Western society, there exists a widely accepted notion that sexuality primarily belongs to the young, healthy, and beautiful (Syme & Cohn, 2016). According to Rubin (1984), a hierarchical system assesses sexuality and determines the sexual value assigned to specific groups. At the summit of this hierarchy are young, married, cis-heterosexual, nondisabled, White individuals. Those whose sexual behaviors fall lower on the scale often find themselves constrained in both social and physical mobility. LGBTQIA+ adults tend to occupy the outer limits of this sexual hierarchy. Consequently, positioned on the "wrong" side of the sexual judgment line, older LGBTQIA+ adults are frequently subjected to desexualization.

Internalization of Ageism and Bias

Consequences related to the stigma and ageism referred to above include the potential internalization of prejudice and discrimination. Internalized homophobia represents the LGBTQIA+ person's negative social attitudes directed toward themselves (Meyer & Dean, 1998). The stigma—and consequently the internalized homophobia—seems even more prevalent among the cohort of older LGBTQIA+ adults and affects several aspects of their lives, including health and self-esteem. When one considers the fact that, currently, more than three million U.S. citizens over the age of 65 identify as part of the LGBTQIA+ community—which is expected to be six million by 2030—many older LGBTQIA+ adults are unseen and affected by a combination of ageism and internalized homophobia. A 2020 study by Fleishman et al. demonstrated that high internalized homophobia among older adults in a same-sex relationship correlates with low resilience and relationship satisfaction levels. In addition, relational and sexual satisfaction are important indicators of quality of life (DeLamater, 2012; Fleishman et al., 2020). In short, the older LGBTQIA+ cohort has a higher chance of experiencing a lower quality of life.

The following represents coauthor Huitema's experience of how older LGBTQIA+ individuals can get trapped by bias in the health-care system:

> I crossed paths with Mr. Baker during his stay at the rehabilitation center where I practiced as a psychologist. He had suffered a stroke and was grappling with feelings of depression. Consequently, I began holding regular conversations with him. Mr. Baker, at 64 years old and in a heterosexual marriage with Mary, revealed to me during our weekly sessions that he was living with a hidden truth—he was secretly gay.
>
> In his candid disclosure, Mr. Baker explained that Mary was aware of his sexual orientation and harbored romantic feelings for him despite this knowledge. To navigate their predicament, they chose to marry and cohabitate without consummating their marriage. Mr. Baker met other gay men discreetly on a near-weekly basis in a wooded setting to satisfy his sexual needs. Simultaneously, he and Mary shared a life together, engaging in vacations and partaking in family events and celebrations.
>
> During his stroke recovery, the medication prescribed by the neurologist and cardiologist, intended to prevent clotting and alleviate his depression, had the unintended consequence of negatively impacting his sexual function. The medical professionals appeared to have not communicated the potential side effects to him, possibly overlooking it because of his age. These side effects left him incapable of continuing his secret encounters, which had become his only means of expressing himself as a gay man.
>
> This sexual dysfunction, a result of the medication, seemed to be the root cause of the depression he was experiencing, as it hindered his ability to embrace his authentic identity. In light of this, we reached out to the medical doctors (MDs) to discuss the medication's side effects and their impact on his sexual life. To our surprise, both MDs were taken aback by Mr. Baker's desire to maintain a fulfilling and active sex life. Consequently, they adjusted his medication to options that did not affect his sexual functioning in the same manner.
>
> The outcome was transformative: Mr. Baker's depression lifted, and he no longer required antidepressants. He returned to his previous state of well-being

and resumed his secret gay encounters. It is worth noting that we discussed the possibility of him revealing his true self to his family and friends. Yet he remained resolute in his belief that his mother would never comprehend his situation, and he was determined to maintain his familial relationships.

Most older patients have internalized societal bias and are ashamed to discuss sexuality with their health-care provider. The consequences can be life altering and cause mental health issues, as in the example of Mr. Baker. Open communication about sexual desires, needs, and limits is lacking for most of this cohort, which ultimately influences their ability to consent.

Inclusive Care for Older LGBTQIA+ Adults: The Route to Sexual Health

Because aging is accompanied by physical, cognitive, and psychological changes, which often result in physical frailty and dependency on others, ageism and other social stigmas have resulted, particularly in Western societies (Barrett & Hinchliff, 2018). The historical and cultural stigma concerning older LGBTQIA+ adults has had a negative impact on available resources for this population. The historical discrimination experienced by older LGBTQIA+ adults creates a barrier for this group when accessing health and social support (Institute of Medicine, 2011). It has made older LGBTQIA+ adults feel skeptical toward health-care professionals in general. This means they are less likely to disclose their sexual orientation or mental and physical health history with a health-care professional. Fear of discrimination has caused older LGBTQIA+ adults to avoid or delay care, which can have negative health consequences.

In addition to older LGBTQIA+ adults being skeptical toward health-care professionals, they also experience barriers, such as a lack of health insurance and a lack of support from family, partners, and friends (Institute of Medicine, 2011). Sometimes same-gender/queer partners are not acknowledged and, therefore, not allowed hospital visits or to be part of medical decision-making. These barriers influence the ability to provide consent for older LGBTQIA+ adults who need or use health-care services.

Sexuality and Long-Term-Care Facilities

With an increased risk of health-care issues, older LGBTQIA+ adults are more likely to become dependent on long-term care. Issues relating to long-term care (LTC) are pivotal for older LGBTQIA+ adults, a disproportionate number of whom are without primary caregivers such as partners or children. Studies have identified that the attitude of staff toward LGBTQ+ residents in LTC is generally negative (Institute of Medicine, 2011). This negative attitude can include refusing permission for selected family, friends, or same-gender/queer partners to visit or refusing to involve a partner or selected family member in medical decision-making—as in the following situation:

> Seventy-year-old Ms. Rita recently moved into the long-term-care facility where I worked. She felt so comfortable and safe that she shared with both the staff and fellow residents that her "niece" visiting her was actually her girlfriend and lover. However, after revealing this, she noticed that others began to shun her. She mentioned feeling isolated during mealtimes as she observed other residents avoiding her. To make matters worse, she overheard a nursing aide saying, "I hope they don't expect me to wash the butt of that old lesbian." After Ms. Rita overheard that, she said, "Whether I die now or not, it doesn't matter, I'm in hell either way."

The case of Ms. Rita demonstrates that when older LGBTQIA+ adults are admitted to LTC, they sometimes feel they have to go back into the closet out of fear of discrimination. Some elderly LGBTQIA+ individuals needing LTC have found inclusive LTC facilities that openly welcome older LGBTQIA+ adults. Unfortunately, not every state or city has LGBTQIA+-friendly facilities.

When older LGBTQIA+ adults live independently and are relatively healthy and capable, they can make their own decisions. However, when they are admitted to LTC, they become more dependent on staff, and the perspective and attitude of the staff toward sexuality, gender, and LGBTQIA+ people can influence the intimate expression of the residents (Benbow & Beeston, 2012; Hajjar & Kamel, 2004). Nevertheless, most LTC facilities do not implement policies or provide training on sexuality and LGBTQIA+ people. Without training, the staff's attitude toward residents' sexual orientation and gender expression depends on personal norms and subjective attitudes (Thys et al., 2019). Consequently, the bias of LTC staff against LGBTQIA+ individuals can affect the care provided and the assessment of sexual consent.

Research on older LGBTQIA+ adults is slowly emerging, as are discussions and policies around sexuality and LTC. Fortunately, being a hidden minority does not mean the situation is unchangeable. We can acknowledge the violent and discriminatory history of today's older LGBTQIA+ adults, including sexual/gender minorities who do not identify as LGBTQIA+, as an essential first step. Additionally, educating health-care professionals on issues relating to older LGBTQIA+ adults will be helpful. We can support the older LGBTQIA+ cohort in being who they are to improve their well-being. Consequently, our recognition and support for the older LGBTQIA+ cohort will benefit their sexual consent potential.

Conclusion

Definitions of healthy sexuality and meaningful consent vary in relation to community, sociopolitical influences, relationships, age, and individual experience. Therefore, our aim for this chapter was to provide a set of experiences, guidelines, values, and skills that touch on multiple areas of sexuality and consent. We hope these ideas and strategies inspire conversations with yourself and others to promote sexual authenticity, safety, and joy!

Chapter 4

Find Your Best Options for LGBTQIA+ Singlehood and Relationships

Moshe-Mordechai (Maurits) van Zuiden, A. Lee Beckstead, Stefano Eleuteri, Erin S. Lavender-Stott, Darren J. Freeman-Coppadge, Tyler Lefevor, Eric Boromisa, Lauren Smithee, Christine Aramburu Alegría, Iva Žegura, and Jeni Wahlig[1]

This chapter is meant for everyone, whether you are happy with your singlehood or relationship status or considering a change. We hope this chapter helps you be more confident about possible transitions, whether or not you choose to pursue them. We hope our ideas, skills, and resources can help you think outside the box, compare and contrast what feels best for you, and have more empathy and care for those with different options/statuses than you.

We wrote this chapter keeping the following two realizations in mind: "[If] so many [people], so many minds, certainly so many hearts, so many kinds of love" (Tolstoy, 1878/2020, p. 158), and "under layers of socialization—and jealousy—there's a deeper wiring that says yes to one or yes to two or yes to many. And relationships should be formed around that yes rather than what society or books say should happen" (brown, 2019, p. 344). In short, let us respect our uniqueness and authenticity and free ourselves from unchecked rigidities and misleading social expectations.

---

[1] The order of authorship does not reflect the amount of content in the chapter but coauthors' combined content and labor on both this book chapter and the e-resource.

To inspire you to be you, we will suggest different ways of being single (noncelibate or celibate) and partnered (exclusive or open regarding romance and sexuality) and ideas that have helped some to feel more secure in monogamous, nonmonogamous, and polyamorous relationships. Ideas and strategies often lack variety. Please see our e-booklet and online resources for more information.

Considering Your Options About Relationships

For some people, the most important thing is to be happy. For some, being as "normal" as possible adds to their happiness. For some, it is crucial not to take risks, while others want to liberate themselves from normalcy. What is most important for you?

People are not all the same; therefore, intimate relationships cannot be "one size fits all." Intimacy is also more than sexuality and romance. What is suitable for one person at a particular time and place may not be as good for another, and it may not be suitable for that person for all time. There are more definitions and choices than one standard option. Also, so-called alternative options don't always fit us. We hope to inspire you with ideas you might not know or not have taken seriously, understood, or appreciated before.

Alternative relationships may be obscured when our family, society, culture, religion, or other factor stigmatizes them as unimportant, harmful, or wrong *for everyone*. What we may consider possible is often limited by what we've seen in the media and around us. Social safety and how well we explore and value ourselves, our relationships, and our life's goals can help us to see what fits us best and choose for ourselves.

How far you succeed in meeting your personal and relational needs will be determined—besides by your ability to live independently and how tolerant your surroundings are—by your choices. These choices could include how much you allow your current relationships to evolve, how much effort you are willing to make in changing what you dislike around you, on what type of relationships you invest in, what kind and how many partner(s) and people you spend time with, and how you choose to behave relationally. Here are a couple of examples:[2]

1. Adrian (they/them) has parents who have a traditional marriage and lifelong respect and support for each other. Family is the primary source of strength. That's what Adrian wants. However, Adrian has struggled to find this with the individuals they have been the most attracted to. Adrian

---

[2] These examples are based on compilations of stories and experiences from people we have encountered in our clinical practice, empirical research, and personal lives. Each one's indicated name is fictitious and is not connected to any specific person.

decided to deemphasize sexual attraction and prioritize family qualities and relationship compatibility. Adrian then found love.

2. Jo (she/he/they) loves being single and polyamorous and has no wish to change despite exposure to many events focused on couples and families. Jo lives alone, is not seeking a primary partner, and spends time being romantic (cuddling and kissing) and enjoying several intimate (sexual and nonsexual) companionships. Jo has considered adopting a child and enjoys caring for the children in friends' and lovers' families.

3. Samantha (she/her) grew up in a family where the expected relationship was a monogamous marriage between a man and woman, preferably with someone from her cultural background and faith. While she has heard of open and polyamorous relationships, she knows these options are too far outside of her culture, comfort, and preferences and would not be good for her. She is also concerned about what her family would think if they knew she was not in a monogamous relationship. Despite social pressures, Samantha feels a committed monogamous relationship with a woman is best for her, preferably someone who shares or at least understands and appreciates her faith and cultural heritage. She is unsure about raising children and plans to explore this option with her future partner.

4. Jeff (he/him) wants a committed relationship but knows he does not want to raise children. His partner's sex characteristics and gender expression don't matter much to him compared to how Jeff likes and feels safe with the person and how the person treats him. Jeff wants his relationship to be sexually open but romantically closed. He wants to participate in his version of kink with others and with a partner who enjoys kink and feels secure within the relationship.

What were your thoughts and emotional reactions reading the above examples? Which experiences fit and don't fit you? What made you curious and want to learn more?

As you consider different relationship ideas, needs, and choices, we encourage you to give yourself time to decide and allow yourself to change your mind or try new things in ways that don't hurt you or others. Consider that it is okay to "hurt" people's *expectations* of you. Their presumptions and insecurities are theirs to grapple with. Consider that their crying and grieving can help reset their expectations. Give them time to grieve and change their old ideas about the path they thought you were on that didn't fit you.

We will discuss that the "sky can be the limit," but let's get down to earth first.

Though improving a relationship takes time, you must get out ASAP when you recognize you're in a relationship with someone abusive, exploitative, or toxic. Feeling good about such a step may come only after you leave. You need to seek power, protection, and support to prioritize yourself (and any children) and distance yourself even if you grapple with guilt, loneliness, and hopelessness. Regaining perspective and making new friends who won't blame you typically take time, too.

Not all relationship options are available to everyone. Circumstances, shame, anxiety, real dangers, and lack of social privilege may limit your opportunities. It makes a difference if you live with your parents, in a boarding school, in a facility, in a close-knit community, with your partner(s) and children, on your own, or with roommates or were thrown into the street or have run away. Options also may depend on your culture and country's laws, how supportive the people around you are, your job, how dependent you are on people who expect agreement or obedience, and how much time and patience you have to see if their rejection will change. One parent/caregiver may accept your authentic self faster than the other(s), and some friends might surprise you with support and others with abandonment or rejection.

Could you choose to dare and do it your way? In that case, strengthen your support from existing and new friends, like-minded people, different communities, and professionals and decide not to rush it if you're not in danger—especially when others pressure you to give up on trusting your thinking and intuition. Some believe following their heart's wishes is their best guide. If this is you, who you engage with can be reality checks to ensure that your heart's desire is not just a short-term impulse that passes and leads to something you don't wish for. Honor how these short-term relationship journeys are meaningful and help you decide your best path. You could determine that your heart's long-term desire is to follow and enjoy short-term impulses and experiences.

Though we are relational beings, to be in a relationship with others, it is first important to be in contact and relationship with ourselves to know our authentic needs and desires.

When you have found peace with who you are and what you need and want, it will be easier for others around you to come to terms with that. If you are still ambivalent, don't pretend you are not. Your honesty might make it safer for others to be less than extreme in their position. More important than changing others' mindsets about your relationship choices is to make yourself independent of their opinions and give them time to experience you in this new relationship option. This may make negotiations on how to proceed easier for everyone involved.

What are your most essential needs and limits? You may set a time limit to try a new adaptation to see if it works for you and others. You don't need to settle for less than what fits you. Yet, sometimes, settling for less than perfect may be better than throwing out something *good enough that can grow or at least be stable* in pursuit of a better future. This reasoning, however, can be part of what keeps people in abusive relationships. Don't make the mistake of expecting your love to change the other person into what you wish them to be. Cutting your losses might be painful but may be your best option if it's not working.

If you find yourself quitting partners over the same reason repeatedly, consider if this indicates an area where you might need to introspect further and improve, especially if your behavior or decisions negatively impact others. Yet this reasoning can be misleading if you are a minority. For example, if you are asexual or demisexual, you don't need to "improve" and be more sexual or pretend to be sexual because all your partners so far were.

We'll next provide a more detailed look at relationship options and their unique issues in two main categories: singlehood and partnered relationships. Later, we'll address options for connection and romantic/sexual exclusivity and openness within singlehood and partnerships.

Singlehood

It used to be that anyone who was not heterosexually married was considered single. This was especially true for lesbian women throughout history, as their sexuality and relationships fell below the radar of heteronormative expectations, making their relationships invisible (Dota, 2017; Lamble, 2009; Lavender-Stott, 2023). We now have different definitions and understandings of singlehood (Lavender-Stott & Allen, 2023). Here are some examples:

- legally single but socially partnered (committed significant relationships, polyamorous relationships, cohabitating, partnered but living apart, etc.)
- legally married but socially single (legal separation, married for benefits or social acceptance, etc.)
- legally and socially single (no committed romantic/sexual partners)

In certain cultures, adults will be single for more of their life than partnered or married (Lavender-Stott et al., 2023). In the United States, a quarter of current young adults will likely remain unpartnered (United States Census, 2017). Even with cultural and demographic changes, some people do not wish to be single, while others are proud of their singlehood (for example, single at heart) (DePaulo, 2006).

In addition to a continuum of happiness of singlehood status, there is a continuum of desire to engage or not engage in sexual/romantic experiences. One common stress that single individuals, regardless of their sexual orientation and gender, may experience is negative judgment from others about singlehood and pressure to "meet the right one" to have equal worth and status. This may be compared to the expectations one may face in raising or not raising children. These stressful expectations may be harder on you depending on how much you have internalized them, how unclear you are about what fits you best, and how many people you have who will take your side.

Next, we'll divide singlehood into being celibate or noncelibate. In doing so, we do not want to imply that having sex or not having sex are central issues of singlehood or that celibacy is the default. We will highlight religious issues in being celibate and, unfortunately, look less at other reasons for celibacy. We also do not focus on how asexual individuals may experience singlehood and how their relationships are not organized around celibacy or noncelibacy. The following sections were developed from the coauthors' research and offered as possible suggestions for how those who are celibate or open to sexual/romantic experiences may increase their well-being and satisfaction. Our companion e-resource provides some suggestions for those whose celibacy is not a choice, and we hope our online resources can provide more guidance for those whose experiences are not covered below.

Single and Celibate

Many Eastern religions venerate celibacy as virtuous. Celibacy as a vocation has its roots in Christian teachings that highlight the virtue of single living to build God's Kingdom (Abbott, 2001). Over the past millennium, celibacy in Europe has been practiced primarily in one-gender communities, such as convents and monasteries, and has provided reverence for single individuals. In communities where same-gender sexuality was taboo, taking a vow of celibacy was admirable and allowed the nun or friar and their families not to talk about anything sensitive. In recent years, increasing attention has been placed on celibacy to reconcile conflicts between sexual orientation and religious identity. Celibacy allows Christians who are sexual minorities to accept and embrace their sexual orientation while also adhering to traditional, orthodox interpretations of the Bible that do not condone sexual activity between two people of the same gender. In this way, celibacy may be a way for traditionally religious sexual minorities to live their values and sexuality in a manner that provides richness and purpose. For the last 70 years, Orthodox rabbis have also advocated this, but recently, more see complete abstinence as unattainable and in contraindication to Judaism's promise of a good life.

Sexual-minority individuals who pursue celibacy face stigma and minority stress from multiple fronts, from many in the queer community who consider celibate individuals deceived by religious control and self-hatred and not free to "live true to themselves" and from heteronormative individuals who criticize these individuals for not being heterosexual and pursuing heterosexual marriage (Freeman-Coppadge & Horne, 2019). This marginalization from both sides can be particularly lonely. The pressure and attempt to resolve sexual conflicts through lifelong celibacy can add additional stressors that, for some people, can become intolerable. Many LGBTQIA+ individuals have been hurt by heteronormative religious leaders and communities and their attempts to encourage and sometimes coerce conformity and, therefore, view celibacy with great skepticism. In the following sections, we discuss research highlighting both the benefits and challenges of being single and celibate.

Gay Celibate Christian Qualitative Study

In a qualitative study investigating the experience of gay celibacy, Freeman-Coppadge and Horne (2019) interviewed seven current gay celibate Christians and five gay Christians who had previously been celibate. The results suggested that celibacy could be positive for some gay Christians, providing them with a sense of freedom and harmony between their sexual and religious identities. Participants spoke of experiencing a deep, vibrant spirituality characterized by closeness to God and others. Their faith provided them with resilience to life's challenges and inspired them to serve those in the community. By not having a romantic partner or children to care for, gay celibate Christians had time, energy, and financial resources to invest in others, which participants found personally and communally rewarding. Some participants expressed that celibacy was an ideal way of life for them that enhanced their well-being as a result of the benefits that they experienced.

Conversely, several participants (current and former celibates) experienced difficulty and even harm related to their pursuit of celibacy. Instead of the freedom and congruence described by others, these participants expressed great dissatisfaction. Some felt compelled to pursue celibacy because of influences from heteronormative culture, homonegative religious communities, and strong internal beliefs that homosexuality and homosexual experiences, expressions, and relationships were always sinful. As such, their experience of celibacy was not beneficial but detrimental to their mental, emotional, and spiritual health. Several described experiencing anxiety, depression, and even suicidality related to the intense loneliness of their celibate living. They found that attempts to remain chaste sometimes contributed to them repressing their sexual/romantic desires in a manner that caused problems in their sexual identity development and friendships. They ignored or were unaware of sexual-risk mitigation strategies that put them at risk of contracting sexually transmitted infections (STIs). Many found celibacy a particularly isolating experience.

Overall, participants highlighted how a broad and singular brushstroke could not characterize celibacy because every individual's experience of it was unique. Celibacy can be life giving and meaningful, torturous and lonely, for always or some time, or anything mixed and in between. There was universal agreement among participants that celibate life comes with challenges, and those challenges could prove unbearable for many who pursued it.

Four Single/Relationship Options Survey

In a survey of 1,782 sexual-minority individuals primarily from conservative religious backgrounds, Lefevor et al. (2019) looked at topics that were most important for satisfaction for individuals who were (a) single and celibate, (b) single and not celibate, (c) in a same-gender relationship, or (d) in a heterosexual mixed-orientation relationship (married to a heterosexual, cisgender person). Most important for single and celibate individuals was resolving any tension between their religious and sexual identities. Meeting needs for connection, intimacy, and mutual understanding; addressing depression; and accepting their same-gender attractions were also identified as necessary for life satisfaction and being single and celibate. In a follow-up analysis, Lefevor et al. (2021) compared satisfied individuals within each of the four options and found that individuals satisfied with celibacy were different from those who were satisfied with the other options due to experiencing their sexual attractions less frequently and experiencing sexual aversion more intensely than any other group. Those satisfied with singlehood and celibacy also reported diminished interest in sex, relative to individuals in the other three options/statuses.

In addition, Lefevor et al. (2021) found that sexual-minority individuals who were satisfied being single and celibate were statistically more religious and morally conservative than others, including those in heterosexual mixed-orientation relationships. Those satisfied with being single and celibate also maintained stronger views that same-gender sexuality was wrong and caused by social factors instead of being innate and less likely to be subject to change.

These findings suggest that some traditionally religious sexual-minority individuals are content with being single and celibate. Yet don't expect everyone experiencing celibacy to continue celibacy or be without conflicts. Those who report being satisfied being celibate feel a solid religious and moral conviction that a life of celibacy is right for them. Having less sexual interest might also help. In contrast, a higher sexual/romantic drive and unmet desire may make pursuing and maintaining abstinence more challenging and perhaps even psychologically harmful.

Individuals living celibately can experience its benefits by finding and connecting with others making similar life choices or at least a community of like-minded individuals who will support them in their identity and needs. Channeling energy into service and developing intimate but nonsexual relationships (for example, celibate partnerships with one or more people) may also be meaningful. Some celibate individuals differentiate between sexual attractions and sexual activity and consider lust, crushes, desire, and masturbation morally neutral, common to humans, and not signs of defectiveness, weakness, or failure (Creek, 2013). Clarifying that all or certain sexual activity is not sinful (for example, masturbation, sexual fantasies, certain forms of physical contact with another person) may increase options for self-congruence, connection, enjoyment, and success.

Some single people are involved in one or more deeply personal, nonromantic, and nonsexual relationships that have some level of life commitment (for example, a nonromantic, nonsexual domestic partnership). Increasing numbers of people of all sexual orientations find these relationships appealing. Their reasons may be varied.

Single and Noncelibate

There are several reasons a sexual minority person might choose to remain single but not celibate. For some, their experiences of being rejected by heteronormative communities inspire them or leave them no choice but to find new ways of relating and meeting their sexual, emotional, romantic, and companionship needs. As such, they reject the notion of dating in pursuit of a committed marriage and instead engage in various forms of sexual and romantic activity with single or multiple partners because it allows them to be sexually and relationally liberated and satisfied. Their relationships can range from being short-lived (for example, a single sexual encounter) to having high levels of fidelity and longevity, sometimes with multiple people (for instance, seeing one or more people separately or being in a polyamorous relationship with multiple partners).

Some sexual minority individuals may be single and noncelibate because they have not yet found a compatible partner. Relatedly, some may have decided to no longer search for a partner and choose a permanent status as single. Regardless of the reason, being single and noncelibate comes with benefits and challenges that can lead to varying levels of life satisfaction, just as with being single and celibate. Hostetler (2009) studied a sample of single gay men from the Midwest and found that while 65% identified as "single by choice," only 14% of the total sample reported being happy and satisfied with being single. Most reporting to be single by choice (83%) preferred to be in a relationship, and many reported being dissatisfied without one. This study suggested that identifying as voluntarily single may be a way for some to make the most of circumstances beyond their control (for example, not being able to be in a romantic relationship or not being able to do so yet) rather than an expression of a desired way of life. Nonetheless, some sexual minorities find singleness, but not celibacy, preferable and satisfactory. While factors contributing to sexual minorities' satisfaction with being single but not celibate have not been well studied, data are beginning to emerge from studies.

From the survey of 1,782 sexual minorities mentioned earlier, Lefevor et al. (2019) found four aspects statistically going together with satisfaction among single but not celibate participants:

1. Most importantly, participants high in satisfaction found ways to meet their needs for connection, intimacy, and mutual understanding. Notably, they might meet these needs separately from or via sexual/romantic activity.
2. Participants who were satisfied with being single and noncelibate indicated they were expressing their sexuality in ways that feel best for them.
3. Those who were satisfied with being single and noncelibate identified their sexual attractions as more strongly same-gender oriented.
4. Finally, those who had proactively addressed their mental health issues tended to be more satisfied.

In the follow-up analysis mentioned earlier (Lefevor et al., 2021), relative to other single/relationship options, those who were satisfied being single and noncelibate were more same-gender oriented, identified more strongly with the LGBTQ+ community, did not expect their attractions to change, and evidenced a strong sex drive. They also reported more favorable views toward same-gender sexuality, more liberal moral values, and less religiousness than those in the other relationship/single options.

These studies suggest that those who are satisfied being single and non-celibate want to stay single and noncelibate (rather than see this as a passing phase). To have a stronger desire for sex and a stronger affiliation with the LGBTQ+ community and feel more same-gender attracted can help in finding sexual partners with similar desires and interests.

Those noncelibate and dissatisfied with being single may consider how much they are meeting their needs for connection and if their sexual encounters are shame-for-intimacy driven and insufficient. A sexual encounter without addressing feelings of shame around identity, authenticity, and intimacy may increase disconnection, shame, guilt, and loneliness. Using sexual encounters to meet long-term needs (self-validation, emotional closeness, etc.) can be like only drinking cola and eating pizza to satisfy you short-term while making you hungry quicker than having a nutritious meal.

Partnered Relationships

A growing body of research (Newcomb, 2020) illustrates that LGBTQIA+ individuals generally experience the same health benefits, satisfaction, and stability in partnered relationships as heterosexual, cisgender individuals. They also face unique stressors that challenge their health and relationship functioning. For example, for binational same-gender couples, where one partner lives in the United States and the other does not, migration, trauma, acculturation, immigration status, access, and scrutiny can increase their anxiety and depression, as they often need to fight harder and develop their resilience to buffer against these stressors (Nakamura & Tsong, 2019). The stress of *internalized stigma* (believing you are inferior and deficient because of your sexual/gender diversity) and *internalized relationship stigma* (believing your relationship is inferior and deficient) also decreases relationship satisfaction (Gamarel et al., 2014).

In contrast, *relationship pride* (valuing the uniqueness and strengths of your relationship) and *relationship resilience* (adapting together to things you and your partner cannot change, experiencing your mutual love stronger than the challenges you face, developing your families of choice, being kind and generous with each other, and doing daily relationship maintenance, etc.) can make you and your relationship less vulnerable to minority stress and relationship stigma (Bin Ibrahim & Barlas, 2021; Haas & Lannutti, 2022).

Next, we'll highlight other similarities and some differences between heterosexual mixed-orientation relationships (MORs)[3] and same-gender relationships (SGRs). Our e-resource will highlight some unique issues for MORs where one partner is cisgender and the other transgender and transitions during the relationship. How much does the following compare to your relationship experiences and cultural values and contexts?

From the Four Options Survey mentioned earlier, Lefevor et al. (2019) found that sexual minorities who reported satisfaction being in an MOR more often reported the following:

- being sexually attracted to some degree to both men and women
- perceiving they did not belong within the LGBTQ+ community
- believing it wrong for a person to have sex with someone of their same sex, regardless of the level of commitment
- not accepting their same-gender attractions
- feeling a strong desire for a child-centered life
- fearing the disappointment of their family
- experiencing more religiosity
- living conservative moral values

Those reporting satisfaction in an SGR more often reported the following:

- experiencing a strong same-gender sexual orientation
- feeling more valued and supported for experiencing same-gender attractions and being LGBTQ+
- feeling like the out/open LGBTQ+ community is a supportive community for them
- having more sex-positive beliefs
- being nonreligious
- living liberal moral values

---

[3] For purposes of the following, MOR represents relationships involving an LGBQ+ person and an exclusively heterosexual cisgender person. Other MORs not discussed here can be between a lesbian woman and bisexual woman, a trans/nonbinary person and cisgender person, an asexual person and a sexual person, or any other mixed relationship.

A recent study (Lefevor, 2023) on individuals associated with the Church of Jesus Christ of Latter-day Saints (LDS) compared current LDS-believing sexual minorities in MORs to former LDS sexual minorities in SGRs and current LDS cisgender heterosexuals in heterosexual relationships. This study found LDS sexual minorities and cisgender heterosexuals varied in sexual activity within their group and between groups. For example, LDS sexual minorities in MORs, in general, reported looking at pornography less often (about once a month) than former LDS sexual minorities in SGRs and much more than LDS cisgender heterosexuals. About 29.9% of LDS sexual minorities in MORs reported looking weekly at pornography, and 53% masturbated weekly. On average, LDS sexual minorities in MORs engaged in other-gender sex (presumably with their spouse) about every other week and engaged in same-gender sex about every other month. About 24% were never sexual with their spouse or looked at pornography, and 13.4% never masturbated. About 21.6% of LDS sexual minorities in MORs reported having the same frequency of same-gender sexual encounters as about 20% of LDS sexual minorities in SGRs (once per year).

- How does reading about the variety of sexual expression in these relationships affect how you feel about your experiences and relationships?

LDS sexual minorities in MORs, in general, endorsed affirming beliefs that integrated their sexual-religious identities (for example, *Jesus Christ is merciful to me because I am LGBTQ+*; *Jesus Christ can help me through the challenges related to being LGBTQ+*; *Because of the Atonement, Jesus Christ knows what it is like to be LGBTQ+*; and *My Heavenly Father and Mother love me*). They disagreed with beliefs that described them as defective, having done something wrong to be LGBTQ+, and being spiritually weaker because of their sexual diversity. In another study (McGraw et al., 2023), these affirming beliefs generally promoted health, and nonaffirming beliefs generally did not promote health (particularly depression and suicidal ideation). However, these associations were not always significant.

Being in an SGR was rated more satisfactorily than the other four single/relationship options in Lefevor et al.'s (2019) sample. J. P. Dehlin et al. (2014) also found that LDS sexual minorities in MORs tended to be less happy and satisfied. The 2023 LDS study also found that LDS sexual minorities in MORs reported less relationship happiness and sexual satisfaction than sexual minorities in SGRs and cis-heterosexuals in heterosexual relationships. However, in the 2023 study, LDS sexual minorities in MORs, on average, reported feeling happy and moderately sexually satisfied.

It's difficult to say if the differences in sexual experiences noted above affected the differences in happiness levels. Cis-het individuals generally report more happiness than LGBTQIA+ individuals, but this is probably due to minority stress rather than masturbation. Yet, in the 2019 Four Options Survey study, the more that sexual minorities in MORs saw masturbation as acceptable, the less happy they were in their relationship. A. J. Dehlin et al. (2019) found that divorced and separated MORs involved a sexual minority spouse having more (a) other-gender physical-sexual aversion, (b) physical-sexual aversion to the spouse, (c) other-gender emotional aversion, and (d) same-gender emotional attraction and less (e) emotional attraction to the spouse. The sexual minority spouse's degree of sexual attraction to same-gender others and sexual aversion to the other gender seems to influence how much the sexual minority spouse can flourish in an MOR (Bridges et al., 2019).

These averages do not mean all sexual minority individuals will, can, or should be more satisfied in an SGR or MOR, as 28% of participants in the 2019 Four Options study reported being very satisfied in an MOR, and 80% reported some satisfaction in this option. Each person needs to decide what fits them and their partner(s) in the short and long term. Enjoyment, trust, and contentment with family and one's partner, monogamy, and life goals may provide enough happiness and relational satisfaction apart from sexual/romantic satisfaction.

Others (Hopwood et al., 2020; Vencill et al., 2018) describe being harmed by being in an MOR, pressured by religion or culture, due to trying to make their MOR work despite personal and relationship distress from denying themselves and their needs. Harms for the sexual/gender minority (SGM) spouse may include higher levels of internalized self-rejection and sexual identity distress; lower self-esteem and quality of life; higher levels of existential distress; isolation/loneliness; identity compartmentalization (living two lives undercover) (A. Walker, 2014); guilt and shame for marital infidelity, including fantasizing about same-gender others during sex with their spouse; and increased frustration, anxiety, and depression.

Some studies (Song et al., 2023; X. Li et al., 2016) report harms for the cis-heterosexual spouse, including increased risk of HIV and other STIs; physical, verbal, and emotional abuse; feelings of inadequacy/self-blame; feelings of gaslighting; isolation/loneliness; depression; and suicidality. As one straight spouse described,[4] "My own identity as a woman was severely damaged by being married to a gay man. Near the end of our marriage, I began to feel like everything feminine about me was repulsive. I wouldn't recommend a mixed-orientation relationship to anyone." Both spouses may feel social and family pressure to remain in their marriage, including fears of exposing the spouse's sexual identity if they divorce and fearing others will consider them spiritually weak (Zulkffli et al., 2022) and view their marriage as a fraud, impossible, and transitional (Adler & Ben-Ari, 2021). Intense anger and acting as adversaries

---

[4]   Personal communication to coauthor Beckstead.

can block either spouse's ability to move on postdisclosure (McCaulley & Coleman, 2022).

These negative social and cultural attitudes marginalize straight and SGM spouses into concealing and distancing from others. Gender inequality perpetuates this disempowerment (Tsang, 2021). These studies suggest that cis-heterosexual spouses in MORs are an invisible minority ((L. Li et al., 2021), like their SGM spouse, and their needs may get overshadowed by their SGM spouse's identity needs and struggles.

Yet many (Wang et al., 2020) find social support and feel empowered to redefine themselves and their spouse (Wolkomir, 2004) and work with their spouse toward reconceptualizing (Reid et al., 2021) and developing their relationship, viewing it as valid and equal to others in whatever form it takes (Adler & Ben-Ari, 2017). The importance of family, community belonging, and living life according to one's sexual orientation, faith, and cultural values will likely influence these decisions and resolutions (Zack & Ben-Ari, 2019).

Results from the Four Options Survey indicate that essential ways to increase satisfaction and well-being, regardless of sexual identity and relationship option, include (a) meeting one's needs for connection, intimacy, and mutual understanding; (b) expressing sexuality in ways that feel best for the person; (c) resolving religious or cultural conflicts in ways that fit the person; and (d) addressing anxiety and depression. Reducing negative internalized beliefs from minority stress and appreciating the positives of being a sexual/gender minority may also increase life satisfaction, regardless of sexual/gender identity.

Options for Connection and Romantic/Sexual Exclusivity and Openness

Each of the following is not to be taken as just one way to do things. There are many ways to implement these options. Even if an option works for you now, it may not work for you later, so you don't need to commit for life. Yet each option will put you on a particular life trajectory. How would it feel to try different styles and return to what you had before?

People often choose labels for themselves to clarify and define their choices. However, in choosing those labels, the ones you use may change over time. Others who use those labels may have similar or different interpretations of what those labels mean. The positive power of a label is that it can help you identify with a community, find an emotional home with people in similar positions, and explain yourself to others. In the future, you may reflect and adopt different, new (or no) labels based on your experiences while keeping other labels for much longer, potentially for your entire life. However, labels may become a limiting factor in your life, putting you in a box that may be difficult to remove yourself from. Choose your labels carefully.

Questions can arise: If the love of your life doesn't like the relationship options and life trajectory you prefer, which would you choose? Which would work best for you and your partner(s)? Do both of you want to make it work? If you or your partner(s) are ambivalent about how to proceed, you may play out different scenarios in your head or on paper or talk about it with an outsider. You could also list plusses and minuses for each option to determine what you both like and identify common-ground desires and limits. Clarifying what each needs for a relationship option to be safe and satisfying might shed light on relationship boundaries and agreements. If you and your partner(s) agree, you could play out each alternative for a week or a month and see how you each like it (keeping in mind that if your options involve others, they may need to be made aware of your "trial" intentions). Potential scenarios may be opening the relationship either sexually or emotionally, doing a trial separation, or sleeping in separate bedrooms but ensuring quality time together.

Therapy, coaching, or support groups might help you clarify your exploration and give you skills to handle your biggest fears. If other partners decide for or before you, you can still make up your mind and try negotiating a change in what was presented as final by others. However, you may ultimately need to land in a place of acceptance, if your partner's needs for themselves do not allow for flexibility in their decision. You can also consider whether there might be anything that would help you change your mind or be more flexible. What are you certain is nonnegotiable for *you* about intimate relationships?

We next describe options organized around levels of high versus low sexual exclusivity and high versus low romantic exclusivity (see Fern, 2020, for more options).

High Sexually Exclusive and High Romantically Exclusive Relationships

Single/Partnered and Celibate

Celibacy can be a choice. Celibacy can be done with or without masturbation. Celibacy can be used as a phase to put a brake on and change unwanted sexual patterns. As described earlier, it can also be a permanent ideal in some cultures. However, permanent sexual abstinence may not be doable for all. That means some people will have sex—by themselves or with others occasionally, periodically, or regularly. Another note to consider is that some people only consider heterosexual intercourse "sex" and label any other sexual practice "not really sex." For Orthodox Jews, striving for celibacy while being fit for a sexual relationship is a sin, not virtuous, as it is seen as the rejection of G-d's gift. Yet, temporarily, abstinence may be the only option if a kosher partner is not found.

Some individuals have trouble never having sex. Being celibate or nonsexual is not an option but a regret, especially if it affects self-esteem. The default of sexual acts as central to one's orientation and worth is problematic and socially constructed. In many instances where one is celibate involuntarily and distressed about it, talking with a mental health professional about unmet needs and internalized self-rejection can interrupt and process negative emotions.

Some sexual-minority celibate Christians create committed (or covenant) partnerships to meet social/emotional needs but without sex. These celibate partnerships help some individuals better deal with celibacy. However, this option can be difficult for those who attempt such relationships because sexual/romantic drives can compromise intentions to remain abstinent, which can negatively impact the relationship (Freeman-Coppadge, 2018).

Monogamy

Monogamy tends to be the most common, preferred, and chosen relationship option. Some choose it because they believe they have to or aren't aware of other options. Monogamy tends to be what many of us grew up believing we must have for a fulfilling relationship and believing it is achievable *for everyone*. One study (Vil et al., 2022) found that most people, regardless of race/ethnicity and gender, believe monogamous relationships are higher quality than consensual nonmonogamous relationships. Yet only 63% of U.S. adults in monogamous relationships have never cheated on a partner; one-third (33%) have cheated emotionally, sexually, or both (Dumitru, 2022).

Research suggests that partners in monogamous, nonmonogamous, and polyamorous relationships are generally more similar than different, especially in their commitment and relationship satisfaction (Balzarini et al., 2019; Flicker & Sancier-Barbosa, 2022). Polyamorous people (who are engaged in more than one steady, intimate relationship) tend to be more content than people in a nonmonogamous open relationship (Scoats & Campbell, 2022), likely because of the need for more communication and empathy to maintain polyamorous relationships. Often, relationship motivations also differ. For example, those who value social conformity tend to have negative attitudes toward people in nonmonogamous relationships and prefer relationships that fulfill long-term practical interests. People who engage in consensual nonmonogamy tend to be more tolerant of uncertainty (Carswell & Impett, 2021). Some people want strict monogamy because they believe in a zero-sum approach to love and sex ("Your gain is my loss") (Burleigh et al., 2017). This results from viewing relationship resources as scarce and that those within a relationship are entitled to all the relationship resources. Some people equate their attachment insecurity with wanting to be sexually exclusive (Moors et al., 2015).

Instead of giving in to compulsory/coerced monogamy expectations, please consider choosing monogamy (or any type of relationship) thoughtfully and intentionally. Typically, choosing monogamy means partners want, prefer, and agree to be sexually and romantically exclusive in a lifelong commitment. However, you and your partner may choose monogamy initially and agree to talk later about opening it up or, conversely, open up your relationship now in some way and agree to talk later about closing it. Many find that sexual interests and needs diminish over time and feel compensated by other fulfilling activities or more intense friendships, but some are not. Some individuals are monogamous with a partner who is polyamorous. Regardless, we encourage you and your partner(s) to consider possibilities and what works best in your situation(s) and for your values and needs rather than simply going with the flow or living up to social norms without seriously admitting doubts, problems, and alternatives. Something not good enough for one is not good enough for their partner(s) too, so don't hesitate to address *your* concerns.

Monogamy can offer important benefits, including a satisfying sex life/ romance, the prevention of STIs, deeper relationship intimacy, greater commitment, less jealousy to handle, focused financial and time investment to the relationship and family, and social support for your relationship (Conley et al., 2013). Long-term monogamy can be satisfying as partners' intimacy and attachment grow within the security of knowing they are with each other and no one else. Both partners are investing in developing this intimacy and connection. "Hot monogamy" (Love & Robinson, 1995) may involve developing mindfulness skills in being attentive and discovering who you and your partner are and who you are together in each sexual/romantic/friendship moment and stage of life, as if you're meeting this person and your experience for the first time, with the added history and knowledge of yourself and this person.

On the other hand, putting all your eggs in one basket and thinking that's the only way can be scary if one partner falls away or there looms a separation. Infidelity against expectations and agreements is often a deal breaker in relationships. Repairing trust after sexual/romantic betrayal is often not easy and not always possible. This process can be helped by understanding together what happened, which aspects of the relationship and agreements need to be updated, and which aspects of each person need to be acknowledged and adapted to (or changed) if the relationship will continue and thrive. It could or could not matter if the cheating was a quick affair or ongoing, romantic or just sexual, with guilt feelings, or unreservedly. Is the partner who cheated willing and able to change their personal traits and relationship dynamics that led to the betrayal? Blaming your infidelity on the other partner seems unlikely to work. If someone cheats on you, don't blame yourself for their lack of reliability and openness. Yet think about how safe you make it for your partner(s) to disclose vulnerable and embarrassing information.

For some, infidelity doesn't start with having sex outside the relationship. Merely looking at someone for too long, talking to someone, laughing with someone, or hugging or flirting with someone is a problem. Infidelities differ between partners but occur when one or both decide to be intimate without the partner's knowledge and consent.

Successful monogamy may be defined as helping each other work through feelings of desire and jealousy through reassurance, commitment, protection, and investment. Although hoped for, monogamy doesn't protect people from dealing with jealousy. Jealousy can happen without connection to sexuality and romance when one partner doesn't want the other to relate in any way to anyone else. This isolation, often from fear of losing the partner, might be so stifling that it backfires and the other just can't stay.

Monogamish

If monogamy holds a strong appeal to you or your partner(s), but you or they are unsure whether you want to or could be sexually/romantically exclusive for life, you may want to consider a restricted form of consensual nonmonogamy, sometimes referred to as a monogam*ish* relationship. Dan Savage coined this term to give people in monogamous relationships a little room to play by bringing another person sexually/romantically into the relationship, according to their preferred types, frequency, and level. This style of nonmonogamy allows committed partners to engage in outside sexual relationships, but those relationships are intended to be sexual only, not emotionally romantic, and short-term, casual, and temporary (Taormino, 2008). The intention of these encounters may be for either one or all partners to meet their sexual needs or fantasies and enhance the primary relationship.

About 20% of U.S. single adults (Haupert, Gesselman, et al., 2017) have engaged in consensual nonmonogamy, and 3–7% of the U.S. population (Haupert, Moors, et al., 2017) are currently in a consensual nonmonogamous relationship. Here is an example: Jack and Ramona occasionally spice up their sex life by finding a male lover to play with in a one-time threesome. Another example: Nancy enjoys being whipped by someone skilled at using a single-tail whip, and because her partner is not into whipping, Nancy sees Gregory (who is very skilled at the single-tail whip) on occasion for "play" dates. Gregory must know from the beginning that this connection will stay sexual and not develop romantically.

Polyfidelitous Relationships

These relationships are similar to monogamous relationships, except that the commitment and fidelity agreement exists between more than two people. For example, Sarah, Kim, and Steve consider themselves married to one another. They live in the same household, raise two biological children (one Sarah's, one Kim's, and both Steve's), and are emotionally and sexually exclusive between them.

Polygamy

Polygamy, being married to more than one person, is frowned on in many communities. Polygamy is common in many parts of the world and is sometimes practiced by certain religious groups or even cults. Some countries have banned the practice because polygamous relationships are statistically associated with violence and considered inequitable. In countries that do not legally recognize polygamy or allow for multiple spouses (including the United States), the practice still exists, often without an official marriage ceremony.

Polygyny means a marriage of one man with several wives. One out of four people in the world lives in a Muslim country where one man marrying up to four wives is common, depending on how many women and children he can support. Often, their households are separate, and there is little contact between the wives of one man. The men are also bound only to be intimate with their wives. In contrast, polyandry is one woman married to several men, who may or may not be related, but the practice is much less common than polygyny. It can complicate finding out who the biological father is in case of pregnancy. Some people don't care about that. Laws may not follow that indifference.

High Sexually Exclusive and Low Romantically Exclusive Relationships

Polyamory is an umbrella term for relationships with multiple partners at the same time at various levels of exclusivity. Ethical polyamory involves choosing and agreeing how many and which people to be intimate with in nonpossessive, honest, and responsible ways (Ve Ard & Veaux, 2005). One out of six single U.S. adults desires to engage in polyamory, and one out of nine has engaged in it (Moors et al., 2021). Although polyamory is sometimes used interchangeably with ethical nonmonogamy, here we want to focus on the relational (as opposed to only sexual) aspect. Being polyam[5] differs from an open relationship and hookups, which can be more transactional and sexual than relational

---

[5] *Poly* is often used as a short form by Polynesian people, so it can be more culturally respectful to refer to polyamory as *polyam*.

and ongoing. Being in a throuple (three people in an intimate relationship), for example, is a form of polyamory. Some or all of the relationships you invest in while living polyamorous can be sexual, romantic, affectionate, spiritual, friendly, committed, fleeting, or fluid, among other possibilities. Two examples of high sexual exclusivity and low romantic/emotional exclusivity would be nonsexual polyamory and polyam-intimate relationships, depending on how the person experiences and defines *sexual*, *love*, and *intimacy*.

Low Sexually Exclusive and High Romantically Exclusive Relationships

Open Marriage/Relationships

Ethical nonmonogamy captures many options for engaging in intimate relationships that are not romantically or sexually exclusive. We use the term *ethical* here to differentiate it from cheating without consent from your partner. The ethical emphasis points to the importance of engaging in this relationship option in considerate, respectful, consensual, and nondamaging ways to yourself and others. For example, ethical nonmonogamy excludes lying to your partner(s), being secretive, or guilting a partner into having sex with another person. It does not mean you must give up on all your privacy. However, it is unethical to withhold from partners how you feel about them. An open relationship requires dialogue and careful consideration for all involved about the actions taken and the consequences they may have. Quick decisions to include another person sexually might mean that not everyone can handle the new setup or where the relationship is going. A partner who used to have no problem with sexual openness may change their mind or be unable to handle it right now or with the particular person you would like to bring in.

Swinging

Swinging is a relationship style in which a couple, typically heterosexual, engages in sex with another couple or group of couples and singles. This relationship style may be similar to partnered nonmonogamy in that, often, couples are exclusive in every way aside from this sexual aspect of their life, which they share and that benefits them individually and their relationship. For many, swinging is confined to specific parties and contexts with deliberate social/sexual scripts and norms that enhance a sense of community identity and belonging.

Dealing with Jealousy

While partners may assume they have no trouble with an open relationship, unexpected jealousy can play up strongly when others enter the relationship.

Feeling secure after jealousy arises might take time, openness, empathy, reassurances, adjustments, or therapy. In silence, jealousy only worsens. If anything wrecks relationships, it is not communicating the feelings, needs, and limits that arise. Things may speed up when the jealous person understands their insecurity needs addressing, not something others "do to them," unless the other person is violating relationship agreements. Jealousy can disappear or be reduced when you feel secure about your value and your relationship and how loved you are. Learn to tell any jealous partner(s), "I still love you more than anyone and won't replace you," with your deepest sincerity and commitment. At the same time, address their concerns and dialogue about past experiences with rejection.

On the other hand, being in an ethical nonmonogamous relationship makes it easier to experiment or play with jealousy inside sexuality. One partner can feel joy (*compersion*) at another partner's joy and be aroused erotically, romantically, or emotionally by watching their partner having a sexual experience with another person or at least learning about it and trusting the experience will not harm them or the relationship. Feeling joy for another's independent joy can enhance the relationship bond. Compersion is experienced on a continuum along with jealousy for a partner's experience (Fern, 2020). For some, the intent to share partners sexually is to experience humiliation, which for that person leads to sexual excitement (*cuckolding*). One study (Lehmiller et al., 2018) found that gay men who enjoy seeing their partner having sex with others tend to have a secure attachment style; have increased sensation seeking, sociosexuality, and agreeableness; and are turned on by group sex and voyeurism.

People who choose ethical nonmonogamy or polyamory sometimes need serious time to go through jealousy, insecurities, and hurt feelings and communicate openly and frequently to keep the relationship going. If nonexclusivity in one, some, or all relational areas is what you both/all want or at least want to explore, give each other the space and time to deal with this. Slow down, talk, and feel to understand and respect each other's needs, process, and limits.

Low Sexual Exclusivity and Low Emotional/Romantic/ Exclusivity Relationships

Hookups, one-night stands, and other noncommittal sexual encounters can be a way for LGBTQIA+ individuals, single or partnered, to cope with minority stress (loneliness, self-rejection, insecurity, lack of sex education and outlets that fit them, gender shame/dysphoria) (Watson et al., 2019). Hookups can promote identity development by (a) providing connection, exploration, experimentation, and self-discovery and (b) increasing involvement with the LGBTQIA+ community (Jaffe et al., 2021).

- How would you describe what makes a good and bad hookup or sexual encounter? Is it the gender/sex of the person, aesthetics of the person, connection, consent, safety, context, trust, risk, conquest, specific sex act(s), power dynamic, orgasm, self-affirmation, easy access, meaningless fun, alcohol/drug use, distraction from stress, pleasure, validation from pleasuring the other person(s), or anything else (Snapp et al., 2023)?

For some, hookups can replace dating. A person's body appreciation versus self-consciousness may affect their sexual functioning when interacting in hookup-culture settings (Ramseyer Winter et al., 2020). A greater propensity for sensation-seeking can affect decision-making when using apps for hookups (Lopes et al., 2019). Make sure you stay safe. Have a backup plan when meeting a total stranger not in a public space.

No-strings-attached sex can also involve coercion and assault due to anonymity; lack of communication; and lack of attention to emotions, personhood, and consent. Some individuals may seek hookups as a reaction to and reenactment of prior unprocessed sexual trauma.

- Which skills must you develop to communicate what you desire and need sexually?
- Which skills must you develop to protect yourself from sex you don't want?
- How sensitive are you to how you and your partner(s) feel(s) in a sexual encounter?
- How comfortable are you telling someone to stop or leave or pushing off someone or leaving if the person ignores your expression of nonconsent?

Many communities, cultures, and families do not teach assertiveness and physical self-defense. Trauma reinforces nonassertiveness. Learning skills to engage in verbal and nonverbal consent and communication before and throughout sex may help you and the other person(s) be happy with the hookup (Lamont et al., 2018).

Friends with benefits may be a bridge from one-night stands to something more relational. These casual sexual friendships share the understanding that repeated sexual encounters do not indicate an obligation for a future relationship (Wentland & Reissing, 2014). If you engage in noncommittal sexual relationships, which needs do you fulfill and what about each relationship works for you? How do you envision your long-term sexual, romantic, and emotional life with these individuals (Kampler, 2022)? If you are someone whose romantic bonding enhances when you are sexual, then having "friends with benefits" may be painful and unrealistic for you, or you may need to find several friends for romance at the same time.

Individuals who enjoy *solo polyamory* tend never to live with another person while they invest in more than one long-term committed relationship. Solo polyamory can mean having similar values, drives, and needs and enjoying the same activities as those in open and polyamorous relationships but wanting to live alone, at least for the time being. Being solo polyam may also involve prioritizing personal reasons and responsibilities (developing one's career, being a caretaker of someone/others, etc.) (Klein, 2022). People who enjoy solo polyamory might even live platonically in a commune and have several dedicated sexual/romantic relations outside the group. The number of options is endless. Folks who engage in *family polyamory* live with, raise children and/or pets with, and even marry one or more of their partners.

Another way of engaging in polyamory is called *hierarchical polyamory*. One crucial aspect of ethical relationship agreements is how the relationship is structured and who gets priority, if any, over others. In this form, one person is the primary partner; other partners are secondary, tertiary, and so on, or central/peripheral. Partners might also have a different primary partner. The words you use to describe the relationships matter less than ensuring all partners know and approve of the relationship hierarchy or nonhierarchy.

Some relationships, particularly those enjoying *relationship anarchy*, eschew hierarchy entirely. In these relationships, every partner and relationship is equal to every other, and each relationship finds its balance relative to the others. The idea behind *free relationships* and relationship anarchy is that all persons are free to engage in relationships whichever way and level they choose; relationships do not need to follow a prescribed set of rules or ideas, nor should people be restricted in relationships because they feel obligated (Veaux, 2017). In this liberated relationship agreement, everyone can do what they like if it doesn't cause unnecessary harm. They are accountable for the consequences of their actions, reactions, and effects on themself and their relationships. Individuals in free relationships engage with all people freely, spontaneously, ethically, authentically, and, therefore, consensually. Free doesn't mean everything goes.

Sometimes, the choices we must make involve letting go of a relationship when it is not working. You can't always know for sure how things will work out. People change, especially in relationships. Needs, preferences, desires, awareness, bodies, and identities can change. This is not to say that changes will always mean a relationship must end. Nor are we implying that you should immediately cut your losses and leave when a relationship is not working for you. Instead, we are reminding you of the possibility and choice you have in weighing your relationship options. If your relationship is not working, consider all your options: win-win solutions or strategies, acceptance, adaptability, growth, help, compromise, and leaving.

If you are terrified of ending a relationship because of social judgments, internalized shame, or hopelessness of finding someone else, focus on developing your self-worth, assertiveness skills, and resources. Then, leaving may be an option or unnecessary after you see how you feel with your empowered self about the relationship. Though difficult and often painful, sometimes ending a relationship may give opportunities for those involved to grow in essential and overdue ways. Above all, if you are in danger, develop your courage and support. If you are used to living with danger, consider quietly getting yourself (and kids) to safety and then think about options.

Conclusion

Choosing your own life and single/relationship style is an activist deed, even if it conforms to social norms or you are saving your life or sanity by being in the closet. Being an activist in ways that feel authentic to you can be an important lifestyle. Don't feel bad for not doing more of what others consider a "proper" activist "should do" because it doesn't speak to you, you don't dare to, or you choose to stay private about what you prefer. Your happy life starts with you being central to it. Whatever life you live, you are writing history, in whatever single/relationship structure fits you because it is your life. This will not always be easy or simple, so we hope to have inspired you with possible and fulfilling options. We wish you enough resources to realize and experience connection and well-being within your life and relationships, if not now, then soon.

Chapter 5

Support for Parents of LGBTQIA+ Persons and for LGBTQIA+ Parents

Susanna M. Gallor, Iraklis Grigoropoulos, Mani B. Mitchell, Denise Steers, Walter R. Schumm, Jeni Wahlig, Alejandro Gepp-Torres, Isabel Lima, Jeannie DiClementi, Amanda Veldorale-Griffin, and Brie Radis[1]

This chapter provides support for parents whose children identify as LGBTQIA+, for parents who identify as LGBTQIA+, and for readers who are both. We describe the parenting needs and skills necessary to provide protection, safety, positive socialization, self-esteem, and connection for all family members (Dahlheimer & Feigal, 1994). We hope this chapter and our companion e-resource help readers acquire the knowledge, empathy, and skills for a wide range of parenting experiences relating to sexual and gender diversity.

The authors of this chapter come from varying backgrounds and perspectives. Although we are not aligned in many aspects of how we conduct ourselves in the world, we are aligned in valuing the intrinsic worth and dignity of each human being, independent of any label, attribute, or characteristic. A second common value we share is our belief that each human being has the right to self-determination and to value the intersectionality and diversity within their life experience. The "who" of each person is much beyond any component of the personal identity, such as sex, gender, race/ethnicity, language, age, disability,

---

[1] Stuart Chen-Hayes, PhD, NCC, LCPC, and Reverend D. Paul Sullins, PhD, contributed to an earlier draft of this chapter and were unable to continue coauthoring and review the final content. The order of authorship does not reflect the amount of content in the chapter but coauthors' combined content and labor on both this book chapter and the e-resource.

health status, cultural affiliation, faith, religion, or any other criteria. These aspects, however, will likely influence parenting and family relationships in some meaningful way.

Safety Issues Important in Parenting

Collaborating with others who likely oppose you politically about parenting can be stressful and lead to conflicting situations. To feel safe working together, as part of our cowriting process, we articulated safety needs that could guide our interactions and what we offered readers about parenting. We hope the following guidelines are helpful to parents (and those who interact with parents) to consider what they, their family, and their community need for safety regarding sexual/gender diversity and parenting issues.

Safety guidelines are not meant to silence angry voices, sterilize conversations, or artificially free them from discomfort. Instead, safety guidelines work best when they are mutually developed and agreed on, to allow for anger, tension, and authenticity. Those involved in this negotiation must feel unrestrained and consent to the values and rules of engagement that make each person accountable for their actions and how they affect both the process and the outcome of the endeavor.

As coauthors, we agreed to honor the multiple cultural identities of others and ourselves and work collectively for common ground. Many of us have witnessed the limitations of cis-heteronormativity—a system based on the attitude that heterosexuality and cisgender identification are the only normal, natural (and therefore superior) expressions of sexuality and gender. We have seen how this often leads to the subversion of healthy conversation and creates feelings of marginalization, resistance, and defiance. In contrast, we value dialogue on sexual and gender issues based on inherent respect for diversity.

In our writing process, we asked for mutual respect and realized that we did not need to be friends but could be respectful of one another. Paul expressed his intentions for friendship in this way: "I will be your friend and not disparage you or be offended, even if you disagree with me. I expect you will be my friend and not disparage me or be offended, even if I disagree. Otherwise, it's hard for us to have a conversation except if we agree completely about everything." Stuart asked the group to challenge a concept but never the person: be aware of how the impact of your words may be harsher than your intent. Walt clarified his safety guidelines in this way:

> I intend to affirm every person I meet as much as possible, but I no longer have expectations of being affirmed by others as I have taken a lot of heat/hatred over the years for my research on a host of topics, not just same-sex parenting issues. I like working with others who are different because you can only

learn, I think, from working within a context of difference. The challenge is to understand apparent differences in a deep way rather than just a superficial one.

Brie asked to support brave spaces to grow by promoting open communication and listening with an intent to understand. Providing feedback in a way that is concrete, kind, and clear also helps this process.

We each affirmed our desire to respect and honor each individual's right to choose the path that seems best for that individual. We agree that it is our collective commitment and responsibility as professionals to inform readers of the science that studies the outcomes of a wide range of options so that readers can make wise choices. Further, we believe that the science we utilize and draw from, as professionals, scientists, researchers, allies, and healers, should be unbiased and rigorous, particularly regarding gender, sexual development, and fluidity. We also recognize that the current research base has privileged monosexual, predominantly White, cisgender male experiences and constrains our understanding of gender and sexuality.

As we may contradict each other, we hoped we would see our differing perspectives as additive. We hoped we would learn together by welcoming ideas that add to our viewpoint. Some individuals and families will greatly benefit from knowing various options and views on these crucial issues.

Next in the chapter, we highlight the experiences, needs, and strengths of parents of LGBTQIA+ children. This is immediately followed by the experiences, needs, and strengths of parents who identify as LGBTQIA+. Many of the ideas and skills for parents of LGBTQIA+ individuals can be helpful for LGBTQIA+ parents and vice versa.

Understanding and Coping With Common Parental/Caregiver Responses

You never really know how you will respond to learning that your child identifies as LGBTQIA+ until it actually happens. For some parents and caregivers, the news is cause for celebration, while for others, it is cause for concern (how did this happen; what does this mean for my child, the family, me, and our future?). You may not know how to feel or have mixed emotions when someone you care about comes out to you. Our hope is that, in the end, your child's disclosure results in connection and growth for all.

Upon finding out that your child is gender-diverse or not exclusively heterosexual or both, you may experience a sense of loss (Wahlig, 2015). Some parents feel they are losing the child they thought they had, their dreams and expectations for their child's future, and their relationship with their child. For other parents, the sense of loss may be unclear or ambiguous. You may feel grief about your child's gender/sexual identity, but you don't know what you are grieving; you can't put your finger on what has been lost for you. Parents with a child who transitions to a different gender than assigned at birth may struggle with their perception that their child is the same but different and physically present but gone because they are developing a new identity (Norwood, 2013). They may miss the gendered aspects of their child and not know how to work through their disenfranchised grief (Canitz & Haberstroh, 2022). This loss and grief can add other levels of stress and make the healing process more difficult (McGuire et al., 2016).

If grief or loss is a part of your experience, you may find it helpful to remember that grief and mourning move through stages. Although some proposed models address family reactions to coming out (most of them based on the grief stages by Kübler Ross, 1970), it is clear that a wide range of responses is expected. Reactions like shock, denial, bargaining, anger, and despair are normal, as is acceptance. Many parents experience joy and pride when their child comes out to them. A study (Savin-Williams & Ream, 2003) of same-gender-attracted individuals between the ages of 17 and 25 found that openly negative reactions by parents (being intolerant, threatening to cut off the child, physically attacking, screaming) were found in 12% to 19% of the sample. Being supportive or very supportive were more common reactions (32% to 44% of the sample). Some parents of LGBTQIA+-identified youth experience pride initially or eventually. Everyone's experience will differ, including how and why a parent feels pride and love.

Each parent, sibling, and extended family member will have their way of reacting to surprises and changes, and this typical reaction will likely extend to how they react to a family member's sexual/gender diversity. From a parent's perspective, being honest about your reactions and any distress you are experiencing is essential. Finding opportunities to express and normalize your emotions is also essential to understand what you need from yourself and others. For example, some parents feel stuck wishing their child was different. This wishing may lead to efforts to convince their child to change or suppress their gender expression or sexuality. These efforts will likely lead to disconnection and distance between parents and their children and increases in mental health issues for the child. Change efforts will also not help parents or their children deal with their grief, pain, confusion, questions, anxiety, and insecurity.

Given a political and social climate that heightens stigma against LGBTQIA+ people, fear about a child's LGBTQIA+ identity is a common parenting response. Some worries may be for your child and their physical well-being and how life may be more challenging. Some fears may be for yourself. There can be social, cultural, community, religious, and family consequences to being the parent of an LGBTQIA+-identified child. You may feel isolated in your experience. You may fear a loss of status or support from your spouse and community. You may feel pain from blaming yourself, feeling ashamed, or believing that you did something or failed to do something to cause your child to be LGBTQIA+. If this is you, we encourage you to reach out and seek sources of support. Having your own space to process your reactions is essential. If parents don't process their distress away from their child, it may impair their child's ability to attend to their self-development (G. M. Diamond et al., 2019). There are people, parents, faith leaders, and professionals who will understand your experience and offer empathy and ways to resolve your pain and shame. Please reference the list of resources on our website[2] for ideas about where to turn for more support.

As mentioned earlier, some parents try to change their child's sexual orientation, sexual behaviors, gender identity, or gender expression. These parents may use their own methods, religious interventions, or professional or unlicensed providers (Ryan et al., 2020). They may believe they are helping their child and not know how else to protect their child. They may believe their child's behaviors are wrong or fear for their child's future and afterlife for not adhering to religious/cultural norms. They may have heard or believe that change is possible and sustainable if their child tries hard enough (Glassgold & Ryan, 2022).

Instead of keeping your child safe, the potential is high for change efforts to reinforce self-hatred, prejudice, shame, anxiety, lying, addictions, and hopelessness and delay your child's identity development. Major mental health organizations strongly discourage providers and parents from trying to change a child's sexual orientation and gender identity/expression due to such efforts reinforcing that your child is flawed, unlovable, worthless, unwanted, and not good enough unless the child changes their likes, dislikes, and mannerisms (Byne et al., 2012).

Change efforts also typically neglect to provide accurate information about LGBTQIA+ individuals, their relationships, and their lives. Change efforts can reinforce false assumptions that everyone can enjoy heterosexuality and that anything but exclusive heterosexuality and traditional gender expression is a symptom of mental illness, addiction, or character defect that can be treated so that the person could enjoy heterosexuality and traditional gender expression. These false assumptions are countered by research and are associated with decreased mental health and functioning (American Psychological Association, 2021a, 2021b). Professional sexual orientation/gender identity change efforts (SO/GICE) are considered consumer fraud. It is illegal for licensed mental health counselors in many states and regions of the United States and in 14 countries to provide methods to change a minor's sexual

---

[2] See www.FindingCongruence.com.

orientation or gender identity. Conversion efforts should not be promoted as an option to consider.

In contrast, research suggests that at least 13 interventions appear reliably useful to sexual minorities who struggle with their sexuality (and may generalize to gender minorities) regardless of their identity and life trajectory (Rosik et al., 2023). These options promote well-being by developing self-acceptance, self-compassion, and social support; reducing shame, trauma, and minority stress; increasing assertiveness to respond to feelings and rejection; and affirming one's own way of expressing gender, sexuality, and faith. These interventions focus on reducing the distress associated with sexual/gender diversity and then assessing the impact, if any, on the individual's sexuality and gender identity.

The Family Acceptance Project (n.d.) has been finding alternatives to change efforts for parents and their families. They want parents to know that actions that support their LGBTQIA+ child(ren)'s well-being do not have to go against faith or cultural beliefs. Since 2002, they have collected and analyzed parent and child reports of rejecting and accepting behaviors and found that rejecting behaviors, similar to change efforts (for example, pressuring your child to act more or less masculine or feminine, telling your child that being LGBTQIA+ is "just a phase," not talking about your child's LGBTQIA+ identity), are associated with a child becoming depressed and suicidal and having substance abuse problems. In contrast, accepting behaviors (for example, telling your child that you're proud of them, telling your child that you will be there for them even if you don't fully understand, believing that your child can be a happy LGBTQIA+-identified adult) are associated with better health, higher self-esteem, and stronger relationships for their child. Studies show that acceptance and support are crucial protective factors against substance use, suicidality, and mental and sexual health problems for LGBTQIA+-identified youth (Russon et al., 2021; Ryan et al., 2009).

Traditionally religious parents may feel torn between supporting their child and supporting their religious/cultural values. Because of this conflict, the Family Acceptance Project resources have been developed to align with parental religious values of compassion, mercy, love, respect, agency, and faith (placing trust in one's higher power to work it out) (Maslowe & Yarhouse, 2015).

Working toward acknowledging what your child is disclosing and sharing with you (turning toward instead of against or away) will provide you with more understanding of your child's experience and what your child needs for safety, exploration, and development. Expressions of acknowledgment, curiosity, and compassion will likely increase your child's trust in you to help. Acceptance can also help parents attend to their own needs, relevance, and autonomy and explore how to adapt and reinvest previous dreams and energies into the reality of their unique child and family.

Give yourself time, space, and opportunities away from your LGBTQIA+-identified child to reflect on your beliefs and feelings about life, yourself, your child, and sexual/gender diversity. Remember that this is new for you, and it is okay if you are unsure how, when, or if you will develop different attitudes and ideas about gender and sexuality. There is no one way for every parent to resolve their unique conflicts and distress with their child's new identity.

Even if your initial responses were difficult, painful, scary, negating, or unsupportive, with time, you likely will be able to repair ruptures with your child. Research studying relationship dynamics suggests that for every negating response expressed in a relationship, there must be three to five affirming responses to maintain relationship commitment, satisfaction, and peace (Coleman et al., 2021). Reducing your negating reactions toward your child and replacing them with any level of acknowledgment, respect, interest, compassion, protection, or celebration will likely feel supportive and positively affect your relationship. It is crucial to note that such support does not require you to change your views on sexuality and gender but rather to express unequivocal love and support for your child.

Parenting that actively seeks to identify an LGBTQIA+ child's strengths, build on what the child is good at, and encourage the child to use their strengths can buffer and help them successfully navigate future trauma and stress (Zavala & Waters, 2020). It can be a delicate balance for parents to guide their LGBTQIA+-identified child in making positive and safe choices while at the same time granting implicit trust and permission to experiment and explore what feels congruent and healthy to them as they develop an independent identity (Nadan, 2021).

Ambiguous loss theory points to another avenue for movement toward resolution: changing your perception (Boss, 2004). You cannot control who your child is or how they choose to live, but you can control how you *perceive* them and their identity and how you relate to them. For some parents, this may mean learning assertiveness skills to manage social stigma, unjustified shame/blame, and conflicting identities (Cassar & Grima Sultana, 2021). For example, developing ***cognitive flexibility*** (the ability to switch from one way of thinking to another and consider issues from various viewpoints) has been shown to help parents navigate the tensions of conflicting situations and be creative in their problem-solving to identify new possibilities for themselves, their child, and their family (Rosenkrantz et al., 2020). Cognitive flexibility is a skill, process, and outcome from being curious, tolerating ambiguity, revising incomplete and false assumptions, and making new meanings. The focus is not on changing cultural/religious beliefs, unless that feels important to you, but examining any inferiority you may feel about yourself or your child and improving how you relate to and connect with your child and yourself.

Many parents discover positive aspects to being a parent of an LGBTQIA+-identified child (K. A. Gonzalez et al., 2013). One of the expected positive responses is personal growth. Being the parent to an LGBTQIA+-identified child can change how you see all people, especially those who experience marginalized and stigmatized identities, and bring about new perspectives, greater awareness of discrimination, more self-compassion and empathy, improved communication skills and ability to deal with conflicts, and a more open mind. You may reflect on and evaluate your beliefs and feelings about gender/sexuality and your cultural beliefs and experiences growing up. This may lead to reinforcing or refining your purpose and meaning in life. You may experience new joys of pride, admiration, and unconditional love. Your child's identity may initiate more social connections and access to new social networks and resources for yourself and your family. You may want to get involved in advocacy efforts and being an ally to your child and the LGBTQIA+ community in ways that fit you and your family. Perhaps most importantly, learning of your child's sexual/gender identity can result in closer and stronger relationships—with your child, yourself, and other members of your family and community.

Responding to Intersexuality

We use the term *intersex* for **diversity of sexual development** or **variations in sex characteristics** (DSD or VSC, for short) when a person's sexual characteristics (external or internal genitalia, chromosomes, hormonal levels) do not fit in our binary categories of male and female. A lack of consensus exists about what is considered to be intersex; therefore, estimates of the number of people born with a DSD/VSC range from 0.018% to 1.7% of the population (Blackless et al., 2000; Sax, 2002).

If a child's intersex condition is first identified during pregnancy, parents and family can spend meaningful time focusing on how to welcome this new child with respect. It is crucial to embrace the baby as a human being by considering who the baby is, not who the baby is not. Seeing your child as equal versus ill or inferior to other children is an essential part of this process.

How this process of receiving an intersex baby is approached can be highly different depending on the medical setting in which the baby is born. Some hospitals have multidisciplinary care teams of relevant subspecialists working in close collaboration. Others might not have the ideal team, leaving parents to figure out their own way into parenthood. Similar to when a child comes out as LGBTQA+, when a parent finds their child is intersex, educating yourself, examining your beliefs about sex and gender, finding peer and professional support, and hearing what intersex people have to say about their raising can make a big difference for both you and your child.

As parents and family consider these possibilities about the intersex fetus during pregnancy, an initial approach can be to work on strengthening the family. A great deal of research has demonstrated that the strength of the parent-child relationship and bonding can affect well-being before, during, and after a child comes out as LGBTQIA+. With this in mind, having open and supportive family communications may contribute to more positive outcomes for parents adjusting to the knowledge of and integration of their intersex child in their family. In addition, consider any medical information and consultation that emphasizes the humanity and integrity of your child. Remember that the attribute of nonbinary sex does not define your newborn's "who" and personhood. Focus on resources and support to help you cope positively with any distress or uncertainty that could affect pregnancy, pre- or postnatal health and well-being, and early development.

Remember that intersex is a wide umbrella of conditions, and most don't pose a medical risk. Surgeries are discouraged when they are not medically required and should be postponed until the person can consent to the procedure (Dickens, 2018). Older minors and adults who are intersex often report adverse mental health effects and resentment regarding discovering they had been put through "corrective" procedures at or near birth, whether they later considered themselves more aligned with the gender/sex role they had been "corrected" toward or not (Human Rights Watch, 2017). Helping an intersex person feel good about their body and uniqueness will help them feel resilient and respond to social stigma about gender-body diversity.

Below are highlights of the subjective dynamics and possibilities for the baby, parents, family, and community that emerge from each child as a new life: who will be born?

1. A baby is born: How does the family relate to the multiprofessional team and vice versa? Genetic information and medical counseling are necessary for specific situations, including if there has been a previous record of intersex in the family.
2. The subjective reactions of the parents: What comes from the idealization of the "perfect child" and the possible frustration about the new circumstance? Which strengths from managing ambiguity and crises in the past does each parent have, and can they draw on both to experience more love and connection?
3. The opportunity for those parents to be in contact with families whose intersex children have been raised and loved: What does it mean? Community resources may promote new relationships and involve a web-based group and restorative practices for sharing, helping, teaching, or giving support.

4. The possible experience of strengthening parents, siblings, and extended family members through the new situation as all grapple with thinking about sex in nonbinary ways.

Moving From the Initial Reaction to Adjustment

More research is needed on how caregivers and families move from their initial reaction to acceptance and integration. In a study of several hundred conservative Christian parents (Yarhouse & Zaporozhets, 2022), changes occurred four to five years postdisclosure of an LGBTQ+ child in three areas: cognitive, emotional, and spiritual. These changes did not always lead to a progressive view of sexuality or gender; many parents remained traditional, but they came to terms with the reality that their child is LGBTQ+ (versus the fantasy of a phase or desire for them to revert/change orientation/gender). Other research and published experiences highlight the role of communication within the family and the community and the collaborative ways family members respond to crises and adapt to change (Herdt & Koff, 2000). If your family has difficulty moving to acceptance and integration or at least a positive coexistence, working with a counselor or mediator on empathic communication, problem-solving for win-win solutions, and imagined possibilities may help you navigate this process.

Various models exist from diverse cultural experiences about LGBTQIA+ identity development and how family members share or do not share their identity with those they feel close to. One aspect all identity models have in common is that "coming out" to the family is rarely at the start of the LGBTQIA+ individual's identity development. It's usually located in the middle stages after much denying, dismissing, bargaining, ruminating, comparing, hiding, exploring, compartmentalizing, self-accepting, and decision-making. Studies about sexual orientation milestones support this, finding that first attractions and self-labeling may occur around five to nine years, respectively, before disclosing to a family member (Martos et al., 2015). Keeping this in mind might help you avoid denial or dismissal of what your child is telling you or is doing ("but he dates girls") and leave room for healthy development in the future. Trans/gender-expansive individuals may come out twice to parents and family members, first as LGBQA+ and then again after understanding their gender identity.

Knowing and feeling positive about one's gender, sexual, religious, cultural, and social identities, as well as learning how to be resilient to prejudice and discrimination, likely do not happen at the same time but sequentially after each other (for example, focusing on career identity and then sexual/gender identity or vice versa and then both).

Like family reaction models, identity development models also show individual differences depending on personal and cultural factors. How do your culture(s) and family of origin typically deal with conflict/crises and gender and sexual topics? How often do cultural and family interactions involve lectures of one person telling the other what not to do or should do or involve dialogues to clarify safety guidelines for personal needs and limits?

Other themes or topics that you might need time to learn (or relearn) include the use of language and terminology, including individuals' self-definitions and labels; gender/sexual identity development, including the wide range of gender identification, transitioning, and coming-out experiences; and adjusting your hopes and dreams for the future of your unique child. There are several ways to find information, and you might consider asking your child who came out to you, if they are an adult, about resources or recommendations—this could serve as a way to show your care and interest in learning. They likely may share what was helpful for their self-development and why they came out to you.

As parents dwell in this new world of sexual/gender diversity, some realize diversity is more common and less unusual than initially thought. The "Who else?" syndrome might happen as you realize not everybody is cisgender and exclusively heterosexual. You may find yourself second-guessing other people's gender or sexuality instead of assuming normativity. This questioning might reflect that you are changing your views about gender and sexuality. Engaging yourself in the LGBTQIA+ aspects of your child's life (for example, meeting their friends or people they date, going together to a pride parade, showing interest in their experiences and views about LGBTQIA+ issues, watching movies with diversity content, shopping for clothes that affirm their gender, etc.) might lead you to realize that life is not radically different and help you find meaningful ways to connect and support your child.

It is vital to note the impact of family resilience on sexual and gender minority youth's well-being and development (Meza Lazaro & Bacio, 2023). LGBTQIA+ individuals of varying racial/ethnic identities may experience family strength, cultural resilience, and coming out differently (for example, to whom they feel they can come out and how they seek harmony and individuality within relationships) (Jhang, 2018). Stronger or weaker identification with one's communities may make a difference in what kind of discrimination and prejudice one experiences and how one copes. Many racialized LGBTQIA+ individuals describe learning from family and community members how to be resilient to social stigma and adversity (Stone et al., 2020).

One tool that may be helpful as you work toward understanding and adapting is expressive writing. This practice has been proven effective in organizing complex emotional experiences, increasing awareness and compassion, and creating positive meaning in distressing situations. In one study (Abreu et al., 2020), Cuban American and Puerto Rican parents wrote about their cultural beliefs and values that facilitated the acceptance of their child's LGBTQIA+ identity. As they reflected on how their beliefs, emotions, and interactions with their child evolved, they spent time reflecting and journaling about the positive impact of the following:

- Developing awareness of systemic and structural oppression toward LGBTQIA+ individuals and their relationships
- Immersing themselves in educational sources and seeking out community connections to understand their child's sexuality and gender identity and expression
- Recalling previous interactions with LGBTQIA+ people and how these interactions helped them have a positive view of their LGBTQIA+ child
- Acknowledging and appreciating their child's positive qualities, traits, and uniqueness
- Recollecting learned lessons from their child about compassion for the LGBTQIA+ community and others
- Reinforcing, revising, or rejecting cultural beliefs about gender and sexual norms to accept and respond positively to their child's sexuality and gender expression

Notably, most parents in this reflective exercise reported that expressive writing led to feelings of happiness, pride, peace, satisfaction, and relief.

Adjusting your hopes and dreams for your child's future may be more possible as diversity rights advance and LGBTQIA+ people can marry, adopt, access assisted fertilization, study, have careers, and choose their affirming environments. It might differ from what you initially imagined, but being LGBTQIA+ does not mean your child will not reach happiness or accomplish typical milestones and their desired life dreams. This adjustment is something most parents have to do independently of their children's sexual orientation and gender identity development, as the idea of a "happy, fulfilling life" usually differs from one individual to another, especially across different families, generations, and cultures.

Finally, suppose you are LGBTQIA+ and a parent of an LGBTQIA+ child. In that case, the above may apply to you but involve its own challenges and strengths in separating your experiences with your sexual/gender identity development as you help your child develop their life course on these issues. You and your child are likely also experiencing different degrees of privilege and stigma. It is a natural parental reaction to want to ease the struggle for your child, but remember, your journey is not theirs. Your best and most caring efforts to help may be perceived as undue pressure to be like you. However, too much noninvolvement can be seen as not caring. As you know, parenting can be a tricky balancing act, and there are no instruction manuals on how to do that. Watch for your child's signals or cues and listen to their questions and those unspoken questions underneath. And, when asking a question, give them time to answer and be aware that answering may take days or weeks.

Routes to LGBTQIA+ Parenthood and Their Social Contexts

The gay baby (gayby) boom started in the 1990s, influenced by the HIV epidemic, as a generation of LGBTQIA+ individuals shifted from fighting for the right to have sex to the right to marry and domesticate (Drescher, 2014). Many LGBTQIA+ individuals continue this desire to become parents, either for the first time or to have more children (Family Equality Council, 2019). LGBTQIA+ parents may enter the world of parenting in a variety of ways (Tornello et al., 2019). These include (a) surrogacy, (b) adoption and foster care, (c) donor insemination, (d) in the context of a previous or current heterosexual relationship, (e) through stepparenthood, or (f) as a bonus caregiver in a committed relationship. These avenues of parenting create both unique opportunities and challenges for LGBTQIA+ parents and may change the needs of these parents and their children (A. E. Goldberg, 2022).

For example, fostering or adopting children from the foster care system frequently involves children from dire circumstances. Abuse and neglect, sexual abuse, abandonment, exposure to drug and alcohol abuse, and the like have varied and severe consequences for the children. These kids need stable homes, and often LGBTQIA+ individuals or couples are the only ones interested and willing to provide a home and family for these youth. These situations bring unique issues that require the parents to navigate a seemingly incomprehensible and often hostile (to the LGBTQIA+ parents) collection of systems to get the services their children need. This is one reason why it is essential to have inclusive and welcoming school settings that support LGBTQIA+ parents and their families.

For those considering foster parenting LGBTQIA+ youth, many issues are associated with LGBTQIA+ child development. Abuse by peers, mental health concerns, oversexualization of identity, institutionalization, targeting by authority figures, abuse by religious institutions or individuals, sexual targeting by adult predators, surgical changes on intersex infants, and rejection of intersex children are just some of the possible concerns (Craig-Oldsen et al., 2006). Such youth may seek invisibility in the foster care system, become chronic runaways, and attempt suicide. These concerns can overwhelm foster parents without strong support from friends, family, professionals, and other foster parents.

If the child(ren) were conceived via donor insemination or surrogacy, the questions that come up with each developmental stage could be, "Where did I come from?"; "Where is my mom (dad)?"; "Susie has a mom and a dad, why don't I?"; and "Whose tummy did I grow in?" For example, one coauthor of this chapter (DiClementi) heard from one of her girls in the first grade, who had found that some friends' parents had divorced and remarried (dad and stepmom and mom and stepdad), asked, "So you're my two moms. Where are my two dads?" It is important to be honest and provide information appropriate for the child's developmental stage.

Surrogacy is the least common and least researched method of entering into parenting (Fantus & Newman, 2022). Because of the high expenses associated with surrogacy, it is generally an option mostly available to wealthy gay men. Because of the inconsistency of laws addressing nonheteronormative methods of becoming parents, such as surrogacy, those parents may need to seek additional protections, such as legal parenting agreements and wills (Gash & Raiskin, 2018). Adoption is a far more common method of family formation (Dente, 2018). Due to laws surrounding both international adoption and domestic adoption in many states, same-gender/queer couples often cannot adopt, effectively excluding one parent from the process as the other pursues adoption as a single parent (Berrick, 2021). The decision to conceive through donor insemination also has considerable legal ramifications and expenses. Specifically, half of all states have no laws supporting second-parent adoption, and in several states, there are laws designed to make second-parent adoption more difficult for LGBTQIA+ parents (A. E. Goldberg et al., 2014).

Regardless of one's sexual orientation and gender, navigating foster care/adoption agencies can be challenging. Prospective parents need to reset their expectations before starting this process. Hiring lawyers skilled in this area to support you in navigating common adoption hurdles may be very helpful. Legal battles over adoption and custody can cost tens of thousands of dollars and are prohibitive for those who cannot afford such expenses.

Because of the vast range of parenting rights between jurisdictions, a same-gender/queer couple can end up with unequal parenting rights (only one is the legal parent) (Kazyak & Park, 2020). For example, coauthor DiClementi and her wife adopted the wife's great-nieces. According to current law, biological adoptions took precedence. Only the wife would have been the legal adoptive parent. At the same time, DiClementi was the primary source of economic support, which set up the possibility that should the legal parent suddenly die, the remaining parent would have no legal rights to the children, and they would end up back in the foster care system. Fortunately, the state in which the children were adopted had enacted a second-parent adoption law during their process that included same-gender couples. Both women became legal adoptive parents and were listed on the new birth certificates. Marriage equality has since simplified this, allowing married parents to be listed on the birth certificate, to adopt jointly, and to apply for stepparent adoption.

Many LGBTQIA+ parents enter into parenthood in the context of a previous heterosexual relationship. This is changing as legal and societal views shift, making parenthood more accessible, and more LGBTQIA+ individuals are coming out earlier in life (Family Equality Council, 2017). Still, this means many LGBTQIA+ parents may experience relationship dissolution as part of their parenting and coming-out process. In particular, transgender/nonbinary parents who transition after having children may face increased family discord and conflict as the couple navigates their relationship after the transgender/nonbinary parent has disclosed their gender identity. In many cases, this conflict will result in divorce or separation. However, this is not a universal outcome; many couples will adapt, stay together, and thrive.

Despite the barriers to parenthood for LGBTQIA+ individuals, many studies report that those homes are just as or more emotionally and psychologically healthy as cis-heterosexual-parent homes (Bos et al., 2016; Farr, 2017). Parents and providers must know that children of LGBTQIA+ parents are as well-adjusted and have equal or higher rates of well-being compared to children of cis-heterosexual parents (Mazrekaj et al., 2020).

Regardless of their route to parenthood, LGBTQIA+ parents face the same challenges that heterosexual, cisgender parents face. They will need to balance their children's needs for closeness and autonomy; negotiate the day-to-day division of parental duties; socialize their children with family, friends, and community; navigate childcare, health care, and educational systems; help their children navigate friendships and romantic relationships; provide for their physical and emotional needs; and all the other tasks incumbent upon parents. This can be more challenging because LGBTQIA + parents must attend to these tasks in a cis-heteronormative climate, which can often be hostile or, at a minimum, unsupportive.

One way this can manifest is in LGBTQIA+ parents feeling less support from their families of origin. It also can be seen in the school context for children with LGBTQIA+ parents who may experience frequent discrimination by teachers and staff related to their parents' gender expression or sexual identity. Age is also a factor in this, as research indicates that bullying is not as common in the early years but becomes so during the middle school years (Gartrell et al., 2005).

Most LGBTQIA+ parents did not have LGBTQIA+ parents to model how to navigate advocacy and social justice issues in their families. LGBTQIA+ parents likely had cisgender heterosexual parents, so they have to negotiate roles and tasks against a backdrop of traditional models of parenting and gender roles. The necessary negotiation and teamwork, however, can become a strength.

Negotiation skills can generalize from the immediate family needs to working with their children's schools and health-care providers, foster care and adoption agencies, and other services. For example, coauthor DiClementi's school district has a school fair every spring for parents to meet school administrators and teachers. DiClementi's opening question has always been, "How do you feel about working with lesbian parents?" One elementary school principal enthusiastically exclaimed, "I *love* my lesbian parents! They're always more involved than the other parents." DiClementi knew then that they had a winner. Negative reactions would have directed DiClementi and her family away from the school to avoid future uncomfortable interactions.

Parents can also negotiate changes in less dramatic situations. While not passing or not being able to conceal being LGBTQIA+ can have its drawbacks, one can use it to one's advantage. DiClementi found that introducing themselves as spouses or their children's moms, with the clear expectation of acceptance, can set the tone for future interactions. Demonstration of self-confidence sends the message that we will not be ignored or stigmatized.

As of November 2022, 11 states still allow agencies to deny adoption or foster care services to LGBTQ individuals based on religious grounds, and nine states do not protect against such discrimination (Movement Advancement Project, 2022). LGBTQIA+ parents may also have more difficulty accessing other kinds of services, such as reliable, affordable, and culturally competent health care, insurance, and mental health counseling, which can increase the likelihood that LGBTQIA+ parents will suffer from adverse health outcomes and make it more challenging to provide appropriate care for their children. Racialized LGBTQIA+ parents are at increased risk for physical and emotional safety and mental health concerns (Radis & Nadan, 2020).

Key LGBTQIA+ family formation issues revolve around the legality and community support or stigma toward family creation practices, including adoption, in vitro fertilization (IVF) treatment, sperm donation, and surrogacy. The legal issues for LGBTQIA+-parented families differ across state and international boundaries. LGBTQIA+-parented families of all belief systems and political backgrounds face legal challenges depending on where they are geographically regarding citizenship and legal documentation when they travel across state and international boundaries. Support issues include the following (Farr & Goldberg, 2015; Levitt et al., 2020; Patterson & Ball, 2018):

1. Lack of universal recognition of marriage licenses/divorce for LGBTQ+ couples and universal protections for single/divorced/widowed LGBTQ+ parents/guardians
2. Lack of universal recognition in health-care settings, public accommodations, and the legal system
3. Variations in child custody and divorce laws (lack of recognition by the state or country)
4. Challenges of rights to family formation by the state or country (bans on parenting, adoption, surrogacy, IVF, egg donation, etc.)
5. Hospitals not granting privileges to providers of reproductive technology
6. Barriers to international adoptions

7. Refusal by judges or jurisdictions to allow second-parent adoptions
8. Countries with conservative family/sexuality/gender policies where the statement or accusation of being LGBTQIA+ can be grounds for death, life in prison, smaller prison sentences, criminal charges, harassment, or ostracization for oneself, one's significant other(s), and one's children, including the threat of forced breakup of the parenting relationship and state control of the children
9. Societal prejudice that a family with children who are biologically/genetically related to the parents is ideal and superior to a family with adopted children (*bionormativity*) (Baker, 2008)

In conservative communities, the resources of the Family Acceptance Project mentioned earlier may help LGBTQIA+ parents guide providers in school and other family settings to affirm and not reject them or their children to increase their children's well-being (Ryan & Chen-Hayes, 2013).

Along those lines, the following section focuses on how heteronormative attitudes, discriminatory laws, and educational biases restrict and impact the experiences of LGBTQIA+ parents and their families. We'll highlight how these issues occur in Greece[3] for you to consider how similar, different, or comprehensive (Goldfarb & Lieberman, 2021) your local and national school systems are regarding sexuality and gender. Parents of LGBTQIA+ children may consider how similar and different their concerns and resources are compared to those described below for LGBTQIA+ parents navigating a stigmatized and marginalized gender/sexual identity.

LGBTQIA+ Parents and School Settings, With a Focus on Greece

Understanding LGBTQIA+ parents' motivations and experiences related to school engagement is paramount since most research on school involvement has largely emphasized those of heterosexual, cisgender parents (A. E. Goldberg & Smith, 2014). Despite the positive outcome research on the well-being of children of LGBTQIA+ parents (American Psychological Association, 2020), research shows that LGBTQIA+ parents and their children are harmed by ongoing stigmatization in the educational setting (I. McDonald & Morgan, 2019). For example, research demonstrates how homophobic stigmatization during adolescence can cause long-term internalizing and externalizing problems for children of lesbian parents (Bos et al., 2021). LGBTQIA+ parents and their children are sometimes outsiders in the school setting, making their involvement even more necessary to create positive school experiences for their children (Nixon, 2011).

---

[3] Many chapters in this book project include a section highlighting an international perspective. We hope this expands readers' global understanding, empathy, and connection and allows readers to consider if and how these experiences and recommendations fit or do not fit for them.

In addition, considering that parents' school involvement and comfort in their children's school communities are strongly associated with better child academic outcomes, it is crucial to consider the constitution of the school environment and how diversity in family types is integrated and welcomed (Jeynes, 2005). Parental concern regarding their children's mistreatment due to their family formation may lead to LGBTQIA+ parents becoming involved to discourage discriminatory actions. On the other hand, LGBTQIA+ parents may avoid interactions with schools and with other parents because of their desire to minimize possible incidents of rejection and stereotyping (Gillborn et al., 2012; Nixon, 2011). This situation echoes the complexity that sexual/gender minority parents may face because they are not included in the dominant societal discourse that reinforces heteronormativity and traditional gender roles and expression (Gato et al., 2020).

Research shows that educational settings in which there is, to some extent, integration of social justice and inclusive perspectives result in beneficial partnerships between the school and home and ensure the most successful outcomes for children (Burt et al., 2010; Fedewa & Clark, 2009). Shared experiences in the school setting can support a sense of connection that could overshadow any differences (Vinjamuri, 2015) and counteract the phenomenon that LGBTQIA+ parents are typically left without a proper peer group in school settings (De Graeve, 2014).

Invitations to participate in or attend school events may be significant for LGBTQIA+ parents who may feel uncertain about their welcome. It is apparent that many school and educational settings still reflect dominant and traditional ideas about sexuality, gender identity, and family forms. This contributes to the real and perceived silencing of some forms of sexuality or gender-related topics in school settings (Gunn, 2011). In addition, discourses that consider children as vulnerable to dangerous knowledge about LGBTQIA+ individuals maintain and reproduce heteronormative/transphobic values within the educational context (Martino & Cumming-Potvin, 2015). Therefore, teachers need to examine their values and knowledge and avoid stigmatization of LGBTQIA-led families (DePalma, 2013). Also, beyond parents' sexual orientation and gender, other factors such as their race/ethnicity, social class positioning, and educational level further shape how they are treated and relate to school communities.

In Greece, discriminatory laws have prohibited[4] adoption or access to assisted reproductive technology for same-gender couples, and this rejection impacts how same-gender couples see themselves and, consequently, their well-being (Grigoropoulos, 2023; Voultsos et al., 2019). The personal biases

---

[4] Greece's Parliament legalized same-sex marriage and adoption February 15, 2024, as this guidebook went to press. We hope our recommendations help with the transition.

of professionals working in education toward LGBTQIA+ parents are scarcely investigated, even though these biases discourage these parents and families from school involvement (Grigoropoulos, 2021).

Greek society is traditionally conservative. Orthodox religion in Greece strongly affects societal attitudes and political legislation, while Greek values overemphasize the importance of heterosexual marriage and traditional gender roles (Voultsos et al., 2019). The Greek cultural context attributes significant value to cisgender, heterosexual parenthood, considering it a prerequisite for personal fulfillment. Heterosexual marriage and parenthood are interconnected in Greece, and this possibly explains the limited cultural tolerance to and respect for LGBTQIA+ parents (Kantsa, 2014). As Kantsa and Chalkidou (2014) noted, being a single mother in Greece is more accepted.

Furthermore, findings from the Greek context show that early childhood teachers may exhibit a homonegativity stance toward marriage equality and same-gender parenting that could affect their interactions with LGBTQIA-parented families and their children, creating a prejudicial school environment (Grigoropoulos, 2022). Greek lesbian mothers, for example, expressed navigating negative experiences in school settings that included being overlooked and feeling unwelcomed because of their family formation ((Grigoropoulos, 2023b). Therefore, educators need to be aware of the harmful impact of homonegative, bi-negative, and transphobic stances in creating a positive school environment. Overall, not only are LGBTQIA+ issues scarcely ever discussed in Greek school settings, it is also somewhat ambiguous whether teachers recognize the negative impact of this invisibility on students and their families (Burt et al., 2010).

Understanding Greek Educational Contexts and Prejudice

In 2016, the Greek Ministry of Education, Research, and Religious Affairs developed a thematic week to familiarize adolescent students with various issues, including sexual orientation and gender identity. However, several political parties and the Greek Orthodox Church strongly opposed those practices as they were considered to undermine patriotic and religious perceptions of Greek society (Sailakis, 2018). In addition, teachers argued that they were not prepared or educated to address issues related to gender, sexuality, and children (Psarra, 2017). Keep in mind that no other additions were made to the curriculum of the other stages of compulsory education (for example, early childhood education and primary educational practices) other than questioning heteronormativity and providing more diverse representations of sexuality and gender. This rejection of making space for LGBTQIA+ parents and youth in education may mean that educators cannot position themselves against LGBTQIA+ prejudice and discrimination and cannot protect LGBTQIA+ children or children with LGBTQIA+ parents in educational settings.

In contrast, research regarding children's gender and sexual development suggests they are most interested during their early years in understanding their own and others' gender and sexuality (Gunn, 2011), making childhood education a central period to respond to gender, sexual, and relationship stereotypes and youth and families who do not fit the norm (Hegde et al., 2013).

The influence and the role of societal beliefs and traditional religion in Greek society become evident because teachers follow normative values about gender, identity, and family forms even though the curriculum has no such apparent intention (Karamouzis, 2015). As Thermos argued, the Greek Orthodox Church opposes queer theory, despite such theory providing educational practices and methods to include in anti-oppressive educational settings (Sailakis, 2018).

Promoting an Inclusive Educational Setting

In Greece, the lack of social visibility, safety, and social education harms the acceptance and health of LGBTQIA+ families. One way to confront this invisibility in school settings is to promote and reinforce continuous education and awareness of educators of all levels on sexual orientation, gender identity, and gender expression.

In particular, emphasis should be placed on challenging stereotypes, social norms, and binary expectations of gender-based behaviors in school settings. School settings should ensure access to textbooks that promote positive references to LGBTQIA+ individuals and their families, using age-appropriate and unbiased language. Counseling support in school settings could counteract prejudice and enable acceptance and positive options for self-development. Further, LGBTQIA+ organizations can collaborate and provide the necessary expertise to implement practices. Any board deciding policy for sexual/gender diversity must be diverse in political affiliations and cultural viewpoints to achieve collaboration, accuracy, and win-win solutions. The absence of personal and humanizing experiences contributes to less positive attitudes toward queer families in school settings (Iliopoulou et al., 2020).

Since each society is distinct because of its different cultural and political characteristics, it is most important to examine the factors that affect the general population's attitude regarding LGBTQIA+ families. This first step is essential but incomplete. Birbili (2014) argued that issues related to sexuality and gender should be of concern in Greek curriculum and classrooms so that children can establish healthy relationships with their own sexuality, gender expression, and self-protection. Research from the cultural context of Greece suggests that LGBTQIA+ issues are not considered important in raising awareness, especially not for society in general (Grigoropoulos, 2021). Research also reports that early childhood educators frame children as immature or uninterested regarding LGBTQIA+ issues and different family formations in classrooms. However, this may echo educators' feelings or unreadiness to address such issues. Teachers may also be confused since there are no guidelines or details of what teachers can do and which topics should be addressed.

Children's and adolescents' understanding of gender expression and sexuality and awareness about sexual/gender minority issues is essential to their identity development, relationships, and health, regardless of their sexual/gender identity. We also do not know which children will grow up and identify as LGBTQIA+. Therefore, school systems, teachers, and families would benefit from implementing LGBTQIA+-affirming pedagogical practices that do not disregard, oppose, discourage, or promote any particular sexual/gender identity but counter prejudice and provide positive role models of healthy relationships and families. Traditional gender roles and heteronormativity in school settings can be maintained while promoting autonomy, equality, and protection for LGBTQIA+ families.

Currently, everyday practice in day care and educational centers is affected by heteronormativity, which continues to reproduce itself (Grigoropoulos, 2021). The absence of nonnormative representations of sexuality and gender in Greek books reflects this exclusion and marginalization (Yiannikopoulou & Sakellaki, 2011). It may be helpful for policy makers and stakeholders to examine and consider age-appropriate LGBTQIA+-themed illustrated books for classrooms and libraries. Any community efforts that (a) destigmatize genderfluid/nonbinary identities, intersex variations, sexual diversity, and sexual/gender questioning and (b) foster openness, exploration, safety, self-acceptance, and self-expression will have a positive effect on all youth (Brömdal et al., 2021; L. M. Diamond, 2020). An Italian school program, for example, designed to reduce homophobic bullying also increased students' empathy, prosociality, and emotional regulation (Iuso et al., 2022).

Government protection for LGBTQIA+ individuals saves lives. Research (Prairie et al., 2020) analyzing responses from 83,000 U.S. high school students found that LGB and questioning students attempted suicide 2.9 to 4.3 times more than their heterosexual peers. Suicide attempts decreased by 1.2% for all students in states with hate crime laws that included LGBQ+ individuals as a protected group, with questioning and bisexual students reporting more reductions in suicide attempts. States that did not have protection for LGBQ+ individuals showed no decrease in student suicide attempts.

Suggestions to Include Gender, Sexual, Faith, and Cultural Diversity

The following tips provide best practices for day care providers, educators, counselors, social workers, therapists, doctors, and related staff to provide LGBTQIA+ culturally competent care. A suggestion for all providers is to practice being curious and compassionate and not make assumptions about families (for example, their needs, priorities, and family makeup). The following suggestions, however, are now outlawed in Florida and other parts of the world, leaving parents and educators empty-handed and without a course of action besides suppression to prepare LGBTQIA+ and cis-heterosexual youth for life (Amos, 2020).

We caution that some suggestions below will lead some traditionally religious parents to not engage in therapy or seek help elsewhere, often from a nonprofessional or parachurch ministry that may not ultimately be as helpful to the family. It's important to know that if LGBTQIA+-affirmative clinicians want to help conservative sexually/gender-diverse youth and adults, they must work with conservative clinicians because conservative clients will likely not go to affirmative clinicians. We need to acknowledge that the stimulus value of certain symbols (a pride flag) may communicate one thing (affirmation/acceptance) to one parent while communicating another thing (an agenda/unwillingness to understand their point of view) to another parent.

Heteronormativity causes queer people to feel like outcasts; aggressive queer messaging causes conservative people to feel like outcasts. Here we are promoting inclusion and collaboration. If a suggestion below doesn't fit you, we hope it inspires self-reflection about which words you would use to incorporate your experiences.

Regarding gender neutrality in language, we suggest this only be employed when caregivers and their children request it. Forms should offer the caregiver the ability to say for themselves what variety, if any, of gendered role they identify with. Provide checkboxes for "mother/mom," "father/dad," "parent," "caregiver," or whatever seems suitable, but it is not the right call to eschew these titles entirely. Gendered words mean something equal or more to transgender/nonbinary individuals than to cis-heterosexuals. Forms should allow people to define for themselves who they are. We hope the following offers other options and paths forward that consider all family diversity.

Tips for Educators

1. Use gender-sensitive language, such as *parents*, *caregivers*, *guardians*, and *child* in addition to *mother and father*, *daughter*, and *son*.
2. Develop an inclusive and comprehensive education (Fantus & Newman, 2021; Kattari et al., 2019; Mata et al., 2022) that involves examples of diverse families, including those with same-gender, queer, and transgender/nonbinary parents and students, caregivers and students with disabilities, and varying gender-expansive identities in readings and resources used in the classroom.

3. Work with staff to create a comprehensive plan for preventing and addressing bullying.
4. Communicate openly with caregivers, providers, and children to address concerns.
5. Immediately address any negative or harassing comments made by students or staff.
6. Involve students in establishing safety codes of conduct for classes, including appropriate language and terms and how to respond to students of diverse backgrounds.
7. Respect and use names and pronouns that feel right for the person. If choosing not to use a person's pronouns, don't disparage what the person shares with you about their identity or use of those pronouns. If using their pronouns violates your integrity, use the person's chosen name to refer to the person (Reconciliation and Growth Project, 2023). Including your pronouns in correspondence is a way to welcome diversity and demonstrate sensitivity to invisibility and marginalization. If others do not want to do this, do not pressure them. Be aware also that pronouns may change, and some individuals may not be ready or want to declare their pronouns openly. Allow for the autonomy of self-expression and self-determination as long as it does not demean, dismiss, or devalue anyone.
8. Include all family variations in celebrations in your classrooms and schools.
9. Create and facilitate support groups for parents across different sexual orientations, genders, and political and cultural experiences to dialogue about common-ground safety needs and how to implement the above to respect differences and collaborate on community safety and growth regarding sexual/gender diversity and cis-heteronormativity.
10. Create affinity and accountability support groups of parents of similar sexual orientations, genders, and political and cultural experiences to meet and understand reactions, social differences, needs, and various levels of social power and disadvantage and work toward shared goals.

Tips for Physical and Mental Health Care Providers

1. Make sure office forms are gender inclusive and provide space for *parents*, *caregivers*, and *guardians* in addition to *mother and father*.
2. Include space on your forms for names and pronouns used. Because of the legal requirements of medical records and insurance reimbursement, legal names must be on the record, but providers can make space to honor their patients' names and pronouns. Ensure nonlegal names are not on any forms that may have to be shared with the insurance company or any other entity requiring access to records.
3. Educate everyone in the office, including the front desk staff, on the physical and mental health needs of LGBTQIA+ individuals, including privacy issues. Access to competent care and support groups can lessen the effects of stigma and discrimination.

4. Inform yourself about child development and the specific family needs of LGBTQIA+ families and various LGBTQIA+ communities.
5. Offer regular in-service opportunities to continue staff education about LGBTQIA+ families and communities; bring in speakers, offer paid time off to attend presentations, and offer Safe Zone ally training.
6. Post signs in offices and waiting areas attesting to commitment to diversity and that your office/clinic is safe for gender, sexual, and faith diversity.
7. Display books and periodicals related to LGBTQIA+ individuals in your office or waiting area. Have brochures and flyers with lists of support resources readily available.
8. Invest in and display an inclusive rainbow flag or other LGBTQIA+ symbol as you also display faith-affirming symbols.

For more about why and how to make changes in educational systems, see the American Psychological Association's (2021c) practice guidelines. Check out our online[5] resource lists and companion e-resources for more support.

Conclusion

Deconstructing the boxes of gender, race, faith, culture, and sexuality is not an impossible hope or goal. Parents can examine their views on these issues, whether ready for it or not, during any crisis and life change, especially when they learn their child is not exclusively heterosexual or gender normative. This deconstruction, reformation, and rebuilding process can be lifelong and becomes possible when it is accepted as an invitation for growth for all family members to share their life experiences. When the invitation is accepted, it becomes possible to be more open by listening to others we live with and encounter. They all communicate their existence, tensions, strengths, and inherent worth.

The tensions that hurt people and relationships are often due to discrimination and rejection when people are excluded and not welcomed. When we express the idea of deconstructing the boxes of gender, race, religion, and sexual identity, it is a metaphor for deconstructing the limits to selfhood and the dignity and individuality of all. In doing so, we propose building the importance of the human condition independently of the imposition of dominating belief systems of sexuality, gender, faith, race, culture, or social background. Above all, we hope parents and caregivers have found some ideas, skills, and resources in this chapter that will help resolve some of their distress related to sexual/gender diversity.

---

[5] At www.FindingCongruence.com.

References

Abbott, E. (2001). *A history of celibacy*. Da Capo.

Abreu, R. L., Gonzalez, K. A., Capielo Rosario, C., Lockett, G. M., Lindley, L., & Lane, S. (2021). "We are our own community": Immigrant Latinx transgender people community experiences. *Journal of Counseling Psychology, 68*(4), 390–403. doi:10.1037/cou0000546

Abreu, R. L., Riggle, E. D. B., & Rostosky, S. S. (2020). Expressive writing intervention with Cuban-American and Puerto Rican parents of LGBTQ individuals. *Counseling Psychologist, 48*(1), 106–34. doi:10.1177/0011000019853240

Adler, A., & Ben-Ari, A. (2017). The myth of openness and secrecy in intimate relationships: The case of spouses of mixed-orientation marriage. *Journal of Homosexuality, 64*, 804–24. doi:10.1080/00918369.2016.1236585

Adler, A., & Ben-Ari, A. (2021). Between mainstream and marginality: The case of men and women of mixed-orientation relationships. *Journal of Homosexuality, 68*, 1813–32. doi:10.1080/00918369.2020.1712139

American Psychological Association. (2005). *Lesbian and gay parenting*. https://www.apa.org/pi/lgbt/resources/parenting-full.pdf

American Psychological Association. (2009). *Appropriate therapeutic responses to sexual orientation*. https://www.apa.org/pi/lgbt/resources/therapeutic-response.pdf

American Psychological Association. (2020). *APA resolution on sexual orientation, gender identity (SOGI), parents and their children*. https://www.apa.org/about/policy/resolution-sexual-orientation-parents-children.pdf

American Psychological Association. (2021a). *APA resolution on gender identity change efforts*. https://www.apa.org/about/policy/resolution-gender-identity-change-efforts.pdf

American Psychological Association. (2021b). *APA resolution on sexual orientation change efforts*. https://www.apa.org/about/policy/resolution-sexual-orientation-change-efforts.pdf

American Psychological Association. (2021c). *Guidelines for psychological practice with sexual minority persons*. https://www.apa.org/about/policy/psychological-sexual-minority-persons.pdf

Amos, C. (Director). (2020). *Hating Peter Tatchell* [Documentary]. Wildbear Entertainment.

Aoki, S. K., Mearns, J., & Kurpius Robinson, S. E. (2017). Social anxiety and assertiveness: The role of self-beliefs in Asian Americans and European Americans *Journal of Mental Health Counseling, 39*(3), 263–74. doi:10.17744/mehc .39.3.06

Aranda, F., Matthews, A. K., Hughes, T. L., Muramatsu, N., Wilsnack, S. C., Johnson, T. P., & Riley, B. B. (2015). Coming out in color: Racial/ethnic differences in the relationship between level of sexual identity disclosure and depression among lesbians. *Cultural Diversity and Ethnic Minority Psychology, 21*(2), 247–57. doi:10.1037/a0037644

Atari, M., Haidt, J., Graham, J., Koleva, S., Stevens, S. T., & Dehghani, M. (2023). Morality beyond the WEIRD: How the nomological network of morality varies across cultures. *Journal of Personality and Social Psychology, 125*(5), 1157–88. doi:10.1037/pspp0000470

Baker, K. K. (2008). Bionormativity and the construction of parenthood. *Georgia Law Review, 42*, 649–716. https://scholarship.kentlaw.iit.edu/fac_schol/49

Balzarini, R. N., Dharma, C., Kohut, T., Campbell, L., Lehmiller, J. J., Harman, J. J., & Holmes, B. M. (2019). Comparing relationship quality across different types of romantic partners in polyamorous and monogamous relationships. *Archives of Sexual Behavior, 48*(6), 1749–67. doi:10.1007/s10508-019-1416-7

Barrett, C., & Hinchliff, S. (2018). *Addressing the sexual rights of older people: Theory, policy and practice.* Routledge.

Beals, K. P., & Peplau, L. A. (2006). Disclosure patterns within the social networks of gay men and lesbians. *Journal of Homosexuality, 51*, 101–20.

Benau, K. (2022). *Shame, pride, and relational trauma: Concepts and psychotherapy.* Routledge.

Benbow, S. M., & Beeston, D. (2012). Sexuality, aging, and dementia. *International Psychogeriatric, 24*(7), 1026–33. doi:10.1017/S1041610212000257.

Berrick, J. D. (2021). Adoption from care: Policy and practice in the United States. In T. Pösö, M Skivenes & J. Thoburn (Eds.), *Adoption from Care* (pp. 67–84). Policy Press.

Bin Ibrahim, M. A., & Barlas, J. (2021). "Making do with things we cannot change": An interpretive phenomenological analysis of relationship resilience among gay men in Singapore. *Journal of Social and Personal Relationships, 38*(9), 2630–52. doi:10.1177/02654075211017988

Birbili, M. (Ed.). (2014). *Odigos Ekpaideftikou yia to programma spoudon tou nipiagogeiou.* [Teacher's guidelines for the curriculum for the kindergarten school]. Institute of Educational Policy.

Bishop, M. D., Fish, J. N., Hammack, P. L., & Russell, S. T. (2020). Sexual identity development milestones in three generations of sexual minority people: A national probability sample. *Developmental Psychology, 56*(11), 2177–93. doi:10.1037/dev0001105

Blackless, M., Charuvastra, A., Derryck, A., Fausto-Sterling, A., Lauzanne, K., & Lee, E. (2000). How sexually dimorphic are we? Review and synthesis. *American Journal of Human Biology, 12*(2), 151–66. doi:10.1002/(SICI)1520 -6300(200003/04)12:2<151::AID-AJHB1>3.0.CO;2-F

Blume, A. W. (2020). *A new psychology based on community, equality, and care of the Earth: An Indigenous American perspective.* Praeger.

Bos, H. M., Carone, N., Rothblum, E. D., Koh, A., & Gartrell, N. (2021). Long-term effects of homophobic stigmatization during adolescence on problem behavior in emerging adult offspring of lesbian parents. *Journal of Youth and Adolescence, 50*(6), 1114–25. doi:10.1007/s10964-020-01364-1

Bos, H. M., Knox, J. R., van Rijn-van Gelderen, L., & Gartrell, N. K. (2016). Same-sex and different-sex parent households and child health outcomes: Findings from the National Survey of Children's Health. *Journal of Developmental and Behavioral Pediatrics, 37*(3), 179–87. doi:10.1097/DBP.0000000000000288

Boss, P. (2004). Ambiguous loss. In F. Walsh & M. McGoldrick (Eds.), *Living beyond loss: Death in the family* (2nd ed., pp. 237–46). Norton.

Bowleg, L., Huang, J., Brooks, K., Black, A., & Burkholder, G. (2003). Triple jeopardy and beyond: Multiple minority stress and resilience among Black lesbians. *Journal of Lesbian Studies, 7*, 87–107.

Bränström, R., & Pachankis, J. E. (2021). Country-level structural stigma, identity concealment, and day-to-day discrimination as determinants of transgender people's life satisfaction. *Social Psychiatry and Psychiatric Epidemiology, 56*, 1537–45. doi:10.1007/s00127-021-02036-6

Braun-Harvey, D., & Vigorito, M. A. (2016). *Treating out of control sexual behavior: Rethinking sex addiction.* Springer. doi:10.1891/9780826196767

Bridges, J. G., Lefevor, G. T., & Schow, R. L. (2019). Sexual satisfaction and mental health in mixed-orientation relationships: A Mormon sample of sexual minority partners. *Journal of Bisexuality, 19*(4), 515–38. doi:10.1080/15299716.2019.1669252

Bridges, S. K., Selvidge, M. M., & Matthews, C. R. (2003). Lesbian women of color: Therapeutic issues and challenges. *Journal of Multicultural Counseling and Development, 31*, 11–30. doi:10.1002/j.2161-1912.2003.tb00537.x

Brömdal, A., Zavros-Orr, A., lisahunter, Hand, K., & Hart, B. (2021). Towards a whole-school approach for sexuality education in supporting and upholding the rights and health of students with intersex variations. *Sex Education, 21*(5), 568–83. doi:10.1080/14681811.2020.1864726

brown, a. m. (2019). *Pleasure activist: The politics of feeling good.* AK Press.

Brown, B. (2017). *Rising strong.* Random House.

Brown, S. S. (2014). *Native self-actualization: Transformation beyond breed.* BookPatch.

Budiman, A., & Ruiz, N. G. (2021) *Asian Americans are the fastest-growing racial or ethnic group in the U.S.* Pew Research Center. https://pewrsr.ch/3tbjILO

Burleigh, T. J., Rubel, A. N., & Meegan, D. V. (2017). Wanting "the whole loaf": Zero-sum thinking about love is associated with prejudice against consensual non-monogamists. *Psychology & Sexuality, 8*(1–2), 24–40. doi:10.1080/19419899.2016.1269020

Burt, T., Gelnaw, A., & Lesser, L. (2010). Creating welcoming and inclusive environments for lesbian, gay, bisexual and transgender (LGBT) families in early childhood settings. *Young Children, 65*(1), 97–102.

Butcher, R. L., Kinney, L. M., Blasdel, G. P., Elwyn, G., Myers, J. B., Boh, B., Luck, K. M., & Moses, R. A. (2023). Decision making in metoidioplasty and phalloplasty gender-affirming surgery: A mixed methods study. *Journal of Sexual Medicine, 20*(7), 1032–43. doi:10.1093/jsxmed/qdad063

Byne, B., Bradley, S. J., Coleman, E., Eyler, A. E., Green, R., Menvielle, E. J., Meyer-Bahlburg, H. F., Pleak, R. R., Tompkins, D. A., & American Psychiatric Association Task Force on Treatment of Gender Identity Disorder. (2012). Report of the American Psychiatric Association Task Force on Treatment of Gender Identity Disorder. *Archives of Sexual Behavior, 41*(4), 759–96. doi:10.1007/s10508-012 -9975-x

Canitz, S. N., & Haberstroh, S. (2022). Navigating loss and grief and constructing new meaning: Therapeutic considerations for caregivers of transgender youth. *Journal of Child and Adolescent Counseling, 8*(3), 168–80. doi:10.1080/ 23727810.2022.2133511

Carswell, K. L., & Impett, E. A. (2021). What fuels passion? An integrative review of competing theories of romantic passion. *Social and Personality Psychology Compass, 15*(8), Article e12629. doi:10.1111/spc3.12629

Cass, V. C. (1979). Homosexual identity formation: A theoretical model. *Journal of Homosexuality, 4*, 219–35. doi:10.1300/J082v04n03_01

Cassar, J., & Grima Sultana, M. (2021). No way am I throwing you out! Adjustments in space and time for parents of gay sons. *Journal of Family Studies, 27*(1), 131–45. doi:10.1080/13229400.2018.1523020

Chang, J., & Chakrabarti, M. (2023, March 09). Journalist Hannah Barnes on the inside story of the collapse of Tavistock's gender identity clinic. WBUR. https://www.wbur.org/onpoint/2023/03/09/the-inside-story-of-the-collapse-of -the-tavistock-gender-service-for-children

Chávez, A. F., & Guido-DiBrito, F. (1999). Racial and ethnic identity and development. *New Direction for Adult and Continuing Education, 84*, 39–47.

Chiongbian, S. F., Ilac, E. J. D., Emata, R. R., & Magno, A. R. C. L. (2023). Finding God alongside trials: Catholicism and resilience among queer Filipino emerging adults. *Psychology of Sexual Orientation and Gender Diversity, 10*(2), 246–56. doi:10.1037/sgd0000508

Chira, S. (2017, June 14). The universal phenomenon of men interrupting women. *New York Times.* https://www.nytimes.com/2017/06/14/business/women-sexism -work-huffington-kamala-harris.html

Coleman, P. T., Fisher, J., Fry, D. P., Liebovitch, L. S., Chen-Carrel, A., & Souillac, G. (2021). How to live in peace? Mapping the science of sustaining peace: A progress report. *American Psychologist, 76*(7), 1113–27. doi:10.1037/amp0000745

Conley, T. D., Ziegler, A., Moors, A. C., Matsick, J. L., & Valentine, B. (2013). A critical examination of popular assumptions about the benefits and outcomes of monogamous relationships. *Personality and Social Psychology Review, 17*(2), 124–41. doi:10.1177/1088868312467087

Cortina, L., Kabat-Farr, D., Leskinen, E., Huerta, M., & Magley, V. (2013). Selective incivility as modern discrimination in organizations. *Journal of Management, 39*(6), 1579–1605. doi:10.1177/0149206311418835

Craig-Oldsen, H., Craig, J. A., & Morton, T. (2006). Issues of shared parenting of LGBTQ children and youth in foster care: Preparing foster parents for new roles. *Child Welfare, 85*(2), 267–80.

Creek, S. J. (2013). "Not getting any because of Jesus": The centrality of desire management to the identity work of gay, celibate Christians. *Symbolic Interaction, 36*(2), 119–36. doi:10.1002/SYMB.58

Dahlheimer, D., & Feigal, J. (1994). Community as family: The multiple-family contexts of gay and lesbian clients. In C. H. Huber (Ed.), *Transitioning from individual to family counseling* (pp. 63–74). American Counseling Association.

Darden, M. C., Ehman, A. C., Lair, E. C., & Gross, A. M. (2019). Sexual compliance: Examining the relationships among sexual want, sexual consent, and sexual assertiveness. *Sexuality & Culture, 23,* 220–35. doi:10.1007/s12119-018-9551-1

De Graeve, K. (2014). Queering the family? A multi-layered analysis of relations of inequality in transnational adoption. *Culture, Health & Sexuality, 16*(6), 683–96. doi:10.1080/13691058.2014.901562

Dehlin, A. J., Galliher, R. V., Legerski, E., Harker, A., & Dehlin, J. P. (2019). Same- and other-sex aversion and attraction as important correlates of quality and outcomes of Mormon mixed-orientation marriages. *Journal of GLBT Family Studies, 15*(1), 22–41. doi:10.1080/1550428X.2017.141672

Dehlin, J. P., Galliher, R. V., Bradshaw, W. S., & Crowell, S. A. (2014). Psychosocial correlates of religious approaches to same-sex attraction: A Mormon perspective. *Journal of Gay & Lesbian Mental Health, 18*(3), 284–311. doi:10.1080/ 19359705.2014.912970

DeLamater, J. (2012). Sexual expression in later life: Review and synthesis. *Journal of Sex Research, 49*(2–3), 125–41. doi:10.1080/00224499.2011.603168

Dente, C. L. (Ed.). (2018). *Social work practice with LGBTQIA populations: An interactional perspective.* Routledge.

DePalma, R. (2013). Choosing to lose our gender expertise: Queering sex/gender in school settings. *Sex Education, 13*(1), 1–15. doi:10.1080/14681811.2011 .634145

DePaulo, B. (2006). *Singled out: How singles are stereotyped, stigmatized, and ignored, and still live happily ever after.* St. Martin's Griffin.

Devor, A. H. (2004). Witnessing and mirroring: A fourteen stage model of transsexual identity formation. *Journal of Gay & Lesbian Psychotherapy, 8*(1–2), 41–67.

Devor, A. H., & Dominic, K. (2015). Trans* sexualities. In J. DeLamater & R. F. Plante (Eds.), *Handbook of the sociology of sexualities* (pp. 181–99). Springer. doi:10.1007/978-3-319-17341-2_11

de Vries, B., & Herdt, G. (2012). Aging in the gay community. In T. M. Witten & A. E. Eyler (Eds.), *Gay, lesbian, bisexual, and transgender aging: Challenges in research, practice, and policy* (pp. 84–129). Johns Hopkins University Press.

Diamond, G. M., Boruchovitz-Zamir, R., Gat, I., & Nir-Gottlieb, O. (2019). Relationship-focused therapy for sexual and gender minority individuals and their parents. In J. E. Pachankis & S. A. Safren (Eds.), *Handbook of evidence-based mental health practice with sexual and gender minorities* (pp. 430–56). Oxford University Press. doi:10.1093/med-psych/9780190669300.003.0019

Diamond, L. M. (2020). Gender fluidity and nonbinary gender identities among children and adolescents. *Child Development Perspectives, 14*(2), 110–15. doi:10 .1111/cdep.12366

Dickens, B. M. (2018). Management of intersex newborns: Legal and ethical developments. *International Journal of Gynecology & Obstetrics, 143*(2), 255–59. doi:10.1002/ijgo.12573

Dota, F. (2017). *Javna i politička povijest muške homoseksualnosti u socijalističkoj Hrvatskoj (1945.–1989.): doktorski rad* [Public and political history of male homosexuality in socialist Croatia (1945–1989), Unpublished doctoral dissertation]. University of Zagreb. http://darhiv.ffzg.unizg.hr/id/eprint/9256

Drazdowski, T. K., Perrin, P. B., Trujillo, M., Sutter, M., Benotsch, E. G., & Snipes, D. J. (2018). Structural equation modeling of the effects of racism, LGBTQIA discrimination, and internalized oppression on illicit drug use in LGBTQIA people of color. *Drug and Alcohol Dependence, 159*, 255–62. doi:10.1016/j.drugalcdep.2015.12.029

Drescher, J. (2014). Are the kids all right? Avuncular reflections on the Gayby Boom. *Journal of Gay & Lesbian Mental Health, 18*(2), 222–29. doi:10.1080/19359705.2014.883959

Dumitru, O. (2022). *How many Americans have cheated on their partners in monogamous relationships?* https://today.yougov.com/topics/society/articles-reports/2022/10/04/how-many-americans-have-cheated-their-partner-poll

Durwood, L., Kuvalanka, K. A., Kahn-Samuelson, S., Jordan, A. E., Rubin, J. D., Schnelzer, P., Devor, A. H., & Olson, K. R. (2022). Retransitioning: The experiences of youth who socially transition genders more than once. *International Journal of Transgender Health, 23*(4), 409–27. doi:10.1080/26895269.2022.2085224

Eckert, A., & McLamore, Q. (2023, May 14). *Detransition, retransition, and what everyone gets wrong.* Science-Based Medicine. https://sciencebasedmedicine.org/detransition-retransition-and-what-everyone-gets-wrong/

Edwards, W. M., & Coleman, E. (2004). Defining sexual health: A descriptive overview. *Archives of Sexual Behavior, 33*(3), 189–95. doi:10.1023/B:ASEB.0000026619.95734.d5

Elm, J. H. L., Lewis, J. P., Walters, K. L., & Self, J. M. (2016). "I'm in this world for a reason": Resilience and recovery among American Indian and Alaska Native two-spirit women. *Journal of Lesbian Studies, 20*(3–4), 352–71. doi:10.1080/10894160.2016.1152813

European Union Agency for Fundamental Rights. (2014). *EU LGBT survey main results.* https://fra.europa.eu/sites/default/files/fra-eu-lgbt-survey-main-results_tk3113640enc_1.pdf

Family Acceptance Project. (n.d.) *Family Acceptance Project.* https://familyproject.sfsu.edu/

Family Equality Council. (2017). *LGBTQ family fact sheet.* https://www2.census.gov/cac/nac/meetings/2017-11/LGBTQ-families-factsheet.pdf

Family Equality Council. (2019). *LGBTQ Family Building Survey.* https://www.familyequality.org/fbs

Fantus, S., & Newman, P. A. (2021). Promoting a positive school climate for sexual and gender minority youth through a systems approach: A theory-informed qualitative study. *American Journal of Orthopsychiatry, 91*(1), 9–19. doi:10.1037/ort0000513

Fantus, S., & Newman, P. A. (2022). The procreative identities of men in same-sex relationships choosing surrogacy: A new theoretical understanding. *Journal of Family Theory & Review, 14*(2), 254–74. doi:10.1111/jftr.12456

Farr, R. H. (2017). Does parental sexual orientation matter? A longitudinal follow-up of adoptive families with school-age children. *Developmental Psychology, 53*(2), 252–64. doi:10.1037/dev0000228

Farr, R. H., & Goldberg, A. E. (2015). Contact between birth and adoptive families during the first year post-placement: Perspectives of lesbian, gay, and heterosexual parents. *Adoption Quarterly, 18*, 11–24. doi:10.1080/10926755.2014.895466

Fattoracci, E. S. M., Revels-Macalinao, M., & Huynh, Q.-L. (2020). Greater than the sum of racism and heterosexism: Intersectional microaggressions toward racial/ethnic and sexual minority group members. *Cultural Diversity and Ethnic Minority Psychology, 27*(2), 176–88. doi:10.1037/cdp0000329

Fedewa, A. L., & Clark, T. P. (2009). Parent practices and home-school partnerships: A differential effect for children with same-sex coupled parents? *Journal of GLBT Family Studies, 5*(4), 312–39. doi:10.1080/15504280903263736

Felipe, L. C., Garrett-Walker, J. J., & Montagno, M. (2022). Monoracial and multiracial LGBTQ+ people: Comparing internalized heterosexism, perceptions of racism, and connection to LGBTQ+ communities. *Psychology of Sexual Orientation and Gender Diversity, 9*(1), 1–11. doi:10.1037/sgd0000440

Fern, J. (2020). *Polycule: Attachment, trauma and consensual nonmonogamy.* Thornapple.

Fleishman, J. M., Crane, B., & Barthalow-Koch, P. (2020). Correlates and predictors of sexual satisfaction for older adults in same-sex relationships. *Journal of Homosexuality, 67*, 1974–98. doi:10.1080/00918369.2019.1618647

Flicker, S. M., & Sancier-Barbosa, F. (2022). Personality predictors of prejudicial attitudes, willingness to engage, and actual engagement in consensual nonmonogamy. *Archives of Sexual Behavior, 51*(8), 3947–61. doi:10.1007/s10508-022-02393-6

Frable, D. E., Wortman, C., & Joseph, J. (1997). Predicting self-esteem, well-being, and distress in a cohort of gay men: The importance of cultural stigma, personal visibility, community networks, and positive identity. *Journal of Personality, 65*(3), 599–624. doi:10.1111/j.1467-6494.1997.tb00328.x

Frank, S. E. (2018). Intersex and intimacy: Presenting concerns about dating and intimate relationships. *Sexuality & Culture: An Interdisciplinary Quarterly, 22*(1), 127–47. doi:10.1007/s12119-017-9456-4

Frankl, V. (1946). *Man's search for meaning.* Beacon Press.

Fredriksen-Goldsen, K. I., & Muraco, A. (2010). Aging and sexual orientation: A 25-year review of the literature. *Research on Aging, 32*(3), 372–413. doi:10.1177/0164027509360355

Freeman-Coppadge, D. J. (2018). *Harmony, dissonance, or harm? The psychological and spiritual promises and perils of gay Christian celibacy* [Unpublished doctoral dissertation]. University of Massachusetts Boston. ProQuest Dissertations and Theses Global Publication No. 10616328.

Freeman-Coppadge, D. J., & Horne, S. G. (2019). "What happens if the cross falls and crushes me?": Psychological and spiritual promises and perils of lesbian and gay Christian celibacy. *Psychology of Sexual Orientation and Gender Diversity, 6*(4), 486–97. doi:10.1037/sgd0000341

Fukuyama, M. A., & Ferguson, A. D. (2000). Lesbian, gay and bisexual people of color: Understanding cultural complexity and managing multiple oppressions. In R. M. Perez, K. A. DeBord & K. J. Bieschke (Eds.), *Handbook of counseling and psychotherapy with lesbians, gay, and bisexual clients.* (pp. 81–105). American Psychological Association.

Gaines, S. (1997). *Culture, ethnicity, and personal relationship process.* Routledge.

Galupo, M. P., Taylor, S. M., & Cole, D. (2019). "I am double the bi": Positive aspects of being both bisexual and biracial. *Journal of Bisexuality, 19*(2), 1–17. doi:10.1080/15299716.2019.1619066

Gamarel, K. E., Reisner, S. L., Laurenceau, J. P., Nemoto, T., & Operario, D. (2014). Gender minority stress, mental health, and relationship quality: A dyadic investigation of transgender women and their cisgender male partners. *Journal of Family Psychology, 28*(4), 437–47. doi:10.1037/a0037171

Gartrell, N., Rodas, C., Deck, A., Peyser, H., & Banks, A. (2005). The National Lesbian Family Study, 4. Interviews with the 10-year-old children. *American Journal of Orthopsychiatry, 75*(4), 518–24. doi:10.1037/0002-9432.75.4.518

Gash, A., & Raiskin, J. (2018). Parenting without protection: How legal status ambiguity affects lesbian and gay parenthood. *Law & Social Inquiry, 43*, 82–118. doi:10.1111/lsi.12233

Gato, J., Leal, D., Coimbra, S., & Tasker, F. (2020). Anticipating parenthood among lesbian, gay, bisexual, and heterosexual young adults without children in Portugal: Predictors and profiles. *Frontiers in Psychology, 11*, 1058. doi:10.3389/fpsyg.2020.01058

Gillborn, D., Rollock, N., Vincent, C., & Ball, S. J. (2012). You got a pass, so what more do you want? Race, class and gender intersections in the educational experiences of the Black middle class. *Race Ethnicity and Education, 15*(1), 121–39. doi:10.1080/13613324.2012.638869

Giwa, S. (2022). *Racism and gay men of color: Living and coping with discrimination.* Rowman & Littlefield.

Glassgold, J. M., & Ryan, C. (2022). The role of families in efforts to change, support, and affirm sexual orientation, gender identity, and expression in children and youth. In D. C. Haldeman (Ed.), *The case against conversion "therapy": Evidence, ethics, and alternatives* (pp. 89–107). APA. doi:10.1037/0000266-005

Goldberg, A. E. (2022). *LGBTQ family building: A guide for prospective parents.* APA. doi:10.1037/0000291-000

Goldberg, A. E., Gartrell, N. K., & Gates, G. (2014). *Research report on LGB-parent families.* Williams Institute. http://williamsinstitute.law.ucla.edu/wp-content/uploads/lgb-parent-families-july-2014.pdf

Goldberg, A. E., & Smith, J. Z. (2014). Preschool selection considerations and experiences of school mistreatment among lesbian, gay, and heterosexual adoptive parents. *Early Childhood Research Quarterly, 29*, 64–75. doi:10.1016/j.ecresq.2013.09.006

Goldberg, S. K., Rothblum, E. D., Russell, S.T., & Meyer, I. H. (2020). Exploring the Q in LGBTQ: Demographic characteristic and sexuality of queer people in a U.S. representative sample of sexual minorities. *Psychology of Sexual Orientation and Gender Diversity, 7*(1), 101–12. doi:10.1037/sgd0000359

Goldfarb, E. S., & Lieberman, L. D. (2021). Three decades of research: The case for comprehensive sex education. *Journal of Adolescent Health, 68*(1), 13–27. doi:10.1016/j.jadohealth.2020.07.036

Gonzalez, A. (2019). Experiences of LGBTQ male students of color in a predominantly White environment. *Ursidae: The Undergraduate Research Journal at the University of Northern Colorado, 6*(2), Article 8. https://digscholarship.unco.edu/urj/vol6/iss2/8/

Gonzalez, K. A., Rostosky, S. S., Odom, R. D., & Riggle, E. D. B. (2013). The positive aspects of being the parent of an LGBTQ child. *Family Process, 52*, 325–37. doi:10.1111/famp.12009

Goodrich, K. M., & Brammer, M. K. (2021). Cass's homosexual identity formation: A critical analysis. *Journal of Multicultural Counseling & Development, 49*(4), 239–53.

Greene, B. (1994). Lesbian women of color: Triple jeopardy. In L. Comas-Diaz & B. Green (Eds.), *Women of color: Integrating ethnic and gender identities in psychotherapy* (pp. 389–427). Guilford Press.

Griffin, B. J., Worthington, E. L., Jr., Leach, J. D., Hook, J. N., Grubbs, J., Exline, J. J., & Davis, D. E. (2016). Sexual congruence moderates the associations of hypersexual behavior with spiritual struggle and sexual self-concept. *Sexual Addiction & Compulsivity, 23*(2–3), 279–95. doi:10.1080/10720162.2016.1150924

Grigoropoulos, I. [Iraklis, G.]. (2021). Subtle forms of prejudice in Greek daycare centres: Early childhood educators' attitudes towards same-sex marriage and children's adjustment in same-sex families. *European Journal of Developmental Psychology, 18*(5), 711–30. doi:10.1080/17405629.2020.1835636

Grigoropoulos, I. (2022). Greek high school teachers' homonegative attitudes towards same-sex parent families. *Sexuality & Culture, 26*, 1132–47. doi:10.1007/s12119-021-09935-5

Grigoropoulos, I. (2023a). Gay fatherhood experiences and challenges through the lens of minority stress theory. *Journal of Homosexuality, 70*(9), 1867–89. doi:10.1080/00918369.2022.2043131

Grigoropoulos, I. [Iraklis, G.]. (2023b). Lesbian motherhood desires and challenges due to minority stress. *Current Psychology, 42*, 11133–11142. doi:10.1007/s12144-021-02376-1

Gunn, A. C. (2011). "Even if you say it three ways, it still doesn't mean it's true": The pervasiveness of heteronormativity in early childhood education. *Journal of Early Childhood Research, 9*(3), 280–90. doi:10.1177/1476718X113985

Guyon, R., Fernet, M., Couture, S., Tardif, M., Cousineau, M. M., & Godbout, N. (2023). "Finding my worth as a sexual being": A qualitative gender analysis of sexual self-concept and coping in survivors of childhood sexual abuse. *Archives of Sexual Behavior, 53*(1), 341–57. doi:10.1007/s10508-023-02693-5

Haas, S. M., & Lannutti, P. J. (2022). Relationship maintenance behaviors, resilience, and relational quality in romantic relationships of LGBTQ+ people. *Couple and Family Psychology: Research and Practice, 11*(2), 117–31. doi:10.1037/cfp0000186

Hajjar, R. R., & Kamel, H. K. (2004). Sexuality in the nursing home, part 1: Attitudes and barriers to sexual expression. *Journal of American Medical Directors Association* (suppl.), s43–s47. doi:10.1097/01.JAM.0000061465.00838.57

Haldeman, D. C. (2006). Queer eye on the straight guy: A case of gay male heterophobia. In M. Englar-Carlson & M. A. Stevens (Eds.), *In the room with men: A casebook of therapeutic change* (pp. 301–17). American Psychological Association. doi:10.1037/11411-016

Harvey, P., Jones, E., & Copulsky, D. (2023). The relational nature of gender, the pervasiveness of heteronormative sexual scripts, and the impact on sexual pleasure. *Archives of Sexual Behavior, 52*(3), 1195–12. doi:10.1007/s10508-023 -02558-x

Hasannia, S. (2017). The relationship between assertiveness and happiness with self-efficacy: Structural equation modeling. *Journal of Psychology, 21*(1), 85–100.

Haupert, M. L., Gesselman, A. N., Moors, A. C., Fisher, H. E., & Garcia, J. R. (2017). Prevalence of experiences with consensual nonmonogamous relationships: Findings from two national samples of single Americans. *Journal of Sex & Marital Therapy, 43*(5), 424–40. doi:10.1080/0092623x.2016.1178675

Haupert, M. L., Moors, A. C., Gesselman, A. N., & Garcia, J. R. (2017). Estimates and correlates of engagement in consensually non-monogamous relationships. *Current Sexual Health Report, 9*, 155–65. doi:10.1007/s11930-017-0121-6

Hegde, A. V., Averett, P., Parker White, C., & Deese, S. (2013). Examining preschool teachers' attitudes, comfort, action orientation and preparation to work with children reared by gay and lesbian parents. *Early Child Development and Care, 184*(7), 963–76. doi:10.1080/03004430.2013.845563

Herdt, G., & Koff, B. (2000). *Something to tell you: The road families travel when a child is gay.* Columbia University Press.

Hobaica, S., & Kwon, P. (2017) "This is how you hetero": Sexual minorities in heteronormative sex education. *American Journal of Sexuality Education, 12*(4), 423–50. doi:10.1080/15546128.2017.1399491

Hopwood, M., Cama, E., de Wit, J., & Treloar, C. (2020). Stigma, anxiety, and depression among gay and bisexual men in mixed-orientation marriages. *Qualitative Health Research, 30*(4), 622–33. doi:10.1177/1049732319862536

Hostetler, A. J. (2009). Single by choice? Assessing and understanding voluntary singlehood among mature gay men. *Journal of Homosexuality, 56*, 499–531. doi:10.1080/00918360902821486

Hotta, M. (2013). Measuring the effectiveness of assertiveness training: An analysis of issues and a proposed model. *Japanese Journal of Educational Psychology, 61*(4), 412–24. doi:10.5926/jjep.61.412

Hsieh, N., & Ruther, P. (2016). Sexual minority health and health risk factors: Intersection effects of gender, race, and sexual identity. *American Journal of Preventive Medicine, 50*(6), 746–55. doi:10.1016/j.amepre.2015.11.016

Human Rights Watch. (2017). *"I want to be like nature made me": Medically unnecessary surgeries on intersex children in the US.* https://www.hrw.org/report/ 2017/07/25/i-want-be-nature-made-me/medically-unnecessary-surgeries-intersex -children-us

Hung, F. N., & Chan, R. C. H. (2022). Differentiation of self, proximal minority stress, and life satisfaction among sexual minorities: Intrapersonal and interpersonal pathways to life satisfaction. *American Journal of Orthopsychiatry, 92*(5), 552–63. doi:10.1037/ort0000638

Hunt, E., & Huang, C. Y. (2020). Mental health of Asian American and Pacific Islander sexual and gender minorities. In E. Rothblum (Ed.), *The Oxford handbook of sexual and gender minority mental health* (pp. 199–207). Oxford University Press. doi:10.1093/oxfordhb/9780190067991.013.18

Iliopoulou, C., Nikolakakis, N., Diakoumakou, F., & Grammenidis, K. (2020). *First Greek National School Climate Survey—results report: The experiences of LGBTQ youth in Greek secondary education.* Colour Youth.

Institute of Medicine, Committee on Lesbian, Gay, Bisexual, and Transgender Health Issues and Research Gaps and Opportunities. (2011). *The health of lesbian, gay, bisexual, and transgender people: Building a foundation for better understanding.* National Academies Press. https://www.ncbi.nlm.nih.gov/books/NBK64806/

Iuso, S., Petito, A., Ventriglio, A., Severo, M., Bellomo, A., & Limone, P. (2022). The impact of psycho-education on school-children's homophobic attitudes. *International Review of Psychiatry, 34*(3–4), 266–73. doi:10.1080/09540261.2022.2034603

Jaffe, A. E., Duckworth, J., Blayney, J. A., Lewis, M. A., & Kaysen, D. (2021). A prospective study of predictors and consequences of hooking up for sexual minority women. *Archives of Sexual Behavior, 50*(4), 1599–1612. doi:10.1007/s10508-020-01896-4

Jeynes, W. H. (2005). Effects of parental involvement and family structure on the academic achievement of adolescents. *Marriage & Family Review, 37*(3), 99–116. doi:10.1300/j002v37n03_06

Jhang, J. (2018). Scaffolding in family relationships: A grounded theory of coming out to family. *Family Relations, 67,* 161–75. doi:10.1111/fare.12302

Jordan, J. V. (2000). The role of mutual empathy in relational/cultural therapy. *Journal of Clinical Psychology, 56*(8), 1005–16. doi:10.1002/1097-4679(200008)56:8<1005::AID-JCLP2>3.0.CO;2-L

Kammrath, L. K., McCarthy, M. H., Cortes, K., & Friesen, C. (2015). Picking one's battles: How assertiveness and unassertiveness abilities are associated with extraversion and agreeableness. *Social Psychological and Personality Science, 6*(6), 622–29. doi:10.1177/1948550615572635

Kampler, B. (2022). Open to more: Queer hookups, temporalities, and life courses. *Sociological Forum, 37*(4), 1063–82. doi:10.1111/socf.12857

Kahneman, D. (2003). Experiences of collaborative research. *American Psychologist, 58*(9), 723–30. doi.org/10.1037/0003-066X.58.9.7 23

Kaniasty, K., & Norris, F. H. (2000). Help-seeking comfort and receiving social support: The role of ethnicity and context of need. *American Journal of Community Psychology, 28,* 545–81.

Kantsa, V. (2014). The price of marriage: Same-sex sexualities and citizenship in Greece. *Sexualities, 17*(7), 818–36. doi:10.1177/13634 60714 544807

Kantsa, V., & Chalkidou, A. (2014). Same-sex mothers: A contradiction in terms? Sexuality and reproduction from an anthropological perspective. In M. Kaifa-Gbanti, E. Kounougeri-Manoledaki & E. Symeonidou-Kastanidou (Eds.), *Assisted reproduction and alternative family forms* (pp. 180–205). Sakkoulas.

Karamouzis, P. (2015). *H koinoniología tis thriskeias metaxi ekpaideysis kai koinonias.* Kallipos, Open Academic Editions. http://hdl.handle.net/11419/3723

Kattari, S. K., Walls, N. E., Atteberry-Ash, B., Klemmer, C., Rusow, J. A., & Kattari, L. (2019). Missing from the conversation: Sexual risk factors across young people by gender identity and sexual orientation. *International Journal of Sexual Health, 31*(4), 394–406. doi:10.1080/19317611.2019.1667938

Katz-Wise, S. L., Rosario, M., Calzo, J. P., Scherer, E. A., Sarda, V., & Austin, S. B. (2017). Endorsement and timing of sexual orientation developmental milestones among sexual minority young adults in the Growing Up Today Study. *Journal of Sex Research, 54*(2), 172–85. doi:10.1080/00224499.2016.1170757

Kavanaugh, S. A., Taylor, A. B., Stuhlsatz, G. L., Neppl, T. K., & Lohman, B. J. (2020). Family and community support among sexual minorities of color: The role of sexual minority identity prominence and outness on psychological well-being. *Journal of GLBT Family Studies, 16*, 1–17. doi:10.1080/1550428X. 2019 .1593279

Kazyak, E., & Park, N. K. (2020). Doing family: The reproduction of heterosexuality in accounts of parenthood. *Journal of Sociology, 56*(4), 646–63. doi:10.1177/ 1440783319888288

King, M. L. (1957). *Loving your enemies*. Martin Luther King, Jr. Research and Education Institute. https://kinginstitute.stanford.edu/king-papers/documents/ loving-your-enemies-sermon-delivered-dexter-avenue-baptist-church

Klein, J. (2022, March 4). Does "solo polyamory" mean having it all? BBC. https:// www.bbc.com/worklife/article/20220301-does-solo-polyamory-mean-having-it -all

Kornfield, J. (2018). *No time like the present: Finding freedom, love, and joy right where you are*. Atria Books.

Kübler-Ross, E. (1970). *On death and dying*. Collier Books/Macmillan.

Lamble, S. (2009). Unknowable bodies, unthinkable sexualities: Lesbian and transgender legal invisibility in the Toronto women's bathhouse raid. *Social & Legal Studies, 18*(1), 111–30. doi:10.1177/0964663908100336

Lamont, E., Roach, T., & Kahn, S. (2018). Navigating campus hookup culture: LGBTQ students and college hookups. *Sociological Forum, 33*(4), 1000–1022. doi:10.1111/socf.12458

Lavender-Stott, E. S. (2023). Queering singlehood: Examining the intersection of sexuality and relationship status from a queer lens. *Journal of Family Theory & Review, 15*(3), 428–43. doi:10.1111/jftr.12521

Lavender-Stott, E. S., & Allen, K. R. (2023). Not alone: Family experiences across the life course of single baby boom sexual minority women. *Family Relations, 72*(1), 140–58. doi:10.1002/fare.12721

Lavender-Stott, E. S., Benjamin, K. B., Brown, S. L., & Manning, W. D. (2023). Kaleidoscopic perspectives on theorizing singlehood. *Journal of Family Theory and Review, 15*(3), 379–88. doi:10.1111/jftr.12532

Le, T. P., Teran, M., & Wang, M. Q. (2023). Latinx sexual minority men, psychological well-being, racial sociopolitical involvement, and discomfort in LGBT community. *Journal of Latinx Psychology, 12*(1), 63–78. doi:10.1037/ lat0000242

Lefevor, G. T. (2023). Sexuality, religiousness, and mental health among sexual minority Latter-day Saints in other-gender relationships. *Journal of Sex & Marital Therapy, 49*(8), 1013–28. doi:10.1080/0092623X.2023.2237957

Lefevor, G. T., Beckstead, A. L., Schow, R. L., Raynes, M., Mansfield, T. R., & Rosik, C. H. (2019). Satisfaction and health within four sexual identity relationship options. *Journal of Sex & Marital Therapy, 45*(5), 355–69. doi:10.1080/ 0092623X.2018.1531333

Lefevor, G. T., Paiz, J. Y., Stone, W.-M., Huynh, K. D., Virk, H. E., Sorrell, S. A., & Gage, S. E. (2020). Homonegativity and the Black church: Is congregational variation the missing link? *Counseling Psychologist, 48*(6), 826–51. doi:10.1177/ 0011000020918558

Lefevor, G. T., Schow, R. L., Beckstead, A. L., Raynes, M., Young, N. T., & Rosik, C. H. (2021). Domains related to four single/relationship options among sexual minorities raised conservatively religious. *Spirituality in Clinical Practice, 8*(2), 112–31. doi:10.1037/scp0000237

Lehmiller, J. J., Ley, D., & Savage, D. (2018). The psychology of gay men's cuckolding fantasies. *Archives of Sexual Behavior, 47*(4), 999–1013. doi:10.1007/s10508 -017-1096-0

Levitt, H. M., Schuyler, S. W., Chickerella. R., Elber, A., White, L., Troeger, R. L., Karter, J. M., Preston. J. M., & Collins, K. M. (2020). How discrimination in adoptive, foster, and medical systems harms LGBTQ+ families: Research on the experiences of prospective parents. *Journal of Gay & Lesbian Social Services, 32*(3), 261–82. doi:10.1080/10538720.2020.1728461

Li, F., Liao, J., Sun, X., Yang, T., Li, T., Wang, Y., & Mei, Y. (2021). Does self-concept clarity relate to depressive symptoms in Chinese gay men? The mediating effects of sexual orientation concealment and gay community connectedness. *Sexuality Research & Social Policy, 19*, 1506–18. doi:10.1007/s13178-021-00666-8

Li, L., Zhu, X., Yang, C., Hu, T., Zhao, X., Li, C., Wu, M., Qiao, G., & Yang, F. (2021). Social support and coping style of Tongqi in China: A cross-sectional study. *Archives of Psychiatric Nursing, 35*(3), 317–22. doi:10.1016/j.apnu.2020 .12.002

Li, X., Zhang, B., Li, Y., Antonio, A. L., Chen, Y., & Williams, A. B. (2016). Mental health and suicidal ideation among Chinese women who have sex with men who have sex with men (MSM). *Women & Health, 56*(8), 940–56. doi:10.1080/ 03630242.2016.1145171

Linden, P. (2018). Body awareness and self-protection training for male sexual abuse survivors. In R. B. Gartner (Ed.). *Healing sexually betrayed men and boys* (pp. 179–200). Routledge.

Lindley, L., & Budge, S. L. (2022). Development and validation of the Trans and Nonbinary Coping Measure (TNCM): A measure of trans and nonbinary specific ways of coping with gender-related stress. *Psychology of Sexual Orientation and Gender Diversity.* Advance online publication. doi:10.1037/sgd0000618

Liu, F., Ren, Z. & Chong, E. S. K. (2023). On the link between reciprocal/authoritarian filial piety and internalized homonegativity: Perceived pressure to get married in a heterosexual marriage as a mediator. *Archives of Sexual Behavior, 52*(3), 957–70. doi:10.1007/s10508-022-02528-9

Liu, G., & An, R. (2021). Applying a yin-yang perspective to the theory of paradox: A review of Chinese management. *Psychology Research and Behavior Management, 14*, 1591–1601. doi:10.2147/PRBM.S330489

Loiacano, D. K. (1989). Gay identity issues among Black Americans: Racism, homophobia, and the need for validation. *Journal of Counseling & Development, 68*, 21–25.

Lopes, A., Skoda, K., & Pedersen, C. L. (2019). Smartphone battery levels and sexual decision-making among men who have sex with men. *Sexuality & Culture, 23*(4), 1301–14. doi:10.1007/s12119-019-09620-8

Lorimer, K., DeAmicis, L., Dalrymple, J., Frankis, J., Jackson, L., Lorgelly, P., McMillan, L., & Ross, J. (2019). A rapid review of sexual wellbeing definitions and measures: Should we now include sexual wellbeing freedom? *Journal of Sex Research, 56*(7), 843–53. doi:10.1080/00224499.2019.1635565

Louie, K. (2014). *Chinese masculinities in a globalizing world*. Routledge.

Louis, C., & Browne, T. (2023, April 22). *Black lives, in mind: Braiding the threads—young, black, and queer* [Webinar]. Connecticut Society for Psychoanalytic Psychology.

Love, P., & Robinson, J. (1995). *Hot monogamy: Essential steps to more passionate, intimate lovemaking*. Plume.

Mallory, A. B., Russell, S. T., & Meyer, I. H. (2023). Intersections of race, gender, and sexual identity attributions toward discrimination and mental health across three cohorts of lesbian, gay, and bisexual adults. *Psychology of Sexual Orientation and Gender Diversity*. Advance online publication. doi:10.1037/sgd0000675

Marcantonio, T. L., O'Neil, A. M., & Jozkowski, K. N. (2022). Sexual consent cues among sexual minority men in the United States. *Psychology & Sexuality, 13*(4), 863–79. doi:10.1080/19419899.2021.1936141

Martin, K. (2023). *Mastering the treatment of complex trauma: Effectively treating "parts"* [Webinar]. http://kmccs.com/webinar.maml?page=webinar_winter_2023

Martino, W. J., & Cumming-Potvin, W. (2015). Teaching about "princess boys" or not: The case of one male elementary school teacher and the polemics of gender expression and embodiment. *Men and Masculinities, 18*(1), 79–99. doi:10.1177/1097184X14551278

Martos, A., Nezhad, S., & Meyer, I. H. (2015). Variations in sexual identity milestones among lesbians, gay men and bisexuals. *Sexuality Research & Social Policy, 12*(1), 24–33. doi:10.1007/s13178-014-0167-4

Maslowe, K. E., & Yarhouse, M. A. (2015). Christian parental reactions when a LGB child comes out. *American Journal of Family Therapy, 43*(4), 352–63. doi:10.1080/01926187.2015.105

Mata, D., Korpak, A. K., Sorensen, B. L., Dodge, B., Mustanski, B., & Feinstein, B. A. (2022). A mixed methods study of sexuality education experiences and preferences among bisexual, pansexual, and queer (bi+) male youth. *Sexuality Research & Social Policy, 19*(2), 806–21. doi:10.1007/s13178-021-00593-8

Matsuno, E., Bricker, N. L., Savarese, E., Mohr, R., Jr., & Balsam, K. F. (2022). "The default is just going to be getting misgendered": Minority stress experiences among nonbinary adults. *Psychology of Sexual Orientation and Gender Diversity*. Advance online publication. doi:10.1037/sgd0000607

Mazrekaj, D., De Witte, K., & Cabus, S. (2020). School outcomes of children raised by same-sex parents: Evidence from administrative panel data. *American Sociological Review, 85*(5), 830–56. doi:10.1177/0003122420957249

McCaulley, G., & Coleman, M. (2022). Gay fathers' coparenting experiences with their ex-wives. *LGBTQ+ Family, 18*(1), 52–70. doi:10.1080/1550428X.2021.2008285

McDonald, I., & Morgan, G. (2019). Same-sex parents' experiences of schools in England. *Journal of GLBT Family Studies, 15*, 486–500. doi:10.1080/1550428X.2019.1568336

McDonald, K. (2018). Social support and mental health in LGBTQ adolescents: A review of the literature. *Issues in Mental Health Nursing, 39*(1), 16–29. doi:10.1080/01612840.2017.1398283

McGraw, J. S., Skidmore, S. J., Lefevor, G. T., Docherty, M., & Mahoney A. (2023). Affirming and nonaffirming religious beliefs predicting depression and suicide risk among Latter-day Saint sexual minorities. *Journal of Counseling Psychologist, 70*(3), 293–306. doi:10.1037/cou0000659

McGuire, J. K., Catalpa, J. M., Lacey, V., & Kuvalanka, K. A. (2016). Ambiguous loss as a framework for interpreting gender transitions in families. *Journal of Family Theory and Review, 8*(3), 373–85. doi:10.1111/jftr.12159

Merighi, J. R., & Grimes, M. D. (2000). Coming out to families in a multicultural context: Families in society. *Journal of Contemporary Human Services, 81*, 32–41.

Meyer, I., & Dean, L. (1998). Internalized homophobia, intimacy and sexual behaviour among gay and bisexual men. In G. Herek (Ed.), *Stigma and sexual orientation* (pp. 160–86). Sage.

Meza Lazaro, Y., & Bacio, G. A. (2023). Determinants of mental health outcomes among transgender Latinas: Minority stress and resilience processes. *Psychology of Sexual Orientation and Gender Diversity, 10*(3), 451–60. doi:10.1037/sgd0000545

Mitamura, T. (2018). Developing the Functional Assertiveness Scale: Measuring dimensions of objective effectiveness and pragmatic politeness. *Japanese Psychological Research, 60*(2), 99–110. doi:10.1111/jpr.12185

Moors, A. C., Conley, T. D., Edelstein, R. S., & Chopik, W. J. (2015). Attached to monogamy? Avoidance predicts willingness to engage (but not actual engagement) in consensual non-monogamy. *Journal of Social and Personal Relationships, 32*(2), 222–40. doi:10.1177/0265407514529065

Moors, A. C., Gesselman, A. N., & Garcia, J. R. (2021). Desire, familiarity, and engagement in polyamory: Results from a national sample of single adults in the United States. *Frontiers in Psychology, 12*. doi:10.3389/fpsyg.2021.619640

Morales, E. (1989). Ethnic minority families and minority gays and lesbians. *Marriage and Family Review, 14*, 217–39.

Movement Advancement Project. (2022). *Foster and adoption laws*. https://www.lgbtmap.org/equality-maps/foster_and_adoption_laws

Muehlenhard, C. L., Humphreys, T. P., Jozkowski, K. N., & Peterson, Z. D. (2016). The complexities of sexual consent among college students: A conceptual and empirical review. *Journal of Sex Research, 53*(4–5), 457–87. doi:10.1080/00224499.2016.1146651

Nadan, Y. (2021). Parenting as a full-time job: The experience of secular middle-class Jewish parents of transgender emerging adults in Israel. *International Journal of Transgender Health, 23*(3), 321–33. doi:10.1080/26895269.2021.1890300

Najdowski, C. J. (2023). How the "Black criminal" stereotype shapes Black people's psychological experience of policing: Evidence of stereotype threat and remaining questions. *American Psychologist, 78*(5), 695–713. doi:10.1037/amp0001159

Nakamura, N., & Tsong, Y. (2019). Perceived stress, psychological functioning, and resilience among individuals in same-sex binational relationships. *Psychology of Sexual Orientation and Gender Diversity, 6*(2), 175–81. doi:10.1037/sgd0000318

National Center for Health Statistics. (2011). *Health, United States, 2011: With special feature on socioeconomic status and health*. https://www.cdc.gov/nchs/data/hus/hus11.pdf

National Center for Transgender Equality. (2022). *The 2015 U. S. Transgender Survey*. https://www.ustranssurvey.org/reports

Newcomb, M. E. (2020). Romantic relationships and sexual minority health: A review and description of the Dyadic Health Model. *Clinical Psychology Review, 82*, 101924. doi:10.1016/j.cpr.2020.101924

Nixon, C. A. (2011). Working-class lesbian parents' emotional engagement with their children's education: Intersections of class and sexuality. *Sexualities, 14*(1), 79–99. doi:10.1177/1363460710390564

Norwood, K. (2013). Grieving gender: Trans-identities, transition, and ambiguous loss. *Communication Monographs, 80*(1), 24–45. doi:10.1080/03637751.2012.739705

Pachankis, J. E. (2007). The psychological implications of concealing a stigma: A cognitive–affective–behavioral model. *Psychological Bulletin, 133*(2), 328–45. doi:10.1037/0033-2909.133.2.328

Pachankis, J. E., Clark, K. A., Burton, C. L., Hughto, J. M. W., Bränström, R., & Keene, D. E. (2020). Sex, status, competition, and exclusion: Intraminority stress from within the gay community and gay and bisexual men's mental health. *Journal of Personality and Social Psychology, 119*(3), 713–40. doi:10.1037/pspp0000282

Parks, C. A., Hughes, T. L., & Matthews, A. K. (2004). Race/ethnicity and sexual orientation: Intersecting identities. *Cultural Diversity & Ethnic Minority Psychology, 10*, 241–28.

Patterson, C. J., & Ball, C.A. (2018). Perspectives on sexual orientation and gender identity in family law. *Family Court Review, 56*, 361–63. doi:10.1111/fcre.12352

Pistella, J., Salvati, M., Ioverno, S., Laghi, F., & Baiocco, R. (2016). Coming-out to family members and internalized sexual stigma in bisexual, lesbian and gay people. *Journal of Child and Family Studies, 25*(12), 3694–701. doi:10.1007/s10826-016-0528-0

Pollitt, A. M., & Mallory, A. B. (2021). Mental and sexual health disparities among bisexual and unsure Latino/a and Black sexual minority youth. *LGBT Health, 8*(4), 254–62. doi:10.1089/lgbt.2020.0374

Poovey, K., de Jong, D. C., & Morey, K. (2022). The roles of body image, sexual motives, and distraction in women's sexual pleasure. *Archives of Sexual Behavior, 51*(3), 1577–89. doi:10.1007/s10508-021-02210-6

Prairie, K., Kivisto, A. J., Gray, S. L., Taylor, N., & Anderson, A. M. (2022). The association between hate crime laws that enumerate sexual orientation and adolescent suicide attempts. *Psychology, Public Policy, and Law, 29*(2), 196–209. doi:10.1037/law0000360

Psarra, A. (2017). Afyles taytóthtes, émfyles antidráseis [Non-gendered identities, gendered reactions]. Efsyn.gr. http://www.efsyn.gr/arthro/afyles-taytotites-emfyles-antidraseis

Pulice-Farrow, L., Bartnik, A., Lindley, L., Flanders, C. E., & Gonzalez, K. A. (2023). Experiences of community connection and belonging for sexual minority trans individuals. *Psychology of Sexual Orientation and Gender Diversity*. Advance online publication. doi:10.1037/sgd0000629

Radis, B., & Nadan, Y. (2020). "Always thinking about safety": African American lesbian mothers' perceptions of risk and well-being. *Family Process, 60*(3), 950–65. doi:10.1111/famp.12607

Rahm-Knigge, R. L., Gleason, N., Mark, K., & Coleman, E. (2023). Identifying relationships between difficulties with emotion regulation and compulsive sexual behavior. *Archives of Sexual Behavior, 52*(8), 3443–55. doi:10.1007/s10508-023 -02690-8

Ramseyer Winter, V., O'Neill, E. A., Cook, M., Rose, K. L., & Hood, A. (2020). Sexual function in hook-up culture: The role of body image. *Body Image, 34*, 135–44. doi:10.1016/j.bodyim.2020.05.010

Reconciliation and Growth Project. (2023). *Clinical common ground for gender, sexual, and faith diversity.* https://reconciliationandgrowth.org/wp-content/uploads/ 2023/08/Clinical-Common-Ground-for-Gender-Sexual-and-Faith-Diversity_ FINAL-2-2023-07-31.pdf

Reid, M., Gamboni, C., & Bailey, L. (2021). Asking for MORE: A phenomenological exploration of the dyadic coming out process in mixed orientation relationships. *Sexual and Relationship Therapy.* Advance online publication. doi:10 .1080/14681994.2021.1998423

Reyes, M. (1998). Latina lesbians and alcohol and other drugs: Social work implications. *Alcoholism Treatment Quarterly, 16*, 179–92.

Reynolds, P. (2021). Consent and sexual literacy for older people. In P. Simpson, P. Reynolds & T. Hafford-Letchfield (Eds.). *Desexualisation in later life: The limits of sex and intimacy* (pp. 17–33). Bristol University.

Roberts, C., Shiman, L. J., Dowling, E. A., Tantay, L., Masdea, J., Pierre, J., Lomax, D., & Bedell, J. (2020). LGBTQ+ students of colour and their experiences and needs in sexual health education: "You belong here just as everybody else." *Sex Education, 20*(3), 267–82. doi:10.1080/14681811.2019.1648248

Robinson, B. B., Bockting, W. O., Rosser, B. R., Miner, M., & Coleman, E. (2002). The Sexual Health Model: Application of a sexological approach to HIV prevention. *Health Education Research, 17*(1), 43–57. doi:10.1093/her/17.1.43

Rosenkrantz, D. E., Rostosky, S. S., Toland, M. D., & Dueber, D. M. (2020). Cognitive-affective and religious values associated with parental acceptance of an LGBT child. *Psychology of Sexual Orientation and Gender Diversity, 7*(1), 55–65. doi:10.1037/sgd0000355

Rosik, C. H., Lefevor, G. T., & Beckstead, A. L. (2023). Sexual minorities responding to sexual orientation distress: Examining 33 methods and the effects of sexual identity labeling and theological viewpoint. *Spirituality in Clinical Practice, 10*(3), 245–60. doi:10.1037/scp0000295

Rowniak, S., & Chesla, C. (2013). Coming out for a third time: Transmen, sexual orientation, and identity. *Archives of Sexual Behavior, 42*(3), 449–61. doi:10 .1007/s10508-012-0036-2

Rubin, G. S. (1984). Thinking sex: Notes for a radical theory of politics of sexuality. In C. S. Vance (Ed.), *Pleasure and danger: Exploring female sexuality* (pp. 267–319). Routledge & Kegan Paul.

Russell, S. T., & Fish, J. N. (2016). Mental health in lesbian, gay, bisexual, and transgender (LGBT) youth. *Annual Review of Clinical Psychology, 12*, 465–87. doi:10.1146/annurev-clinpsy-021815-093153

Russell, S. T., Pollitt, A. M., Li, G., & Grossman, A. H. (2018). Chosen name use is linked to reduced depressive symptoms, suicidal ideation, and suicidal behavior among transgender youth. *Journal of Adolescent Health, 63*(4), 503–5. doi:10 .1016/j.jadohealth.2018.02.003

Russon, J., Washington, R., Machado, A., Smithee, L., & Dellinger, J. (2021). Suicide among LGBTQIA+ youth: A review of the treatment literature. *Aggression and Violent Behavior, 64*, 101578. doi10.1016/j.avb.2021.101578

Ryan, C., & Chen-Hayes, S. F. (2013). Educating and empowering families of lesbian, gay, bisexual, transgender, and questioning students. In E. S. Fisher & K. Komosa-Hawkins (Eds.), *Creating safe and supportive learning environments: A guide for working with lesbian, gay, bisexual, transgender, and questioning youth and families* (pp. 209–29). Routledge.

Ryan, C., Huebner, D., Diaz, R. M., & Sanchez, J. (2009). Family rejection as a predictor of negative health outcomes in White and Latino lesbian, gay, and bisexual young adults. *Pediatrics, 123*(1), 346–52. doi:10.1542/peds.2007-3524

Ryan, C., Russell, S. T., Huebner, D., Diaz, R., & Sanchez, J. (2010). Family acceptance in adolescence and the health of LGBT young adults. *Journal of Child and Adolescent Psychiatric Nursing, 23*(4), 205–13. doi:10.1111/j.1744-6171.2010.00246.x

Ryan, C., Toomey, R., Diaz, R. M., & Russell, S. T. (2020). Parent-initiated sexual orientation change efforts with LGBT adolescents: Implications for young adult mental health and adjustment. *Journal of Homosexuality, 67*, 159–73. doi:10.1080/00918369.2018.1538407

Sailakis, I. (2018). *Bibliographic review about queer studies in English bibliography (2000–2017): Research in Greece* [Unpublished master's thesis]. University of Western Macedonia. https://dspace.uowm.gr/xmlui/handle/123456789/993

Saiz, E. G., Sarda, V., Pletta, D. R., Reisner, S. L., & Katz-Wise, S. L. (2021). Family functioning as a protective factor for sexual risk behaviors among gender minority adolescents. *Archives of Sexual Behavior, 50*(7), 3023–33. doi:10.1007/s10508-021-02079-5

Sanders, T., du Plessis, C., Mullens, A. B., & Brömdal, A. (2023). Navigating detransition borders: An exploration of social media narratives. *Archives of Sexual Behavior, 52*(3), 1061–72. doi:10.1007/s10508-023-02556-z

Saraff, S., Singh, T., Kaur, H., & Biswal, R. (2022). Stigma and health of Indian LGBT population: A systematic review. *Stigma and Health, 7*(2), 178–95. doi:10.1037/sah0000361

Savin-Williams, R. C., & Ream, G. L. (2003). Sex variations in the disclosure to parents of same-sex attractions. *Journal of Family Psychology, 17*(3), 429–38. doi:10.1037/0893-3200.17.3.429

Sax, L. (2002). How common is intersex? A response to Anne Fausto-Sterling. *Journal of Sex Research, 39*(3), 174–78. doi:10.1080/00224490209552139

Schalk, S. (2019). Bodyminds reimagined: A conversation with Sami Schalk. In a. m. brown, *Pleasure activist: The politics of feeling good* (pp. 144–50). AK Press.

Scoats, R., & Campbell, C. (2022). What do we know about consensual non-monogamy? *Current Opinion in Psychology, 48*, 101468. https://www.sciencedirect.com/science/article/pii/S2352250X22001890#bib14

Shapiro, F. (2017). *Eye movement, desensitization, and reprocessing (EMDR) therapy: Basic principles, protocols, and procedures* (3rd ed.). Guilford Press.

Shulruf, B., Hattie, J., & Dixon, R. (2007). Development of a new measurement tool for individualism and collectivism. *Journal of Psychoeducational Assessment, 25*(4), 385–401. doi:10.1177/0734282906298992

Siegel, D. (2019). *Aware: The science and practice of presence—the groundbreaking meditation practice*. TarcherPerigee.

Snapp, S., Ching, T. H. W., Miranda-Ramirez, M. A., Gallik, C., Duenaz, U., & Watson, R. J. (2023). Queering hookup motives in a diverse sample of LGBTQ+ young adults. *Journal of Sex Research, 61*(1), 133–43. doi:10.1080/00224499.2023.2183175

Society for Adolescent Health and Medicine. (2017). Abstinence-only-until-marriage policies and programs: An updated position paper of the Society for Adolescent Health and Medicine. *Journal of Adolescent Health, 61*(3), 400–403. doi:10.1016/j.jadohealth.2017.06.001

Son, D., & Updegraff, K. A. (2023). Sexual minority adolescents' disclosure of sexual identity to family: A systematic review and conceptual framework. *Adolescent Research Review, 8*(1), 75–95. doi:10.1007/s40894-021-00177-y

Song, C., Xie, H., Ding, R., & Phuengsamran, D. (2023). HIV-positive, heterosexually married men who have sex with men in China: HIV status disclosure and sexual behaviors. *Sexuality Research & Social Policy*. Advance online publication. doi:10.1007/s13178-023-00864-6

Stone, A. L., Nimmons, E. A., Salcido, R., & Schnarrs, P. (2020). "My meemaw is a cool ass person": Family members as role models of resilience for sexual and gender diverse people of color. *Journal of GLBT Family Studies, 16*, 241–57. doi:10.1080/1550428X.2020.1724148

Štulhofer, A., Wiessner, C., Koletić, G., Pietras, L., & Briken, P. (2022). Religiosity, perceived effects of pornography use on personal sex life, and moral incongruence: Insights from the German Health and Sexuality Survey (GeSiD). *Journal of Sex Research, 59*(6), 720–30. doi:10.1080/00224499.2021.1916422

Suh, E. M., & Lee, H. (2017). Collectivistic cultures. In V. Zeigler-Hill & T. Shackelford (Eds.), *Encyclopedia of personality and individual differences*. Springer. doi:10.1007/978-3-319-28099-8_2017-1

Syme, M. L. (2021). "I need a little sugar in my bowl": Prioritizing the sexual rights and wellness of older adults, *Clinical Gerontologist, 44*(3), 207–9. doi:10.1080/07317115.2021.1902651

Syme, M. L., & Cohn, T. J. (2016). Examining aging sexual stigma attitudes among adults by gender, age, and generational status. *Aging & Mental Health, 20*(1), 36–45. doi:10.1080/13607863.2015.1012044

Taormino, T. (2008). *Opening up: A guide to creating and sustaining open relationships*. Cleis.

Teach Democracy. (2024). *Bringing down an empire: Gandhi and civil disobedience*. https://www.crf-usa.org/bill-of-rights-in-action/bria-16-3-b-bringing-down-an-empire-gandhi-and-civil-disobedience

Tebbe, E. A., Bell, H. L., Cassidy, K., Lindner, S., Wilson, E., & Budge, S. (2022). "It's loving yourself for you": Happiness in trans and nonbinary adults. *Psychology of Sexual Orientation and Gender Diversity*. Advance online publication. doi:10.1037/sgd0000613

Thompson, M. (1994). *Gay soul: Finding the heart of gay spirit and nature with sixteen writers, healers, teachers, and visionaries*. HarperCollins.

Thöni, C., Eisner, L., & Hässler, T. (2022). Not straight enough, nor queer enough: Identity denial, stigmatization, and negative affect among bisexual and pansexual people. *Psychology of Sexual Orientation and Gender Diversity.* Advance online publication. doi:10.1037/sgd0000606

Thys, K., Mahieu, L., Cavolo, A., Hensen, C., Dierkx de Casterlé, B., & Gastmans, C. (2019). Nurses' experiences and reactions towards intimacy and sexuality expressions by nursing home residents: A qualitative study. *Journal of Clinical Nursing, 28*(5–6), 836–49. doi:10.1111/jocn.14680

Tierney, D., Spengler, E. S., Schuch, E., & Grzanka, P. R. (2021). Sexual orientation beliefs and identity development: A person-centered analysis among sexual minorities. *Journal of Sex Research, 58*(5), 625–37. doi:10.1080/00224499.2021.1878344

Tilley, D. S., Kolodetsky, A., Cottrell, D., & Tilton, A. (2020). Correlates to increased risk of sexual assault and sexual harassment among LGBT+ university students. *Journal of Forensic Nursing, 16*(2), 63–72. doi:10.1097/JFN.0000000000000284

Tolstoy, L. (2020). *Anna Karenina* (C. Garnett, Trans.). Instaread. (Original work published 1878)

Tordoff, D. M., Haley, S. G., Shook, A., Kantor, A., Crouch, J. M., & Ahrens, K. (2021). "Talk about bodies": Recommendations for using transgender-inclusive language in sex education curricula. *Sex Roles, 84*, 152–65. doi:10.1007/s11199-020-01160-y

Tornello, S. L., Riskind, R. G., & Babić, A. (2019). Transgender and gender non-binary parents' pathways to parenthood. *Psychology of Sexual Orientation and Gender Diversity, 6*(2), 232–41. doi:10.1037/sgd0000323

Tsang, E. Y. H. (2021). A "phoenix" rising from the ashes: China's *Tongqi*, marriage fraud, and resistance. *British Journal of Sociology, 72*(3), 793–807. doi:10.1111/1468-4446.12812

United States Census. (2017). *Unmarried and Single Americans Week.* https://www.census.gov/content/dam/Census/newsroom/facts-for-features/2017/cb17-ff16.pdf

Vagos, P., & Pereira, A. (2016). A cognitive perspective for understanding and training assertiveness. *European Psychologist, 21*(2), 109–21. doi:10.1027/1016-9040/a000250

Valentine, S. E., & Shipherd, J. C. (2018). A systematic review of social stress and mental health among transgender and gender non-conforming people in the United States. *Clinical Psychology Review, 66*, 24–38. doi:10.1016/j.cpr.2018.03.003

Ve Ard, C., & Veaux, F. (2005). *Polyamory 101.* http://www.xeromag.com/poly101.pdf

Veaux, F. (2017). *Glossary of poly terms: Learning the lingo.* https://lovingwithout-boundaries.com/resources/glossary/

Vencill, J. A., Carlson, S., Iantaffi, A., & Miner, M. (2018). Mental health, relationships, and sex: Exploring patterns among bisexual individuals in mixed orientation relationships. *Sexual and Relationship Therapy, 33*(1–2), 14–33. doi:10.1080/14681994.2017.1419570

Vil, N. M. S., Bay-Cheng, L. Y., Ginn, H. G., & Chen, Z. (2022). Perceptions of monogamy, nonconsensual nonmonogamy and consensual nonmonogamy at the intersections of race and gender. *Culture, Health & Sexuality, 24*(1), 109–24. doi:10.1080/13691058.2020.1817561

Vincke, J., & Bolton, R. (1994). Social support, depression, and self-acceptance among gay men. *Human Relations, 47*, 1049–62.

Vinjamuri, M. (2015). Reminders of heteronormativity: Gay adoptive fathers navigating uninvited social interactions. *Family Relations, 64*(2), 263–77. doi:10.1111/fare.12118

Voultsos, P., Zymvragou, C.-E., Raikos, N., & Spiliopoulou, C. C. (2019). Lesbians' experiences and attitudes towards parenthood in Greece. *Culture, Health & Sexuality, 21*(1), 108–20. doi:10.1080/13691058.2018.1442021

Wade, B. (2021). *Grieving while Black: An antiracist take on oppression and sorrow*. North Atlantic.

Wahlig, J. L. (2015). Losing the child they thought they had: Therapeutic suggestions for an ambiguous loss perspective with parents of a transgender child. *Journal of GLBT Family Studies, 11*(4), 305–26. doi:10.1080/1550428X.2014.945676

Walker, A. (2014). "I'm not a lesbian; I'm just a freak": A pilot study of the experiences of women in assumed-monogamous other-sex unions seeking secret same-sex encounters online, their negotiation of sexual desire, and meaning-making of sexual identity. *Sexuality & Culture, 18*(4), 911–35. doi:10.1007/s12119-014-9226-5

Walker, J. J., & Longmire-Avital, B. (2013). The impact of religious faith and internalized homonegativity on resiliency for Black lesbian, gay, and bisexual emerging adults. *Developmental Psychology, 49*(9), 1723–31. doi:10.1037/a0031059

Wang, Y., Wilson, A., Chen, R., Hu, Z., Peng, K., & Xu, S. (2020). Behind the rainbow, "Tongqi" wives of men who have sex with men in China: A systematic review. *Frontiers in Psychology, 10*, Article 2929. doi:10.3389/fpsyg.2019.02929

Watson, R. J., Shahin, Y. M., & Arbeit, M. R. (2019). Hookup initiation and emotional outcomes differ across LGB young men and women. *Sexualities, 22*(5–6), 932–50. doi:10.1177/1363460718774528

Wentland, J. J., & Reissing, E. (2014). Casual sexual relationships: Identifying definitions for one night stands, booty calls, fuck buddies, and friends with benefits. *Canadian Journal of Human Sexuality, 23*(3), 167–77. doi:10.3138/cjhs.2744

Wilson, B. D. M., & Miller, R. L. (2002). Strategies for managing heterosexism used among African American gay and bisexual men. *Journal of Black Psychology, 28*, 371–91.

Wolkomir, M. (2004). "Giving it up to God": Negotiating femininity in support groups for wives of ex-gay Christian men. *Gender & Society, 18*(6), 735–55. doi:10.1177/0891243204268772

Yarhouse, M. A., Dean, J. B., Lastoria, M., & Stratton, S. P. (2018). *Listening to sexual minorities*. InterVarsity Press Academic.

Yarhouse, M. A., & Sadusky, J. (2021). Best practices in ministry to youth navigating gender identity and faith. *Christian Education Journal, 18*(2), 263–74. doi:10.1177/0739891320952807

Yarhouse, M. A., & Zaporozhets, O. (2022). *When children come out*. InterVarsity Press Academic.

Yiannikopoulou, A., & Sakellaki, K. (2011). Omophilophilos gonios sto ikonographimeno paidiko vivlio? Den iparkhi!!!! [Gay/lesbian parents in children's books? This does not exist!!!!]. *Kimena, 14*, 1–17.

Zack, E., & Ben-Ari, A. (2019). "Men are for sex and women are for marriage": On the duality in the lives of Jewish religious gay men married to women. *Journal of GLBT Family Studies, 15*(4), 395–413. doi:10.1080/1550428X.2018.1506374

Zamantakis, A. (2022). Queering intimate emotions: Trans/nonbinary people negotiating emotional expectations in intimate relationships. *Sexualities, 25*(5–6), 581–97. doi:10.1177/1363460720979307

Zavala, C., & Waters, L. (2020). Coming out as LGBTQ+: The role strength-based parenting on posttraumatic stress and posttraumatic growth. *Journal of Happiness Studies, 22*(3), 1359–83. doi:10.1007/s10902-020-00276-y

Zulkffli, M. A., Ab Rashid, R., Kamarul Azlan, M. A., & Ismail, H. H. (2022). The interplay of infidelity, sexuality, and religiosity in the discourse of mixed-orientation marriages: A discursive psychological analysis. *Frontiers in Psychology, 13*, 784675. doi:10.3389/fpsyg.2022.784675

Index

Each coeditor and coauthor listed in their bios what they considered their primary social labels, locations, or characteristics of how they personally experience the world. This is to inform you and other readers about our potential biases, expertise, privileges, and disadvantages on the subject. We also hope it dismantles some stereotypes.

Editors

A. Lee Beckstead (he/him), PhD, is white-Peruvian, gay, cisgender, currently nondisabled, and spiritual; was excommunicated from the Church of Jesus Christ of Latter-day Saints; and has been in a primary relationship with a man since 1997. He has been a psychologist in private practice since 2003 in Salt Lake City, Utah. He conducted a qualitative study from 1998 to 2001 on 50 individuals who tried to change their sexual orientation through psychotherapy. Half reported benefits, half reported harms, and many reported mixed results. Since 2005, he has co-facilitated weekend retreats for male survivors of sexual abuse (MenHealing.org). He served on the 2009 American Psychological Association task force making recommendations for those seeking therapy to change their sexual orientation. In 2012, he initiated the LGBTQ-affirmative Psychotherapist Guild of Utah to file ethical complaints against Utah clinicians providing sexual orientation change efforts (SOCE). In 2013, he shifted focus and organized a workshop to foster dialogue and understanding with these individuals. Since then, he's been meeting twice per month with therapists and educators holding differing views on sexual orientation, gender, and religion (ReconciliationAndGrowth.org). He testified as an expert witness in a 2015 New Jersey legal case against a Jewish organization accused of consumer fraud due to offering SOCE. From 2016, he's been part of a diverse research team studying the health and satisfaction of individuals who are single and celibate or noncelibate or in a same-gender/queer or mixed-orientation relationship

(4OptionsSurvey.com). He is also the lead coeditor of the LGBTQIA+ Peace-making Book Project.

Jacks Cheng (tā [他]/he/they), PhD, EdM, is a queer migrant of Taiwanese heritage to Canada and the United States. Tā works as a supervising psychologist at NYC Health + Hospitals/Jacobi and assistant professor of psychiatry and behavioral sciences at Albert Einstein College of Medicine. Tā is also the 2023 chair of the Committee on Early Career Psychologists of the American Psychological Association. Tā received a doctorate in counseling psychology from Indiana University and is passionate about cultural-affirmative and anticolonialist approaches in research and practice, with a particular interest in empowering sexual and gender diverse, migrant, and people of color communities in oppressive spaces.

Sulaimon Giwa (he/him/his), PhD, is an associate professor and interim dean of social work at Memorial University of Newfoundland and Labrador in Canada. Sulaimon is a scholar-activist who self-identifies as Black, Muslim, and gay. His intersectional identity adds depth to his contributions in the field of LGBTQ+ studies, demonstrating his unwavering commitment to fostering inclusive discourse from diverse perspectives. Through his academic and community pursuits, Sulaimon demonstrates his astute understanding of the intricacies surrounding identity and representation within the LGBTQ+ community, promoting crucial conversations on equity and social justice. He authored the 2022 book *Racism and Gay Men of Color: Living and Coping with Discrimination.*

Mark A. Yarhouse, PsyD, is a clinical psychologist who specializes in conflicts tied to religious identity and sexual and gender identity. He assists people who are navigating the complex relationship between their sexual or gender identity and Christian faith. He is the Dr. Arthur P. and Mrs. Jean May Rech Chair in Psychology at Wheaton College, where he runs the Sexual and Gender Identity (SGI) Institute. He is an award-winning teacher and researcher and is the past recipient of the Gary Collins Award for Excellence in Christian Counseling. He was a past participant with the Ethics and Public Policy Center think tank in Washington, DC, and he was named senior fellow with the Council of Christian Colleges and Universities to conduct a study of students navigating sexual identity concerns at Christian colleges and universities. He has been a consultant to the National Institute of Corrections to address issues facing sexual minorities in corrections, and he was part of a consensus panel from the American Psychological Association on sexual orientation and gender identity change efforts that convened to provide input to the Substance Abuse and Mental Health Services Administration (SAMHSA) in Washington, DC. He is currently the chair of the task force on LGBT issues for Division 36 (Psychology of Religion and Spirituality) of the American Psychological Association. He was also invited to write the featured white paper on sexual identity for the Christ on Campus Initiative, edited by Don A. Carson for the Gospel Coalition. He has published over 80 peer-reviewed journal articles and book chapters and is author or coauthor of several books, including *Understanding Sexual Identity: A Resource for Youth Ministers* and *Understanding Gender Dysphoria: Navigating Transgender Issues in a Changing Culture*. His most recent books are *Sexual Identity and Faith* and *Costly Obedience: Listening to and Learning from Celibate Gay Christians*.

Iva Žegura (she/her) graduated from and specialized in clinical psychology at the Department of Psychology, Faculty of Philosophy, in Zagreb and is currently pursuing doctoral studies at Sigmund Freud University Vienna, Austria. She is a licensed clinical psychologist and is educated in gestalt integrative therapy, cybernetic psychotherapy, and sexual therapy. She works at the University Psychiatric Hospital Vrapče in Zagreb, and collaborates with several national universities and departments of psychology. She introduced the concept of affirmative and sensitive LGBTAIQ+ mental health practice in Croatia and the region. The Section for Psychology of Sexuality and Psychology of Gender of the Croatian Psychological Association was established on her initiative in 2007. In 2015, she facilitated the implementation of legalization and health care for trans people based on SOC WPATH within the Croatian health-care system. She is a member of the national list of experts for transgender health care at the Croatian Ministry of Health. She is the president of the Section for Clinical Psychology and Section for Psychology and Human Rights, and vice president of the Section for Psychology of Sexuality and Psychology of Gender. From 2021, she has been a member of the board of directors of the European Professional Association for Transgender Health (EPATH) and now she is president-elect. She collaborates with the Global Education Institute of WPATH and APA IPsy Net. She is a member of several national, European, and international professional associations. In 2022, she received the APA Division 52 International Psychology Global Citizen Psychologist Citation Award for exceptional volunteer professional engagement and contribution to increasing visibility and strengthening the availability of psychological scientific and practical knowledge both in local and international community related to LGBTQ+ mental health. In 2024, she received the highest professional award in Croatia "Ramiro Bujas" from the Croatian Psychological Association for exceptional achievements in the social affirmation of psychology.

Authors

Christine Aramburu Alegría, PhD, RN, is associate professor emerita at the University of Nevada, Reno. She holds a PhD in social psychology. She identifies as a cisgender Spanish-Basque woman. Her work focuses on transgender/gender-nonconforming persons and their families.

Frances Aranda (she/her), PhD, MPH, MS, is a third-generation Mexican American, cisgender lesbian. She has been a senior research specialist at a large university in Chicago, Illinois, for the past 26 years. She completed her PhD in public health (community health sciences) in 2010. She has two master's degrees (in human service administration and in public health [gerontology concentration]) and a bachelor's degree in psychology. She completed a postdoctoral fellowship in 2013, which was funded through a Diversity Supplement by the National Institute on Alcohol Abuse and Alcoholism at the University of Illinois, College of Nursing. She has a broad range of research experience gained over 26 years of working in a university and health-care setting. Dr. Aranda was the project manager for three NIH-funded longitudinal studies, several cross-sectional studies, and intervention studies. These studies focused on breast cancer among low-income racial/ethnic minority women, cervical and breast cancer in Korean immigrant women, alcohol use among lesbians, and smoking cessation among LGBT individuals. Her research interests include racial/ethnic differences in various physical and mental health conditions (e.g., depression, chronic pain, PTSD, alcohol use, and smoking). Additional research interests include aging and measurement issues among racial/ethnic and sexual minorities.

Eric Boromisa is a consultant with a background in neuroscience who teaches workshops on consent, nonverbal communication, social skills, and affirmative attraction. He is a member of the RAHM LGBTQ+ Professional Leadership Community, identifies as White and gay/bisexual and resides in Berlin, Germany.

Don L. Braegger (he/him), dual BS, is a father of seven and grandfather of 10 and a very happy, well-adjusted, mature gay man. He started out life as a good little "Mormon boy" from rural Utah but has spent the last eight years as a full-time nomad roaming the lower 48 states of the United States and enjoying gay sex at every opportunity!

João Paulo Mendes Carvalho (he/him), MA, is a doctoral student in critical social/personality psychology at the Graduate Center, City University of New York. He holds a master's in family and gender studies from the University of Lisbon. His research interests focus on queer immigrants' experiences, community and personal networks, structural inequalities, queer theory, and decoloniality. He is Brazilian, gay, cisgender, and currently nondisabled.

Jeannie DiClementi (she/her/hers), PsyD, is a White, cisgender, lesbian, wife, mother, grandmother, great-grandmother, licensed psychologist, community activist, and boat rocker. She has worked in academia for nearly 30 years and is in the process of retiring from Purdue University Fort Wayne. She has worked as a clinician with LGBTQIA+ clients since the mid-1980s and with HIV+ clients during the peak years of the HIV pandemic. In her current university faculty position, she created the campus Safe Zone training, the LGBTQIA+ Resource Center, the LGBTQIA+ Task Force, and mental health education and suicide prevention programming. She mentors LGBTQIA+ graduate students for the American Psychological Association's Graduate Student Association. She provides consultation and training on clinical work with LGBTQIA+ clients for Northeast Indiana area mental health centers, including clinical psychology internship programs.

Stefano Eleuteri (he/him/his), clinical psychology PhD, is a lecturer at Sapienza University, Lumsa University, and Mercatorum University, all in Rome. Currently, he is member of the Advisory Committee of the World Association for Sexual Health and of the Executive Committee of the European Federation for Sexology. He is a White, European cisgender man and resides in Rome, Italy.

Alison Feit, PhD, can be found most easily

- Teaching at her psychoanalytic homes (Saint Louis Psychoanalytic Institute, William Alanson White Institute, China American Psychoanalytic Alliance)
- Hanging with her psychoanalytic pals (William Alanson White Institute's Artist Group, Sexual Abuse Service, LGBTQ Service)
- On her podcast (*Ask Freudina*, available on most platforms)
- At her offices in Atlanta, New York City, or somewhere on the Zoom-zoom.

The most easily accessible introduction to her writing can be found at

- "A Letter to My Sons, July 2020," *International Journal of Controversial Discussions* (https://ijcd.internationalpsychoanalysis.net/wp-content/uploads/2020/09/ijcd-issue-3-September-2020.pdf)
- "On the Joys and Frustrations of the Human Need for Contact," *Psychoanalysis Today* (https://www.psychoanalysis.today/en-GB/PT-Articles/Feit171179/Is-six-feet-too-much-to-ask-On-the-joys-and-frustr.aspx)

Darren J. Freeman-Coppadge (he/him/his), PhD, PharmD, BCPP, is a counseling psychologist and board-certified psychiatric clinical pharmacist. He is the CEO of Congruence Counseling & Psychology, LLC, which provides psychotherapy, consultation, and educational services. His clinical and research interests include identity conflicts and development, cultural humility, and intersectionality, particularly the intersections of sexuality, religion/spirituality, and race/ethnicity. He frequently speaks, teaches, and writes on these topics and provides psychotherapy to clients who are affected by them. He also engages in these issues professionally in the American Psychological Association as an active member of Division 17 (Society of Counseling Psychology) and a cochair of the Task Force on Religion and Spirituality in Division 44 (Society for the Psychology of Sexual Orientation and Gender Diversity). He identifies as a non-disabled, Black, cisgender, gay man of faith (Christian upbringing).

Susanna M. Gallor (she/her), PhD, is a senior lecturer at UMass Boston and a clinical faculty member of the UMass Boston Clinical Psychology PhD Program. She is a White, Cuban American, cisgender, nondisabled, Jewish lesbian woman. Susanna previously worked as a staff psychologist in various university mental health centers, and she has served in several roles related to promoting mental health and well-being on college campuses. At UMass Boston, Susanna supervises prevention-oriented, outreach and assessment services provided by UMB-UR-BEST (University Resources for Behavioral and Educational Skills Training). In addition to her graduate teaching and supervision, Susanna teaches undergraduate courses and has served on department and program committees that focus on their ongoing commitment to antiracist and social justice–oriented teaching, research, and supervision. Broadly, Susanna serves her students, clients, and communities from an intersectional and justice-oriented perspective, and this is reflected in the consultation and outreach work she has engaged in, including presenting to a variety of audiences about a range of topics, such as equity issues in the discipline of psychology, understanding gender identity development and expression, supporting student mental health and wellness during the COVID-19 pandemic, and coming-out issues and experiences for diverse LGBTQ+ individuals.

Alejandro Gepp-Torres (he/él), MD, is a child and adolescent psychiatrist and gender, sex, and relationship diversity therapist from Valparaíso, Chile. He studied medicine at Universidad de Valparaíso. After that, he enrolled in the Child and Adolescent Psychiatry Program at the same university. At the same time, he worked with adolescents with substance abuse disorders. After graduating, he started working at Hospital Carlos van Buren, taking charge of the Gender Identity Program, and teaching consultation psychiatry and developmental psychology. Eventually, he became the chief of the Mental Health Unit in the same hospital. He also works with a foundation called Diversalud, where a group of medical professionals who work with gender diversity do activism to give access to affirming care to people across the country. He was raised in a Catholic family and identifies as a proud and happy gay man.

Iraklis Grigoropoulos (he/him) earned his PhD in social psychology from Aristotle University Greece, his MSc in developmental psychopathology from the medical school at Aristotle University Greece, his MSc in counseling psychology from Manchester Metropolitan University in the United Kingdom, and his psychology degree from Aristotle University Greece. He serves as full-time laboratory teaching staff in the Early Childhood Education and Care Department at the International Hellenic University, teaching psychology courses at the undergraduate and postgraduate levels.

Nathalie Huitema (she/her), PhD, is a registered sexologist, sex therapist for Dutch expats, and dissertation advisor for the Human Sexuality Department at the California Institute of Integral Studies. She is also a sex educator, having developed diverse sexuality training programs for long-term care. Nathalie serves as a consultant and presenter at (inter)national conferences, expressing her love for sharing knowledge and passion. Additionally, she is a (co)author of several journal articles and book chapters. Specializing in sexuality, aging, and consent, Nathalie is a Dutch, cisgender, partnered mother.

Jay Jacobsen (he/him/they) is a gay, cisgender White man from the U.S. northwest, a secular humanist, and a former Latter-day Saint of 30 years. He currently works as an ecommerce director in Utah and has focused years of community volunteer work on bridge-building efforts. With three others, he cofounded North Star, a nonprofit intended to help those at the intersection of the Mormon and LGBTQ+ experience to build community around authentically, honestly, and openly finding their way. Motivated by fundamentally changed beliefs, he stepped down from its governing committee and away from his Latter-day Saint home religious community. With loss of spiritual community and relationships destabilized by significant repositioning, he found a sense of community in the shared values and purpose of Circling the Wagons Conferences, focused on dialogue and conflict resolution across diverse LGBTQ+ and Mormon experience, eventually codirecting the organization for two years. He also became a regular contributor as the self-dubbed "token heathen" on the *Out in Zion* podcast.

Erin S. Lavender-Stott (she/they), PhD, is an Appalachian queer single person who currently resides in the rural great plains. Professionally, she is currently an assistant professor in the Human Development and Family Studies Program within the School of Education, Counseling, and Human Development at South

Dakota State University. She has worked with LGBTQ+ individuals across the life course, most recently in her university and local community, in addition to a recent research focus on single LBQ older women. Her research on single LBQ older women explored how they understood family, expectations for aging, and the connections between singlehood and sexuality. She continues to expand her work on singlehood and comes to it from a strength-based perspective.

Tyler Lefevor, PhD, identifies as a White cisgender, gay/queer Mormon man. He is an associate professor of psychology at Utah State University. His work focuses primarily on understanding how and when religiousness relates to health for sexual and gender minorities. In addition, he maintains a small private therapy practice focused on helping sexual and gender minorities to thrive, particularly those raised in conservative religious traditions.

Isabel Maria Sampaio Oliveira Lima is a retired judge from the Bahia State Court and a public health doctor, human rights educator, and restorative justice specialist. Dr. Lima retired as a professor from the Catholic University of Salvador (Bahia-Brazil) at the Doctorate Program in Family in the Contemporary Society, where she coordinated the Research Group on Human Rights, Family, and Rights to Health. She works at Moinho de Paz (www.moinhodepaz .com.br) on peacebuilding circles, restorative practices, and restorative justice programs.

Paul Linden, PhD, has been practicing and teaching aikido for over 50 years and holds a sixth-degree black belt. He also holds a black belt in Isshin-ryū karate and a certificate as an instructor of the Feldenkrais method of somatic education. Paul has a BA in philosophy and PhD in physical education. He developed Being In Movement mind-body education as a way of living from an integrated mind-body state of power and love. He has applied it in areas such as sports, computer use, attention disorders, trauma recovery, and conflict resolution. He has taught internationally—in places from Russia to Israel and Ecuador. He has had Parkinson's for 20 years and has found that the body awareness methods he has developed have allowed him to stay functional. His particular passion right now is saving the planet, so his grandchildren will have someplace to live. Through body awareness education, people can develop the power, courage, and love they will need to create a peaceful and sustainable civilization.

Julia Mackaronis (she/her/they/them), PhD, has been a licensed clinical psychologist since 2015 and currently works with the Quinault Indian Nation and in her own small consultation practice. Her work involves a blend of therapy, supervision of other mental health providers, and community engagement. She continues to participate in research on interpersonal processes involved in therapy, sleep, and suicidality, among other topics. She is a former president of the Washington State Psychological Association (WSPA) and current member of the WSPA Good Trouble (Social Justice) Committee. As a bisexual member of the LGBTQIA2S+ community, contributing to this book is a form of advocacy for her. She tries to understand and engage with the world as intersectionally as possible, which involves grounding her efforts toward social justice with awareness that certain aspects of her identity (e.g., she is White, cisgender, and currently nondisabled) mean she benefits from systemic forms of oppression that harm others. She made her contributions to this book from where she currently lives on what has been the land of the Quinault people since time immemorial, where Quinault people continue to live and thrive.

Mani B. Mitchell (Mx, they/them) is a pakeha (White New Zealander), change agent, nonbinary, intersex, and queer-identifying person. Born in the shadows of the Second World War, Mx. Mitchell's parents—loving, remote rural conservative people—were poorly equipped to deal with the reality their birth brought to their parents' life. Mx. Mitchell did not deal with the trauma of their childhood until their 40s. They had trained as an educator, gone onto local government emergency management, and specialized in critical incident stress management, management, and then psychotherapy. Once Mx. Mitchell started to "deal" with their own birth reality, own trauma, and own suicidal ideation, they made the decision they could not change the past but could assist with changing the future. So they have used all their training, lived experience, *aroha*, stubbornness, pain, and sadness to bring awareness and visibility of intersex realities to the world. They seek to find people to collaborate with, work beside, and inspire locally, nationally, and internationally. Mx. Mitchell's dream is that we will, as a global collective, achieve critical mass and change the model, and that trauma, stigma, shame, and secrecy will be relegated to history as a sad artifact of the past, and that intersex persons will be free to be the magnificent humans we are all entitled to be.

Eduardo Morales (he/him/él), PhD, is a cisgender gay man of Puerto Rican descent who is a distinguished professor emeritus of Alliant International University. He was one of the founders and is the current executive director of AGUILAS, an award-winning behavioral health and leadership development program for Latinx LGBTQ+. He received numerous distinguished awards, including the APA Award for Distinguished Professional Contributions to Institutional Practice, and is a fellow of 12 Divisions of the American Psychological Association. He is the 2024 chair of the APA Commission of Ethnic Minority

Recruitment, Retention, and Training in Psychology Task Force-2. Dr. Morales is very active in obtaining research, program evaluation, and service grants. He was president of various psychological associations and founded many programs for various ethnic groups. Areas of expertise include health prevention and promotion, HIV, substance use, community interventions, juvenile delinquency prevention, program evaluation research, and strategic planning and policy development for various types of multicultural communities and organizations locally and nationally. The first person in Manhattan to receive the Pope Pius XII Award at St Patrick's Cathedral, as well as an Eagle Scout with a gold palm as of 1967, he was frequently called on for public relations. An active musician and singer, he directed and performed with various arts organizations, toured the United States with the San Francisco Gay Men's Chorus in its first national concert tour in 1981 and performed solo for the 2014 APA Council's opening session. These experiences provided the basis of his passion, advocacy, and motivation to serve and build teams for addressing community empowerment, embracing collaboration, and realizing dreams. He has had a regular column in the *San Francisco Bay Times* since 2021.

Brie Radis, LCSW, identifies as a strength-based antioppressive trauma-informed educator, clinical social worker, and researcher. She is an associate professor of social work at West Chester University. Brie has worked in the field of community mental health, substance use, homelessness, and housing first. Brie is a White, cisgender, queer mother to two kids, one of whom identifies as nonbinary.

Alex Rivera (she/they) is a mixed Chinese American queer woman and licensed psychologist in the Bay Area. She is director of a community-minded group practice that focuses on treatment for queer and trans BIPOC. She recently wrote the book *The Intersectional Other: Reimagining Power in the Margins*, which was published by Lexington Books in 2022.

Christopher H. Rosik, PhD, is a Phi Beta Kappa graduate of the University of Oregon and earned his doctorate in clinical psychology from Fuller Graduate School of Psychology. He is currently a psychologist and director of research at Link Care Foundation in Fresno, California, as well as a clinical faculty member of Fresno Pacific University. Dr. Rosik has professional interests that include the psychological care of missionaries and clergy, dissociative disorders, and sexual orientation, with an emphasis on understanding the experiences of nonheterosexual persons who remain in traditional faith communities and often do not identify as LGBT+. He has published more than 60 articles in peer-reviewed journals on these and other topics and has made presentations across America and in Europe. Dr. Rosik has served as president of the Western Region of the Christian Association for Psychological Studies and the Alliance for Therapeutic Choice and Scientific Integrity. He is a member of the American Psychological Association, International Society for the Study of Trauma and Dissociation, and National Association of Social Workers.

Jordan Rullo, PhD, ABPP, is a board-certified clinical health psychologist, AASECT-certified sex therapist and supervisor, and certified Gottman therapist. She is an adjunct assistant professor in clinical psychology at the University of Utah and also in private practice in Salt Lake City, Utah. She specializes in sexual health and wellness for individuals and couples.

Walter R. Schumm (he/him), PhD, is emeritus professor of applied family science, Department of Applied Human Sciences, College of Health and Human Sciences, Kansas State University, retiring in 2021 after 42 years of teaching and research there. His degrees include a BS in physics, College of William and Mary in Virginia (1972); an MS in family and child development, Kansas State University (1976); and a PhD in family studies, Purdue University (1979). He served as editor of the journal *Marriage & Family Review* (2010–2020) and continues to review for numerous journals. He is a fellow of the National Council on Family Relations and is a certified family life educator. He retired as a colonel from the U.S. Army in 2002 after nearly 30 years of service. His primary research interests include military families, LGBT families, and research methodology. He is a Colson Fellow (2021–). Walter and his wife, Kimberly, have seven grown children living in Kansas, Texas, Iowa, and Wyoming. He is White, heterosexual, cisgender, and disabled (Veterans Administration) and has served as a substitute pastor at Ashland Community Church of Manhattan since 2010.

Samuel Skidmore (he/him), MS, is a fifth-year PhD student of clinical/counseling psychology at Utah State University. He is a White, cisgender, gay, currently nondisabled agnostic with an LDS upbringing.

Lauren Smithee (she/they) is a White, cisgender, queer, and neurodivergent woman. She is a marriage and family therapist (LMFT) who maintains a private practice in Bountiful, Utah. Her work focuses on the mental health and well-being of transgender, gender-diverse, and queer people and their relationships. She has personal, clinical, and research experience with navigating the transition of a transgender life partner.

Kersti Spjut (she/her), PhD, is an assistant clinical professor at Brigham Young University Counseling and Psychological Services and a psychologist in private practice. Her clinical and research interests include sex therapy, sexual health and identity, out-of-control sexual behaviors, perfectionism, body image, fat liberation, and the integration of mental health and chronic illness. Dr. Spjut received a BA in neuroscience from Dartmouth College in 2009 and a doctorate in clinical psychology from Brigham Young University in 2017. She is White, cisgender, partnered, and lives with type 1 diabetes.

Denise Steers (she/her) is a clinical psychologist and researcher with over 30 years working with children, teens, and young adults and their families in Aotearoa/New Zealand. She has worked in the public mental health system and at the University of Otago Medical School, where she completed her PhD and postdoc in the field of intersex/variations in sex characteristics. Denise is a cisgender, White lesbian who has a partner of 27 years and a teenage son.

Jim Struve (he/him), LCSW, has been working with male victims of sexual violence and issues of social justice since the mid-1970s. He is currently executive director for MenHealing (www.menhealing.org), and he was a cofounding member of the LGBTQ-Affirmative Psychotherapy Guild of Utah in 2004 and served as guild coordinator until 2018. He is a nationally known speaker and workshop presenter and has a number of publications focused on patriarchy and the politics of sexual abuse, gender and sexually diverse male survivors of sexual abuse, and the cultural and historical context of gender regarding clinical perspectives about male sexual victimization.

Tim van Wanrooij (he/him), is a chartered doctor of psychology and White (Dutch), queer/gay, cisgender, and neurodivergent (dyslexic). He was born and raised in the Netherlands and studied social work before completing his psychology training at Trinity College Dublin in Ireland. Tim has a private practice in Dublin, Ireland, in which he primarily focuses on relationships, sexuality, and intersectionality experiences.

Moshe-Mordechai (Maurits) van Zuiden lives in Jerusalem, Israel, is an Orthodox Jew raised socialist, formerly from Amsterdam, with 45+ years of experience in co-counseling (RC) with extra awareness around oppressions, abuse, and sexuality. He learned some nonviolent communication (NVC) and medicine (BSc), raised children, and is an activist and blogger (ToI).

Amanda Veldorale-Griffin (she/they) is a licensed marriage and family therapist in the state of Florida and an AAMFT-approved supervisor. She is also a professor of marriage and family sciences at National University and has a small private practice serving predominantly trans* clients and their families. Dr. Veldorale-Griffin holds a PhD in family and child sciences from Florida State

University and an MS in family studies with a concentration in marriage and family therapy from the University of Kentucky. Their area of research is transgender parenting and barriers to care for gender-expansive clients. Personally, she is White, Jewish, cisgender, and nondisabled and has a deep connection to the LGBTQ+ community as a pansexual individual and the daughter of a trans woman.

Jeni Wahlig (she/they), PhD, LMFT, is a relationship transformation coach, licensed couple and family therapist, teacher, author, and public speaker. She identifies as graysexual queer, genderqueer-femme, polyamorous, White, nondisabled, and a parent. A self-proclaimed "relationship nerd," Jeni has dedicated her career to studying relationships and supporting couples, particularly within the queer and trans communities. In partnership with her soulmate, Jeni offers critically conscious relationship education and coaching through their business, PowerfuLove. Their mission is to empower couples with the knowledge and skills they need to move beyond struggles and consciously create an extraordinary relationship.

Josephine Pui-Hing Wong (佢/lui/she/they), RN, PhD, FCAN, is a cisgender racialized immigrant settler, professor, and Research Chair in Urban Health in the Daphne Cockwell School of Nursing, Toronto Metropolitan University, with extensive experience in critical public health and community-centered action research in partnership with racialized and LGBTQ+ communities.

www.ingramcontent.com/pod-product-compliance
Lightning Source LLC
Chambersburg PA
CBHW031136270326
41929CB00011B/1654